日本語
NihonGO NOW!

NihonGO NOW! Level 2 is an intermediate-level courseware package that takes a performed-culture approach to learning Japanese. This approach balances the need for an intellectual understanding of structural elements with multiple opportunities to experience the language within its cultural context.

From the outset, learners are presented with samples of authentic language that are context-sensitive and culturally coherent. Instructional time is used primarily to rehearse interactions that learners of Japanese are likely to encounter in the future, whether they involve speaking, listening, writing, or reading.

Level 2 comprises two textbooks with accompanying activity books. These four books in combination with audio and video files allow instructors to adapt an intermediate-level course, such as the second or third year of college Japanese, to their students' needs. They focus on language and modeled behavior, providing opportunities for learners to acquire language through performance templates. Online resources provide additional support for both students and instructors. Audio files, videos, supplementary exercises, and a teachers' manual are available at www.routledge.com/9781138305304.

NihonGO NOW! Level 2 Volume 2 Textbook is ideally accompanied by the *Level 2 Volume 2 Activity Book*.

Mari Noda is Professor of Japanese at The Ohio State University.

Patricia J. Wetzel is Emerita Professor of Japanese at Portland State University.

Ginger Marcus is Professor of the Practice of Japanese Language at Washington University in St. Louis.

Stephen D. Luft is Lecturer of Japanese at the University of Pittsburgh.

Shinsuke Tsuchiya is Assistant Professor of Japanese at Brigham Young University.

日本語 NOW! NihonGO NOW!

Performing Japanese Culture
Level 2 Volume 2
Textbook

Mari Noda, Patricia J. Wetzel, Ginger Marcus, Stephen D. Luft, and Shinsuke Tsuchiya

LONDON AND NEW YORK

First published 2021
by Routledge
2 Park Square, Milton Park, Abingdon, Oxon OX14 4RN

and by Routledge
52 Vanderbilt Avenue, New York, NY 10017

Routledge is an imprint of the Taylor & Francis Group, an informa business

© 2021 Mari Noda, Patricia J. Wetzel, Ginger Marcus, Stephen D. Luft, and Shinsuke Tsuchiya

The right of Mari Noda, Patricia J. Wetzel, Ginger Marcus, Stephen D. Luft, and Shinsuke Tsuchiya to be identified as authors of this work has been asserted by them in accordance with sections 77 and 78 of the Copyright, Designs and Patents Act 1988.

All rights reserved. No part of this book may be reprinted or reproduced or utilised in any form or by any electronic, mechanical, or other means, now known or hereafter invented, including photocopying and recording, or in any information storage or retrieval system, without permission in writing from the publishers.

Trademark notice: Product or corporate names may be trademarks or registered trademarks, and are used only for identification and explanation without intent to infringe.

British Library Cataloguing-in-Publication Data
A catalogue record for this book is available from the British Library

Library of Congress Cataloging-in-Publication Data
Names: Noda, Mari, author.
Title: Nihongo now! : performing Japanese culture / Mari Noda, Patricia J. Wetzel, Ginger Marcus, Stephen D. Luft, Shinsuke Tsuchiya, Masayuki Itomitsu.
Description: New York : Routledge, 2020. | Includes bibliographical references. | Contents: Level 1, volume 1. Textbook – Level 1, volume 1. Activity book – Level 1, volume 2. Textbook – Level 1, volume 2. Activity book. | In English and Japanese.
Identifiers: LCCN 2020026010 (print) | LCCN 2020026011 (ebook) | ISBN 9780367509279 (level 1, volume 1 ; set ; hardback) | ISBN 9780367508494 (level 1, volume 1 ; set ; paperback) | ISBN 9781138304123 (level 1, volume 1 ; textbook ; hardback) | ISBN 9781138304147 (level 1, volume 1 ; textbook ; paperback) | ISBN 9781138304277 (level 1, volume 1 ; activity book ; hardback) | ISBN 9781138304314 (level 1, volume 1 ; activity book ; paperback) | ISBN 9780367509309 (level 1, volume 2 ; set ; hardback) | ISBN 9780367508531 (level 1, volume 2 ; set ; paperback) | ISBN 9780367483241 (level 1, volume 2 ; textbook ; hardback) | ISBN 9780367483210 (level 1, volume 2 ; textbook ; paperback) | ISBN 9780367483494 (level 1, volume 2 ; activity book ; hardback) | ISBN 9780367483364 (level 1, volume 2 ; activity book ; paperback) | ISBN 9780203730249 (level 1, volume 1 ; ebook) | ISBN 9780203730362 (level 1, volume 1 ; ebook) | ISBN 9781003051855 (level 1, volume 1 ; ebook) | ISBN 9781003039334 (level 1, volume 2 ; ebook) | ISBN 9781003039471 (level 1, volume 2 ; ebook) | ISBN 9781003051879 (level 1, volume 2 ; ebook)
Subjects: LCSH: Japanese language—Textbooks for foreign speakers—English. | Japanese language – Study and teaching – English speakers.
Classification: LCC PL539.5.E5 N554 2020 (print) | LCC PL539.5.E5 (ebook) | DDC 495.682/421—dc23
LC record available at https://lccn.loc.gov/2020026010
LC ebook record available at https://lccn.loc.gov/2020026011

ISBN: 978-0-367-74340-6 (hbk)
ISBN: 978-0-367-74339-0 (pbk)
ISBN: 978-1-003-15733-5 (ebk)

Typeset in Times New Roman
by Apex CoVantage, LLC

Access the Support Material: www.routledge.com/9781138305304

Contents

Act 19　そういうわけにはいきませんし……。
　　　　It's not as if 1

話す・聞く　Speaking and listening..3

シーン 19-1　「乗り換えるのには……。In order to transfer 3

　　　　BTS 1　Non-past Verb + のに(は)..5
　　　　BTS 2　Sentence + わけ・訳..6
　　　　BTS 3　〜としては・も..6

シーン 19-2　わけわかんない。I don't get the point............................8

　　　　BTS 4　Sentence + わけでは・も ない...................................10
　　　　BTS 5　わかんない 10

シーン 19-3　外すわけにもいきませんし……。
　　　　We can't take her off the team either. 11

　　　　BTS 6　Sentence + くせに...13
　　　　BTS 7　Sentence + わけに(は・も)いかない........................13

シーン 19-4　遅れるわけないですよね。It can't be that she's late, surely..........14

　　　　BTS 8　Sentence + わけ・訳 (が)ない.....................................15

シーン 19-5　もしあと５分遅れて(い)たら……。
　　　　If we had been five minutes later 16

　　　　BTS 9　Sentence + からいいようなものの..............................17

シーン 19-6　ブライアンの話 (予想外の展開) Brian's story (an unexpected
　　　　development)..18

　　　　BTS 10　More on storytelling 20

v

読み書き　Reading and writing 22

シーン 19-7R　トピックとしてはいいけど……。It's good as a topic, but 22
BTL 1 Script choice 23

シーン 19-8R　大人(おとな)のくせに…… You are an adult, yet 28
BTL 2 Innovative vocabulary 29

シーン 19-9R　けが人(にん)が出(で)なかったからいいようなものの
Good thing there were no injuries. 33
BTL 3 Listening to and reading news stories 34
BTL 4 Becoming proficient in reading by using multiple reading strategies ... 34
BTL 5 Using online resources and apps 35

Act 20　聞(き)かずにはいられなくなって……。
I couldn't help but ask 41

話す・聞く　Speaking and listening 43

シーン 20-1　お帰(かえ)りになりました。 She went home. 43
BTS 1 Honorific お + Verb stem + に + なる↑ 45
BTS 2 Verb stem ～かける 45
BTS 3 Negative Verb form ～ず(に)・ない(で) 45

シーン 20-2　かえってよくないよ。On the contrary, it's not good. 47
BTS 4 ことわざ: Using proverbs 49

シーン 20-3　治(なお)してはくれないけど……。It won't cure you, but 50
BTS 5 Sentence + だけ 51

シーン 20-4　肺(はい)が弱(よわ)ってるとか。I heard your lungs are weak. 53
BTS 6 Physical conditions 55

シーン 20-5　やればやるほど楽(たの)しくなってくる。
The more you do it the more fun it gets to be. 56
BTS 7 ～れば……～ほど 57

シーン 20-6　ブライアンの話(はなし) (思(おも)い違(ちが)い) Brian's story (a misunderstanding) 59
BTS 8 Sentence Particle わ 61

vi

　　　　BTS 9 Contractions 61
　　　　BTS 10 More on storytelling 62

読み書き　Reading and writing 63

シーン 20-7R 起承転結 Introduction, development, twist, conclusion 63
　　　　BTL 1 起承転結 64
　　　　BTL 2 Onomatopoeia in manga 65
　　　　BTL 3 Creative sentence endings: キャラ語尾 65

シーン 20-8R 寝耳に水 An astonishing surprise 71
　　　　BTL 4 名詞止め Ending with noun 72
　　　　BTL 5 Identifying and describing kanji: 部首 72

シーン 20-9R ミステリートマト The mystery tomato 77
　　　　BTL 6 Choosing words to refer to yourself 78
　　　　BTL 7 Usernames 78
　　　　BTL 8 Reading manga and watching anime 79

Act 21　典型的な夜型です。
I'm a typical night owl. 85

話す・聞く　Speaking and listening 87

シーン 21-1 つまり……っていうこと。In other words, it means 87
　　　　BTS 1 Being creative with language 89

シーン 21-2 私なりの健康管理です。It's my way of health management. 90
　　　　BTS 2 X なりに; X なりの Y 92
　　　　BTS 3 X というと 92

シーン 21-3 誰にでも当てはまるとは限らないんじゃないですか？
Isn't it the case that it doesn't apply to everyone? 94
　　　　BTS 4 Passive for general description 96
　　　　BTS 5 必ずしも + negative 96

シーン 21-4 答え合わせしていきましょう。Let's check our answers. 97
　　　　BTS 6 Verb 〜ていく 98
　　　　BTS 7 Sentence particle ぞ 99
　　　　BTS 8 その [Modifier] + noun (discourse strategy) 99

vii

シーン 21-5　エイミーの話 (難しいこと) Amy's story ... 100

    BTS 9 Constructing a narration with multiple participants ... 102

シーン 21-6　孝の話 (ことば遊び) Takashi's story (language play) ... 103

    BTS 10 言ってやった ... 104
    BTS 11 Empathy-seeking intonation: 古くない？ ... 104
    BTS 12 だから as a discourse connector ... 105

読み書き　Reading and writing ... 106

シーン 21-7R 自分なりに考えよう。Let's think for ourselves. ... 106

    BTL 1 Including 平仮名 and カタカナ as part of search words ... 107
    BTL 2 Using online resources to study Japanese ... 107
    BTL 3 Composing catchy headlines and titles in Japanese ... 107
    BTL 4 キラキラネーム ... 108

シーン 21-8R 「勉強は朝するべきではない」
    "Study should not be done in the morning" ... 113

    BTL 5 How to use 原稿用紙 ... 114
    BTL 6 Compositions and papers: 作文、小論文 ... 114
    BTL 7 More on written style ... 115

シーン 21-9R SF映画の歴史が変わる。 Changes in the history of sci-fi movies ... 120

Act 22　これさえできれば大丈夫。
If we can do just this much it will be fine ... 127

話す・聞く　Speaking and listening ... 129

シーン 22-1　プリントしたばっかりだったのに。
    Even though I just finished printing it now ... 129

    BTS 1 Past sentence + ばかり・ばっかり ... 130
    BTS 2 Expressing frustration in a professional setting ... 130

シーン 22-2　コンビニ弁当ばかり……。
    Nothing but convenience store bento 132

    BTS 3 Exclusivity: Noun + ばかり・ばっかり ... 133
    BTS 4 むしろ ... 134
    BTS 5 など ... 134
    BTS 6 かしら ... 135

シーン 22-3	コピーさえできれば……。 If we can just get the copies done 136
	BTS 7 Special humble nouns: 拝借(はいしゃく) 137
	BTS 8 Noun ＋ さえ ＋ 〜ば 138

シーン 22-4	社長(しゃちょう)がいいって言いさえすれば……。 If only the president would just say okay 139
	BTS 9 Non-past Sentence ＋ ばかり 141
	BTS 10 Verb stem ＋ さえ 141

シーン 22-5	そう言えば……。Come to think of it 142
	BTS 11 Connectives.................143

シーン 22-6	池辺(いけべ)さんの話(はなし) (失敗談(しっぱいだん)) Ikebe-san's story (explaining failure) 144
	BTS 12 Verb 〜て ＋ ばかり・ばっかり 146
	BTS 13 〜て ＋ さえ 146
	BTS 14 〜たって 147

読み書き Reading and writing.................149

シーン 22-7R	発送(はっそう)のお知(し)らせ Shipping notice 149
	BTL 1 にて・まで in business writing.................150
	BTL 2 Japanese addresses.................151

シーン 22-8R	履歴書(りれきしょ) Resume 157
	BTL 3 履歴書(りれきしょ).................159

シーン 22-9R	自己(じこ) PR Promoting your strengths.................165
	BTL 4 Talking about your strengths in Japanese.................167
	BTL 5 Using the appropriate terms of address: 当社(とうしゃ) vs. 弊社(へいしゃ) and 御社(おんしゃ) vs. 貴社(きしゃ).................168
	BTL 6 Verb stem 〜得(う)る・得(え)る 171

Act 23 理想(りそう)を言えばキリがないけど……。
When it comes to ideals, there is no end, but 173

話す・聞く Speaking and listening.................175

シーン 23-1	10時以降(いこう)は洗濯(せんたく)するな。It is forbidden to do laundry after 10:00......175
	BTS 1 Negative imperative: Verb ＋ な.................177
	BTS 2 Rules and regulations.................178

シーン 23-2　行け！ Go!..179
　　　BTS 3 Affirmative imperative..181
　　　BTS 4 Sentence particle ぜ...182

シーン 23-3　おんなじことばっかりさせられて……。
　　　　　　Being made to do the same thing 183
　　　BTS 5 Causative passive..184

シーン 23-4　LDK にこだわるの？ You are set on an LDK?.........................186
　　　BTS 6 キリ..188

シーン 23-5　こんなに払わせられるくらいなら
　　　　　　If I'm to be made to pay this much.......................................189
　　　BTS 7 Sentence + くらい...190

シーン 23-6　ブライアンの話 (新情報) Brian's story (new information)................192
　　　BTS 8 X に関して..194
　　　BTS 9 X に始まって、Y、Z...194

読み書き　Reading and writing 195

シーン 23-7R　ゴミを捨てるな Don't throw away trash here.......................195
　　　BTL 1 Sorting trash: ゴミの分別..196

シーン 23-8R　残業させられることナシ！
　　　　　　You won't be forced to work overtime!.................................202
　　　BTL 2 Job hunting...203
　　　BTL 3 More on より..203
　　　BTL 4 のみ...204

シーン 23-9R　スカイタワーズナウ Sky Towers NOW..................................209

Act 24　挨拶 Formal speeches **215**

話す・聞く　Speaking and listening...217

シーン 24-1　ブライアンの挨拶 (感謝) Brian's remarks (gratitude) 217
　　　BTS 1 Structure of a simple gratitude speech..............................219

シーン 24-2　乾杯の音頭 Leading a toast 220
    BTS 2 Leading a toast (discourse structure) 223
    BTS 3 X に Y に 223
    BTS 4 X はもとより、Y、Z 224

シーン 24-3　サーシャの挨拶 (新たな出発) Sasha's farewell (moving on) 225
    BTS 5 Formal speech when moving on (discourse structure) 227
    BTS 6 X (を)始めY、Z 227

シーン 24-4　孝の挨拶 (振り返り) Takashi's reflection 229
    BTS 7 Impromptu farewell speech structure 230
    BTS 8 Non-past Sentence + とともに 230
    BTS 9 X、または Y 231

シーン 24-5　エイミーの挨拶 (自己紹介) Amy's remarks (self-introduction) 232
    BTS 10 Workplace self-introduction (discourse structure) 234

読み書き Reading and writing 235

シーン 24-6R　失敗談 Learning experiences 235
    BTL 1 恩と義理 236

シーン 24-7R　お祝いの言葉 Congratulatory words 241

Appendix A: Japanese-English glossary in *gojuuon* order 247
Index 368

第 19 幕
Act 19

そういうわけにはいきませんし……。
It's not as if . . .

寝る子は育つ。
A child who sleeps well grows up well.

◆ 話す・聞く

Scene 19-1 乗(の)り換(か)えるのには……。
In order to transfer . . .

Sasha and Kanda-san are making a transfer from the subway to a JR train.

The script

神田	サーシャ
ええっと、JRに乗(の)り換(か)えるのにはどっちへ行けばいいのかな。	工事中(こうじちゅう)で、わかりにくいですね。どこかに書(か)いてあるはずですけど……。
あ、あそこ！	ああ、反対側(はんたいがわ)なんだ。
ああ、そういうわけですか。	工事中(こうじちゅう)としても、これはややこしいですね。

Kanda	Sasha
Uhhh, in order to transfer to JR, which way should we go, I wonder.	It's under construction so it's hard to figure out. It should be written somewhere, but . . .
Oh, over there!	Oh, so it's on the other side.
Oh, so that's it.	Yeah, even for a construction site this is confusing.

単語と表現

名詞

JR	Japan Railway
在来線(ざいらいせん)	conventional train (as opposed to shinkansen)

方向 (ほうこう)	direction, district
ホーム	platform
手前 (てまえ)	this side (of a location); a little before reaching (a location, a situation)
工事 (こうじ)	construction
工事中 (こうじちゅう)	under construction
切符売り場 (きっぷうりば)	ticket window
券売機 (けんばいき)	ticket machine
改札口 (かいさつぐち)	ticket gate, wicket
窓口 (まどぐち)	ticket window
みどりの窓口 (まどぐち)	JR ticket office (lit. 'green window')
チャージ(する)	charge
精算(する) (せいさん)	calculation adjustment
わけ・訳 (わけ)	reason, judgement based on evidence

動詞

降りる (-RU; 降りた)	disembark
問い合わせる (-RU; 問い合わせた)	inquire (for information)
確かめる (-RU; 確かめた)	make sure
起こす (-U; 起こした)	wake (someone) up
離す (-U; 離した)	divide X, separate, put distance between two things
倒す (-U; 倒した)	throw down, knock down, defeat
進む (-U; 進んだ)	go forward, improve
下がる (-U; 下がった)	dangle, step back

形容詞

| ややこしい | confusing, perplexing |

表現

| 〜のには | in order to . . . |
| 〜としては・も | for an X; even for X |

Behind the scenes

BTS 1 Non-past Verb + のに (は)

The combination of a non-past Verb with のに indicates that what follows is needed for the purpose of the Verb.

これ、売るのにコストはどのぐらいかかります？	In order to sell these, about how much should the cost be?
完全に書き換えるのには1週間以上かかります。	It'll take over a week in order to completely rewrite it.
お客様に喜んでいただくのに一生懸命で、遅くまで残って仕事をしていました。	I stayed late working really hard to make sure the clients would be satisfied.

When のに is followed by は, it has its usual limiting function, as when Kanda-san asks: JRに乗り換えるのにはどっちへ行けばいい？ 'In order to transfer to JR (at least, nothing more), which way should we go?' You will find that の is often dropped in this combination: JRに乗り換えるにはどっちへ行けばいい？

| A: インターネットは情報を集めるのに便利です。 | A: The internet is convenient for gathering information. |
| B: 情報を集めるのには便利ですが、本当かどうか、考えなければなりませんね。 | B: It's convenient for gathering information, but you have to consider whether it's true or not. |

There is a good deal of overlap between this のに and ために, which you have seen in earlier Acts. All of the forgoing examples are acceptable with ために. But ために indicates purpose more explicitly, so when vagueness is appropriate のに is preferred.

BTS 2 Sentence + わけ・訳

わけ is a Noun that occurs in a number of patterns that come up in this Act. The simplest of these is [Sentence + わけです] (where だ changes to な), which is used to state or sum up a conclusion based on some sort of evidence. In this respect it can overlap with [Sentence + んです] that came up earlier. 卒業してからすぐ帰国するわけですか。 'So that means you'll be coming back after you graduate?' is very close in meaning to 卒業してからすぐ帰国するんですか。 [Sentence + わけです] is more definite and thus a bit more formal than [Sentence + んです].

The question どういう訳ですか。 is an explicit request for justification: 'How did this come about?' Note that [Sentence + と・って いうわけ] is nearly equivalent to [Sentence + わけ]. The addition of と・って いう makes the conclusion sound like hearsay, so it is more likely to occur in summations of other people's speech. This と・って いうわけ can also be shortened to と・って わけ.

「不安だ」って言っていますが、それって、やりたくないというわけですか。	She says she feels anxious, but does that mean she doesn't want to do it?
「できない」って、どういうわけでしょうか。説明していただけますか？	What do you mean you can't do it? Please explain.
空調が故障なわけではないけど、暑いですよね、ここ。	It's not that the air conditioning is broken, but it's hot here, isn't it?

BTS 3 〜としては・も

You saw [Noun として] in an earlier Act meaning 'as, in the capacity of.'

部長として何か言ってくださいよ。	Please say something in your role as division chief.
今日は妻としてじゃなく、お客様として来てますから、もっと丁寧に話してください。	I'm here today not as your wife but as a customer. So please speak to me more politely.

When も is added (Noun としても) it means 'even for an X.'

アルバイトとしても知らな過ぎますよ。お客様に失礼でしょ？	Even for a part-time worker there's too much he doesn't know. It's rude to the client, isn't it?

When は is added (Noun としては) it contrasts the Noun with more commonly held expectations about that Noun.

１年生としてはめちゃくちゃ上手（うま）くてびっくりだよ。	For a first-year student she is so insanely good I am astonished.

Now go to the Activity Book for 練習 and 腕試し.

Scene 19-2 わけわかんない。 I don't get the point.

Ichiro is eager to get Brian's reaction to the latest film that Brian just saw.

The script

一郎	ブライアン
映画どうだった？	うん。アクション映画としてはすごくよかったよ。だけどストーリーはイマイチかな。
イマイチか。	というより、わけわかんない。
そうか。じゃあ、止めとくか。	あ、でも全くつまんないってわけでもないよ。

Ichiro	Brian
How was the movie?	Yeah. For an action movie it was really good. But the story wasn't much.
Not great, huh?	Or should I say, I don't get the point.
I see. Well then, maybe I'll pass.	Oh, but it's not as if it was a complete waste of time!

単語と表現

名詞

アクション	action
コメディ	comedy
ユーモア	humor
サイエンスフィクション	science fiction
ミステリー	mystery

ストーリー	story
筋(すじ)	plot
CG	computer graphics
構成(こうせい)	organization, composition
演出(えんしゅつ)	(theater, film) direction
役者(やくしゃ)	actor, actress
批判(ひはん)(する)	criticism
批判的(ひはんてき)(な)	critical
評価(ひょうか)(する)	assessment, evaluation
感動(かんどう)(する)	strong emotion
感動的(かんどうてき)(な)	emotionally moving

動詞

比(くら)べる (-RU; 比べた)	compare

形容詞

つまんない	boring

表現

というより	rather than
わけ(が)わからない	doesn't make sense, has no point
全(まった)く	completely, entirely
〜わけでは・もない	doesn't mean X; doesn't mean X either

拡張

What genres of films do you tend to watch? Discuss movies with your Japanese friend/colleague to learn how those genres are identified in Japanese.

Behind the scenes

BTS 4 Sentence + わけで は・も ない

The combination [Sentence + わけで は・も ない] negates an assertion or assumption. Thus an affirmative [Sentence + わけで は・も ない] means 'I don't mean that Sentence,' while a negative [Sentence + わけで は・も ない] means 'I don't mean that negative Sentence.' The appearance of は here, as usual, indicates that there are other possibilities for Sentence. Compare すぐ使うわけではない. 'I don't mean that I'll use it right away (although I may do other things with it).' and いらないわけではない ' I don't mean that I don't need it (although I could use it if it were available).' The use of も in these examples would indicate that the Sentence is in addition to others that may be understood from context or have already been mentioned: すぐ使うわけでもない. 'Nor do I mean that I'll use it right away.' and いらないわけでもない ' Nor do I mean that I don't need it.'

工事中でも、通れないわけではありませんから。	Even if it's under construction, it doesn't mean you can't go through.
ああ、この特急が全部このホームに止まるっていうわけでもないんですね。	Oh, it also doesn't mean that all these express trains stop at this platform, right?
ちょっと……。あ、間違っているっていうわけじゃないですよ！	Hold on. . . . Oh, I don't mean that it's a mistake!

BTS 5 わかんない

In rapid casual speech a ら syllable before な is often contracted to ん. Thus つまらない becomes つまんない, and わからない becomes わかんない.

そんなに時間かかんないじゃん。	C'mon, it doesn't take that much time.

Now go to the Activity Book for 練習 and 腕試し.

Scene 19-3 外すわけにもいきませんし……。
We can't take her off the team either...

Ikebe-san, a part-time worker, is not being terribly effective as a project team member.

The script

神田	サーシャ
池辺さん、相変わらず問題が多いようですね。	はい。頼まれた時には「はい、はい」と返事するくせに、口だけで、ちっとも実行に移してくれないんです。
そう。それはまずいですね。	だからと言って、チームから外すわけにもいきませんし……。
いや、そんなことだったら辞めてもらいましょうか。	え？いや、もうしばらく様子見て報告させてもらえますか。

Kanda	Sasha
As usual Ikebe-san seems to have a lot of problems, doesn't she.	Yes. Even though she answers, "yes, yes" when she's asked, it's just talk, and it doesn't show up one bit in her performance.
Right. It's unfortunate, isn't it.	Nevertheless, we can't very well take her off the team either, so . . .
If that's the case, should we have her resign?	What? No, would you let me report back to you after watching her for a bit longer?

単語と表現

名詞

返事(する)	answer, reply
くせ	habit, tendency

実行(する)	performance, practice
行動(する)	behavior, conduct
満足(な)・(する)	satisfaction
かわいそう(な)	pitiful, pathetic
チーム	team
様子	situation, circumstances

動詞

引き受ける (-RU; 引き受けた)	take on, undertake
守る (-U; 守った)	guard, watch over
外す (-U; 外した)	take off, remove, unfasten
怠ける (-RU; 怠けた)	neglect a job or task
除く (-U; 除いた)	exclude, eliminate
悩む (-U; 悩んだ)	worry about
頼る (-U; 頼った)	depend on, count on

表現

相変わらず	as usual, as ever
〜くせに	even though, in spite of
口だけ (です)	just words, just talk
ちっとも	not a bit, not at all
実行に移す	put into practice, put into effect
だからと言って	nevertheless, while it may be true that

Behind the scenes

BTS 6 Sentence + くせに

A Sentence in combination with くせに means 'even though' or 'in spite of the fact that,' usually in a negative sense.

「はい、はい」と返事するくせに、口だけです。	Even though he says "yes, yes" it's just talk.
自分で作ったことないくせに、知ったような顔で話す人、いますよね。	There are people who act as if they know even though they've never made it themselves.
弱気なくせに、言うことは結構強いですね。	Even though he's fainthearted, what he says is pretty forceful.

The word くせ alone means 'habit.'

彼女、考える前に話すくせがある。	She has a habit of speaking before she thinks.

You will also hear the combination くせになる 'something becomes a habit' or 'one gets used to something.'

おいしいでしょう？くせになりますよね、これ。	Delicious, right? You could get addicted to this.

BTS 7 Sentence + わけに(は・も)いかない

The combination [Sentence + わけに(は・も)いかない] indicates that there is no justification for Sentence, or circumstances do not allow Sentence: 'One can't very well do X (given the circumstances).'

社長がそのままでいいって言うんでしょう？変えるわけにはいきませんよね。	The company president said it's fine as it is, right? We can't very well change it, can we?
こんなボロボロの車で、お客様をご案内するわけにはいきませんから……。	One can't very well take guests around in a car as beat up as this.

Now go to the Activity Book for 練習 and 腕試し.

そういうわけにはいきませんし……。

Scene 19-4 遅れるわけないですよね。
It can't be that she's late, surely.

Sasha and Kanda-san are waiting for Ikebe-san to show up.

The script

サーシャ	神田
まだ来ませんねぇ、池辺さん。もしかして、また遅刻なんて。	さすがにそれはあり得ないでしょう。この間部長からも注意されたところですから。
そうですよねぇ。それでまた遅れるわけないですよね。	あ、来た、来た！
あ〜、よかった。	

Sasha	Kanda
Ikebe-san still isn't here. Surely she can't be delayed again.	Even for her, that couldn't be possible. Because she was just cautioned by the division chief recently.
That's true. So it wouldn't be that she's late again.	Oh, here she is! Here she is!
What a relief.	

単語と表現

名詞

遅刻(する)	delay, lateness
早退(する)	leaving early
直帰(する)	going directly home
通勤(する)	commuting to work

通学(する)	commuting to school
状況	circumstances
理由	reason, motive
原因	cause, origin

表現

もしかして	maybe, by some chance
さすがに	still, even so
〜訳(が)ない	there's no reason to suppose that X

Behind the scenes

BTS 8 Sentence + わけ・訳(が)ない

The combination [Sentence + わけ(が)ない] indicates a conclusion that arises from reasoning: '(given the circumstances) there's no way that . . .'

こんな難しい本、読める訳がないですよ。	There's no reason to expect that I could read a book as difficult as this.
こんなに準備したんですから、失敗する訳ありませんよ。	We did all this preparation so there's no way we could fail.

Now go to the Activity Book for 練習 and 腕試し.

Scene 19-5 もしあと5分遅れて(い)たら……。
If we had been five minutes later . . .

Ichiro and Brian were delayed getting to a concert but made it just in time.

The script

一郎	ブライアン
間に合った！	よかった！もしあと5分遅れてたらアウトだった。
本当。なんとか間に合ったからいいようなものの……。	しかし、危ないところだったね。

Ichiro	Brian
We made it!	Great! If we had been five minutes later we'd have been out (of luck)!
True. Good thing we made it, because . . .	. . . that was close, huh.

単語と表現

名詞

アウト	out (from baseball)
セーフ	safe (from baseball)

動詞

閉まる (-U; 閉まった)	X closes

表現

やっと	narrowly, at last
何とか・なんとか	something-or-other
〜からいいようなものの	good thing that . . .
ギリギリ	just barely
しかし	but

Behind the scenes

BTS 9 Sentence ＋ からいいようなものの

The combination of [Sentence ＋からいいようなものの] presents a near-miss situation while suggesting the possibility that the reverse might have happened: 'It's a good thing that . . .' There is no need to finish the sentence – in this Scene, Ichiro leaves the alternative unstated, but Brian finishes it.

カバンが見つかったからいいようなものの、もし見つからなかったら大変なことになっていた。	Good thing that the bag was found; it would have been a disaster if it hadn't.
お母さんが気づかなかったからいいようなものの、もし気づいていたらカミナリが落ちているところだったよね。	Good thing that mom didn't notice; lightning (lit. 'thunder') would have struck (us) had she noticed (what we'd done), you know.

Now go to the Activity Book for 練習 and 腕試し.

Scene 19-6 ブライアンの話（予想外の展開）
Brian's story (an unexpected development)

Brian is having lunch with Kawamura-senpai and decides to tell him about his recent adventure.

 The script

ブライアン	川村
２週間ほど前にコンサートに行ったんですけどね。	うん。
あ、ホームステイの家族の一郎くんと一緒に。	うん、うん。
途中で電車が止まっちゃって……。	ああ、よくあるんだよね、この頃。
で１時間も缶詰状態だったんですよ。	へえ、間に合った？
それが、駅に着いた時はもう開演予定の１０分前で……。	ああ、
でもせっかく買ったチケット、無駄にするわけにはいかないじゃないですか。	そりゃそうだよね。
だから、２人で飛び出して、ダッシュしました。	そう。
で、会場に飛び込んだらぁ、	飛び込んだら？
開演も２０分遅れますっていうんで、もうホッとして。	じゃ、間に合ったんだね。
なんとか。	

Brian	Kawamura
About two weeks ago I went to a concert but...	Uh-huh.
With Ichiro from my homestay family...	Uh-huh. Uh-huh.
The train stopped on the way...	That happens a lot these days.

We were stuck for an hour.	You made it in time?
In fact, when we got to the station, it was already ten minutes before the start of the performance . . .	Ohhh.
But it's not as if we can waste the tickets that we went to all the trouble of buying, right?	That's right.
Both of us dashed, rushing.	Right.
So then when we went rushing into the theater . . .	Rushing in?
The start was 20 minutes delayed so we breathed a sigh of relief.	So you made it in time.
Somehow.	

単語と表現

名詞

予想(する)	prediction, expectation
予想外	unexpected
展開(する)	expansion, development
途中	on the way, in the middle of
渋滞(する)	(traffic) congestion
缶詰	stuck in a confined space
状態	status, circumstances
缶詰状態	backed up, clogged (traffic)
開演(する)	curtain (of a performance)
無駄(な)	waste, futility
ダッシュ(する)	dash, run
会場	assembly hall, theater
ビル	building

動詞

飛び出す (-U; 飛び出した)	rush out
飛び込む (-U; 飛び込んだ)	rush in
焦る (-U; 焦った)	hurry
止まる (-U; 止まった)	come to a halt, stop
動く (-U; 動いた)	move (one's position)

助詞

[quantity] + ほど	about, as many as

表現

そりゃそうだ	that's right
で、	so then, and then
ホッとする	feel relieved

Behind the scenes

BTS 10 More on storytelling

In this Scene you see strategies for telling a story or anecdote. Note that the speakers together "frame" the reported events and give a new description to keep the conversation going in certain directions. Try to think of your narration in the following progression. The listener should also assist in developing the story and adding a conclusion.

a. Frame 1: Brian sets up the first frame for his story by introducing the event – going to the concert. ～んです sets the frame and けど signals that he is going to say something about it.
b. An unexpected or unwelcome event is described with ～ちゃって.
c. Frame 2: Kawamura-senpai sets up his comment with よくあるんだ, acknowledging Brian's description of the event (the train stopped operating). His contribution – よくある、この頃 – expands the narrative. His role in Brian's narration is crucial. Listeners help to facilitate story development by helping to co-construct the story.

d. Frame 3: Brian then tells what resulted from (a) and (b), beginning this phase with で, and ending with だったんですよ, using 缶詰状態(かんづめじょうたい) to frame the next part of the story.
e. Reason(s): Brian gives the reason for the next action, using 〜じゃないですか.
f. Action: Brian then tells what he and Ichiro did next, using 〜しました. The action culminates with Brian and Ichiro rushing into the venue. Brian uses the 〜たら form (飛(と)び込(こ)んだら) to introduce what they discover after the culminating action.
g. Discovery: What the speaker sets up as a discovery is often the punchline of the story. Here, it is that the opening of the show was also delayed by 20 minutes.
h. Frame 4: Brian frames this discovery (〜んで) with the announcement that the opening was delayed by 20 minutes and follows it with his sense of relief.
i. Frame 5: Kawamura-san further frames this final situation (〜んだね) with a conclusion – that they made it.

Now go to the Activity Book for 練習 and 腕試し.

Then do 評価 activities.

◆ 読み書き

シーン 19-7R　トピックとしてはいいけど……。
It's good as a topic, but . . .

Amy is consulting with Takashi via text message about her upcoming presentation for the JLC.

 テキスト Text

Think about problems of discrimination in the U.S. and Japan
#usjapan #discrimination
A big problem in recent years . . .
Do you think I can use this problem as a topic for my JLC presentation?

Hmm. I'm not sure.
It's good as a topic, but it might be a little complicated to use for a presentation.

You're right.

We have only ten minutes from start to finish, and we also need to move the tables.
Simple is the best after all.

You're right. Thanks.

(Sorry to) change the subject, but weren't you saying the other day that you might quit your part-time job?

Oh, I just meant that I might take some time off, not that I'm quitting.

Oh, was that it.

BTL 1 Script choice

Recall that katakana may be used to add emphasis by making text stand out (e.g., 頑張ろうニッポン！ as opposed to 日本) or making it look less formal (e.g., アルバイト as opposed to 非正規雇用者; テスト as opposed to 試験). When you begin writing academic papers, you will probably use more 漢語, in which case the number of kanji will increase. But in casual settings, katakana and hiragana provide a softer impression and may be preferred over kanji that are more formal. For instance, Amy's writing would appear a little rigid if she were to write 確かに instead of たしかに in the text above. For the same reason, under ordinary circumstances, hiragana script is preferred over kanji for some of the vocabulary you have learned so far (e.g., いろいろ vs. 色々; たとえば vs. 例えば; とき vs. 時; わけ vs. 訳). On the other hand, using too much hiragana can look childish (as this is common in children's books).

The standards for how to mix kanji, hiragana, and katakana are different depending on the setting as well as individual preferences. As you explore different styles of writing, pay attention to how hiragana, katakana, and kanji characters are incorporated to effectively convey the intended message.

文字と例 Kanji with examples

296. 始　はじ(める)　はじ(まる)　シ　start, begin　始

1. 始める　　　　　　　　　　　　　start (something)
2. 始めるのにどのぐらいかかる？　　About how long does it take to start?

3.		いつでも始められるわけじゃないし、今がチャンスだよ。	It's not possible to just start at any time, so now is the chance.
4.		始まる	start
5.	+	始め	beginning
6.	+	始まり	beginning, origin
7.		始まりとしてはいいね。	It's good as a beginning.
8.	+	開始(する)	start

297. 終 お(える) お(わる) シュウ finish 終

1.		終える	finish (something)
2.		終わる	is finished; finish (something)
3.	+	終わり	end
4.		話を終わらせようと思ってるんだけど、なかなか終わらない。	I'm trying to end the story, but it just doesn't quite end.
5.		僕としてはここで終わってほしくないんだけど。	As for me, I don't want it to end here.
6.	#	終了(する)	end
7.	#	一部始終	from beginning to end

298. 止 と(める) と(まる) や(める) シ   stop, quit   止

1.	+	止める	stop X
2.		手をあげてタクシーを止めた。	I stopped the taxi by raising my hand.
3.		水が止められてしまいました。	The water was cut off.
4.		止まる	stop
5.		ここで止まってください。	Please stop here.
6.		止める	quit (something)
7.		ゲームもう止めちゃうんですか。	Are you already quitting the game?

8. +	中止(する)		cancellation
10.	残念ながら、明日のツアーは台風で中止になりました。		Unfortunately, tomorrow's tour is cancelled due to the typhoon.

299. 辞 や(める) ジ　quit　辞

1.	辞める	quit (e.g., job)
2.	しばらく休むだけで辞めるわけではないよ。	I'm only going to take some time off so it doesn't mean I'm quitting.
3.	あの先月始めたバイト、もう辞めるらしいよ。	It seems that that part-timer who started working last month is already quitting.
4.	私としては辞めないでほしいんだけど。	As for me, I don't want you to quit.
5.	今月末で辞めさせてください。	Please allow me to quit by the end of this month.
6.	辞めたくてもまだ辞められないんです。	Even though I want to quit, I can't yet.
7. #	辞任(する)	resignation

300. 動 うご(く) うご(かす) ドウ　move　動

1.	動く	move
2.	動かないわけじゃないけど……。	It's not that it won't move, but . . .
3.	動かす	move (something)
4.	これを動かすのに何人手伝えばいいかな。	How many people would we need in order to move this?
5.	動かせるかどうかわかんないけどやってみよう。	I'm not sure whether we can move it or not, but let's give it a try.
6. +	運動(する)	exercise
7.	この場所、運動するのにいいですね。	This place is suited for exercising.
8.	行動(する)	act
9.	早く行動しないと間に合わなくなっちゃうよ。	If we don't act early, we won't make it in time.

そういうわけにはいきません……。

10.	+	動物(どうぶつ)	animal
11.		動物の中ではやっぱりペンギンが一番好きです。	Of course, among animals I like penguins the best.

301. 確　たしか(める)　カク　　check, confirm　　確

1.		確(たし)かめる	check (something)
2.		まだ確かめなくちゃならないことがあるんです。	I still have things that I must check.
3.		確かめさせてもらえなくて困ってます。	I'm troubled that they are not allowing me to check it.
4.		確か(な)	certain
5.		確かに or たしかに	certainly
6.		確かに今終(お)わらせないと間に合わなくなりますね。	You are right – we won't make it in time if we don't end now.
7.		うん、それは確かにありえますね。	Yes, that is certainly a possibility.
8.	¥	確認(かくにん)(する)	confirmation

302. 問　と(う)　モン　　ask　　問

1.	#	問(と)う[1]	question (something)
2.	+	問(とい)	question
3.		問１．次の漢字の読み方を_____に書きましょう。	Q 1. Write the readings of the following kanji on the line.
4.		問(と)い合(あ)わせる	inquire
5.	+	(お)問い合わせ	inquiry
6.		お問い合わせのご案内です。	Here is information regarding the inquiry.
7.		問題(もんだい)	problem
8.		問題はその日にだれも来られないということです。	The problem is that no one can come on that day.

[1] The past form of 問う is 問うた, an old Japanese conjugation; the negative form is 問わない

303. 必 かなら(ず)　ヒツ (See kanji certainty #304.)　必

1. 必ず — without fail, always
2. あの駅で必ず降りないといけないよ。 — You must get off at that station.
3. 安くしたって、必ず売れるわけでもない。 — Even if we make it cheap, it doesn't guarantee that it will sell for sure.

304. 要　い(る)　ヨウ　need　要

1. お金が要る — need money
2. 要らないわけじゃないけど、今必要ってわけでもない。 — It's not that I don't need it, but I don't necessarily need it now.
3. + 要 X — X needed
4. 要注意 — requires attention, needs special attention
5. 必要(な) — need
6. 国としても考えていく必要があるというふうに考えています。 — I'm thinking that there is a need to think about it as a nation, too.
7. 必要とされる — is deemed necessary
8. 会社で必要とされる人になりたい。 — I want to be a person who is needed in the company.
9. グローバル社会で必要とされているスキル — skills needed in a globalized society

Now go to the Activity Book for 練習.

そういうわけにはいきませんし……。

シーン 19-8R 大人(おとな)のくせに……
You are an adult, yet . . .

Takashi wrote the following post on his SNS ('social networking service').

 テキスト Text

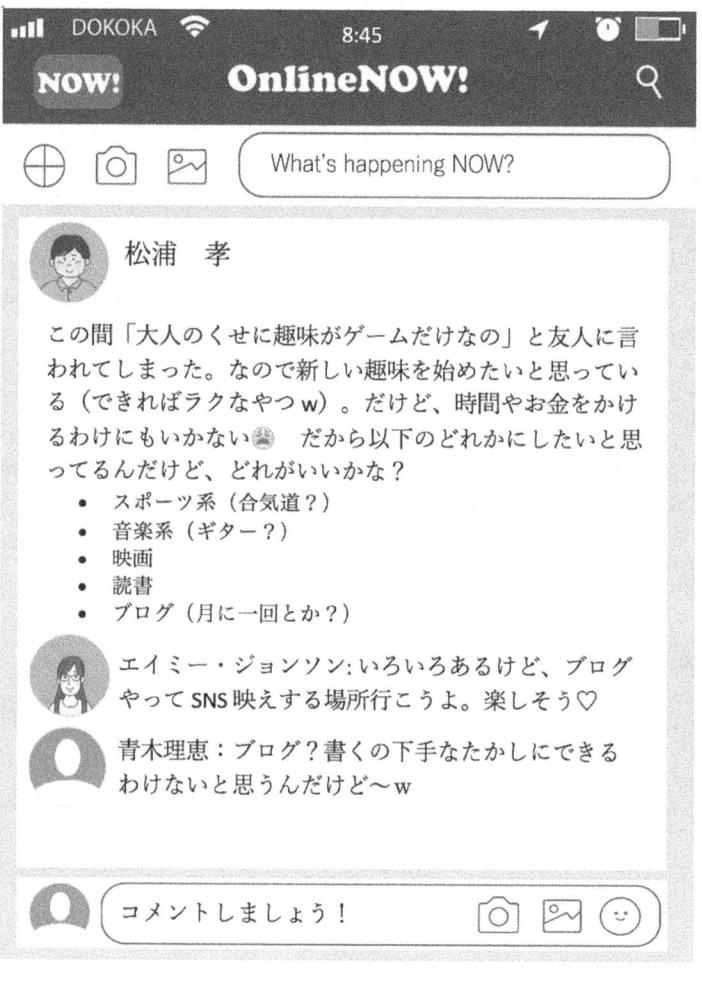

\+ 　　　　　だけど　　　　　but, however

Takashi Matsuura
I was told by my friend the other day, "You are an adult, yet your only hobby is playing videogames," so I'd like to start a new hobby (if possible something that is easy to do, lol). I can't spend too much time or money, so I'm thinking of doing one of the following. Which one would be good?

- Some kind of sport (aikido?)
- Something to do with music (guitar?)
- Movies
- Reading
- Blog (maybe once a month?)

Amy: There are a variety of options, but let's do a blog and go to places that will look good on SNS. That would be fun ♡

Rie Aoki: Blog? I don't think it's possible for Takashi considering he's bad at writing (lol).

BTL 2 Innovative vocabulary

Innovative vocabulary, such as SNS 映え used in the text above, are common in Japanese. They are made by borrowing from (and often changing the meaning of) other languages, compounding, shortening, adding suffixes, inverting, etc. Some examples include:

- ネチケット 'netiquette' (internet + etiquette)
- アベノミクス 'Abenomics' (Prime Minister Abe Shinzo + economics)
- 食育 'nutrition education' (食事 'meal' + 教育 'education')
- サボる 'skip (a class or meeting)' (sabotage + -る)
- ワイシャツ 'business shirt' (overgeneralization of 'white shirt')
- ラムネ '*ramune*' (early borrowing of 'lemonade')
- カミハエール 'a product for growing hair' (髪 'hair' + 生える 'grow')
- セキナオール 'a product for treating a cough' (咳 'cough' + 治す 'cure')
- オタッキー 'an *otaku*-like person' (オタク '*otaku*' + -y)
- グラサン 'sunglasses' (inversion of サン and グラ from サングラス 'sunglasses')

文字と例 Kanji with examples

305. 返 かえ(す) ヘン   return   返

1. 手紙を返す   return a letter

2. 返すわけにもいかないなあ。   I can't very well return it. Considering
    せっかく買ってもらったんだ   that she bought it for me . . .
    し……。

3.		返事(へんじ)(する)	response
4.		あの人メール見ないから返事するわけないと思うよ。	That person doesn't check his email so I don't expect he'll reply.
5.		昨日までに返事するって言ってたくせにまだ返事してないの。	Even though he said he would reply by yesterday, he hasn't yet.
6.	+	返送(へんそう)(する)	return, sending back
7.		できれば来週までに返送したいんですが、間に合わせられますか。	If possible I'd like to return this by next week, but will you be able to manage okay?

306. 映 うつ(す) は(える) ば(え) エイ (See kanji #307.)   project, shine   映

1.	#	映(は)える	shine, be noticeable
2.	+	X 映(ば)え	X-worthy
3.		写真映え(する)	picture worthy
4.		SNS 映え(する)	SNS worthy
8.		SNS 映えする人気のスポット	a popular spot that is SNS worthy
9.	#	映(うつ)す	project (something)

307. 画 カク ガ   image, stroke   画

1.		映画(えいが)	movie
2.		待ち合わせ場所は映画館でいいかな。	Is it okay if the movie theater is the place to meet?
3.	+	画(かく)	draw, paint, sketch, stroke of a kanji
4.		この漢字って何画かわかんない？	Do you know how many strokes this kanji has?
5.	+	動画(どうが)	motion picture, movie
6.		この動画めっちゃおもしろいよ。	This movie is very interesting.
7.	#	洋画(ようが)	Western movie

308. 音 おと オン   sound   音

1.		音(おと)	sound
2.		音読(おんよ)み	Chinese reading (of a character)

3.		長音 (ちょうおん)		long vowel	
4.		五十音 (ごじゅうおん)		Japanese syllabary	
5.		発音(する) (はつおん)		pronunciation	
6.		これってどう発音すればいいの？		How should I pronounce this?	

309. 楽　　たの(しい)　ガク　ラク　　fun, enjoyable　　楽

1.	楽しい (たの)		fun, enjoyable
2. +	楽しむ (たの)		enjoy (something)
3.	今日はみんなとの時間を楽しむために来ました。		I came for the purpose of enjoying the time with everyone.
4.	音楽 (おんがく)		music
5.	楽(な) (らく)		comfortable
6. +	洋楽 (ようがく)		Western music
7.	洋楽のアーティストで好きなのはだれ？		Among Western music artists, who do you like?

310. 絵　　え　カイ　　drawing, picture　　絵

1.	絵 (え)		drawing, picture
2.	アマチュアなのに絵が上手なんです。		Despite being an amateur, his drawing is good.
3.	プロのくせに絵が下手なんです。		Despite being a pro, his drawing is bad.
4. +	理絵 (りえ)		[female given name]
5.	理絵ちゃんにまかせるわけにはいかないよ。		I can't very well leave it up to Rie.
6.	理絵ちゃんにはできるわけないよ。		There is no way Rie can do it.
7. #	絵画 (かいが)		picture

311. 道　　みち　ドウ　　road, way　　道

1.	道 (みち)		road, way
2.	どうすんのよ。道もわかんないくせに。		What will you do? You don't even know the way.
3.	ナビがないんだから、道分かるわけないじゃん。		I don't have GPS, so no way do I know how to get there.

4.		茶道		tea ceremony
5.		茶道部に入らせてもらいたいと思っています。		I'm thinking of joining the tea club.
6. +		書道		calligraphy
7.		合気道		aikido
8.		合気道を始めて5年になりました。		It's been five years since I started aikido.

312. 取 と(る) シュ　　　　　take　　　　取

1. お皿を取る — take a plate
2. それ、取ってもらえますか。 — Can I have you take that for me?
3. 聞き取り — listening
4. 明日の聞き取りクイズってどのレッスンだったか覚えてる？ — Do you remember which lesson was for tomorrow's listening quiz?
5. + 取り急ぎ — in haste
6. 取り急ぎのご連絡をさせていただきます。 — Allow me to inform you in haste.
7. 取り急ぎ、ご連絡まで。 — In haste, just to keep you informed.
8. # 取得(する) — acquisition

313. 趣 シュ　　　　　interest　　　　趣

1. 趣味 — hobby
2. 趣味: 絵、映画、音楽 (洋楽) — hobbies: drawing, movies, music (Western music)
3. プロみたいにできるんだから趣味でやってるわけないよ。 — She can do it like a pro, so it's unlikely that she is just doing it as a hobby.
4. ゲームが趣味のくせにこのゲームクリアしてないんだって。 — His hobby is video games, but I heard he hasn't beat this game yet.
5. 趣味で先月から合気道を始めました。 — I started aikido as a hobby starting last month.
6. コスプレを趣味としている人はコスプレイヤーって呼ばれています。 — A person whose hobby is cosplay is called a cosplayer.

Now go to the Activity Book for 練習.

シーン 19-9R　けが人が出なかったからいいようなものの
Good thing there were no injuries

This is a local news article that Hiroshi shared online.

テキスト Text

川村　博

福沢大学　改装工事中の７号館で火事　けが人なし

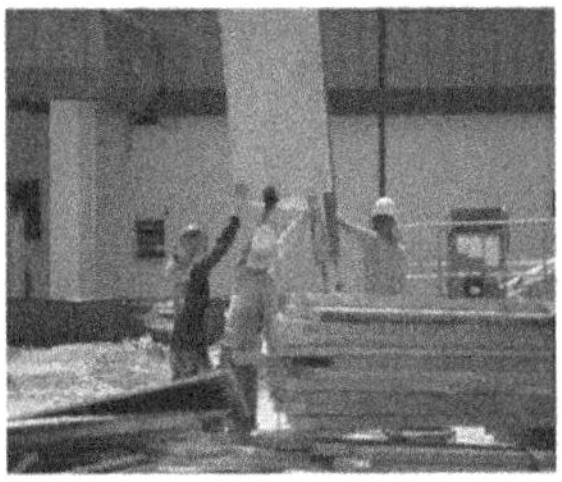

５日朝、福沢大学で改装工事中の７号館で火事が起きました。
けが人はなく、火は午前９時に消し止められました。
５日午前８時半ごろ、福沢市にある福沢大学で、「改装工事中の７号館から煙が出ている」という通報が消防にありました。

改装工事中の七号館で火事。けが人が出なかったからいいようなものの、すぐ反対の六号館のクラスは予定より２時間遅れてスタート。実は先週も事故があったらしい。ここの工事の危なさは、もう他人事とは思えないし、個人的にはあり得ない。

リアクション　　コメント

ブライアン・ワン: え〜！マジですか？

コメントしましょう！

そういうわけにはいきませんし……。

#改装工事(かいそうこうじ)	renovation
+〜号館(ごうかん)	classifier for naming buildings
+火事(かじ)	fire
#煙(けむり)	smoke
#通報(つうほう)(する)	report to the police
+けが人(にん)	injured person
#事故(じこ)	accident

Hiroshi Kawamura
Fire at Renovation Construction of Building No. 7 at Fukuzawa University – No Injuries
On the morning of the fifth, a fire broke out in Building No. 7, which is undergoing renovation, at Fukuzawa University.
There were no injuries and the fire was extinguished at 9:00 a.m.
Around 8:30 a.m. on the 5th, a call was made to the fire department saying that
"smoke is coming out of Building No. 7 under renovation" at Fukuzawa University in Fukuzawa City . . .

A fire in Building No. 7 under renovation. Good thing there were no injuries, but classes at Building No. 6 just opposite (of Building No. 7) started two hours behind schedule. I heard there was actually an accident last week, too. I can't think about the dangers involved in this construction as someone else's problem, and personally find it unacceptable.

Brian: What? Really?

Between the lines

BTL 3 Listening to and reading news stories

There are many podcasts and online articles to practice listening and reading in Japanese. Listening to and reading news stories in Japanese is a good habit to take up as it allows you to be familiar with topics that are relevant to Japanese people – giving you something to talk about when you speak with them. Knowing how news stories are formatted is helpful for understanding articles and podcasts that seem to be difficult at first. Whether you are listening to or reading news stories, the first part of a news story almost always summarizes the key points such as what happened, when it happened, where it happened, and who is involved, etc. Do not worry if you do not understand everything at first; key facts are often repeated with additional details later.

BTL 4 Becoming proficient in reading by using multiple reading strategies

Inexperienced readers have a tendency to rely on a limited number of reading strategies. For instance, it takes a long time for some language learners to read because they feel "responsible" for understanding all "assignments" word for word and so they look up every word they do not know. While it is not a bad strategy to look up words, reading can become a daunting and boring task if it is the only strategy you are relying on.

Proficient readers are selective and rarely read word for word when they read things like novels, newspapers, social media, and manga. Consider using some of the following reading strategies that proficient readers use:

- (if possible) listen to the text before reading
- get accustomed to natural reading speed by listening to the audio (if available) while following the text
- take the time to read the title and guess the contents
- gather background information about the topic and author
- think about the intent behind the text
- scan for key ideas and words
- read the introduction and summary to identify the most relevant section for you to read
- gauge your own reading ability and interests by asking questions such as "What percentage of the reading am I understanding?" and "How is this topic relevant to me or others?"
- make time in your daily schedule to discuss what you read with others

If you are struggling to read in Japanese, seek advice from others by asking what kind of reading strategies and resources they are using.

BTL 5 Using online resources and apps

There are many online resources and apps that can be used as dictionaries, translators, and furigana generators. Proficient readers make use of these resources effectively. While inexperienced readers may think it's enough to just determine English equivalents, proficient readers take the time to investigate how words are used in the target language by paying attention to things like word class, formality, and word combinations.

While online translations are accessible, it is difficult for translation devices to take into account background factors such as the intent of the writer and the intended reader. Proficient readers may make use of online translations to confirm their understanding, but they know when and how to doubt the accuracy of online translations.

文字と例 Kanji with examples

314.	他 ほか　タ		other	他
	1.	他の人		other people
	2.	すみません。その日は他の人に頼まれていることがあって……。		Sorry, I have something I was asked to do by another person on that day.

3.		その他(た)	other
4.	+	他人(たにん)	others, outsider
5.	+	他人事(たにんごと)	other person's affairs
6.		家族だったからいいようなもの、他人だったら大変なことになってたよ。	Good thing that it was (just) family, but it would have been terrible if it was someone else.

315. 実 み・ジツ　　fruit　　実

1.		実(じつ)は	actually
2.		実は絵が趣味なんです。	Actually, my hobby is drawing.
3.		これって実は動かせるんじゃないの？	This is actually movable, right?
4.	+	実(じつ)を言うと	to tell the truth
5.		実を言うと、仕事は先週辞めたんだ。	To tell the truth, I quit work last week.
6.	+	実(じつ)に	truly
7.		この映画は音楽が実にすばらしい！	The music of this movie is truly wonderful!
8.	#	真実(しんじつ)	truth
9.	#	木の実(き・み)	fruit

316. 的 てき　　-like, target　　的

1.		目的(もくてき)	purpose
2.		個人の学習目的に合ったカリキュラム	a curriculum that is suited for individualized study
3.		X 的(てき)	-like, -ic
4.		日本的な考え方	a Japanese way of thinking
5.		僕的には、て言うか僕としては合気道の方が楽しいと思うな。	Personally, well, as for me, I think aikido is more fun.
6.		社会的(な)	social
7.		文学的(な)	literary
8.	+	個人的(こじんてき)(な)	personal

9.	個人的には問題ないはずだけど……。		Personally, there should be no problem, but . . .
10. ¥	実用的(な)		practical
11. ¥	積極的(な)		active, positive, optimistic

317. 予 よ　　　foresee

1.	予約(する)	reservation
2.	実は予約があるわけではないんです。	Actually it's not that I have an appointment.
3.	今から予約を取るわけにもいかないしなあ。	And I can't make a reservation now either.
4.	予約するの忘れていたくせに。	Even though I had forgotten to make a reservation.
5.	今日はもう終わっちゃったから、明日予約するしかないね。	It is already finished today, so there is no other option but to make a reservation for tomorrow.
6.	要予約	reservation/appointment needed
7.	NEW! スカイビルナウ見学要予約	NEW! Sky Building Now reservation needed for visit
8. ¥	天気予報	weather forecast
9. #	予言(する)	vision

318. 定　さだ(める)　テイ　　　set, decide

1.	予定	plan
2.	予定よりかなり遅れてしまい申し訳ありませんでした。	I'm terribly sorry that it was quite behind schedule.
3.	予定としては来月から始めたいと思ってるんだけど……。	As for the schedule, I'm thinking that I'd like to start it next month.
4.	他の人の予定も確かめておくべきだったんじゃない？	You should have checked others' schedules, right?
5.	冬の予定ってもう決まってますか。	Is the schedule for winter already decided?
6.	夏休みなのに予定がなくて、つまんないな。	It's summer vacation but I don't have plans . . . bor-ing.
7. #	定める	set (something)

37

319. 工 コウ ク　work　工

1. 工事(する) — construction
2. 工事する必要って本当にある？ — Is there really a need for construction?
3. 工事中のため要注意！ — It's under construction, so pay attention.
4. 工学 — engineering
5. 大学では工学を勉強するつもりです。 — I plan to study engineering in college.
6. 工場 — factory, workshop
7. この工場に行くのにはどの道を行けばいいですか。 — Which way should I go in order to get to this factory?
8. # 大工 — carpenter

320. 危 あぶな(い) キ　dangerous　危

1. 危ない — dangerous
2. 危ないよ！歩きながらのスマートフォン — It's dangerous (to use) a smartphone while walking
3. ベビーカーに子どもを乗せたままエレベーターは危ない。 — It's dangerous to get on an elevator with the children in a stroller.
4. 危ないっ！車は急に止まれない。 — Watch out! Cars can't stop suddenly.
5. 危な過ぎる若者のセルフィー — selfies by young people that are too dangerous
6. 一人で降りるのは大人でも危ない。 — It's dangerous to disembark alone even for adults.
7. だれにも当たらなかったからいいようなものの、本当に危なかったよ。 — It's good that it didn't hit anyone, but it was really dangerous.
8. # 危険(な) — danger

321. 反 ハン (See kanji #322.)　opposite　反

322. 対 タイ　compete, versus　対

1. 3対1 — 3-1 (score)
2. ジャイアンツ対カープ — Giants vs. Carps

3.	反対(する)	oppose
4.	この問題のこと、昨日は反対してたくせに、どうして？	You were against (us) on this problem yesterday, but how come?
5.	他の人に反対されるわけないよ。	There is no way that it will be opposed by others.
6. ¥	絶対(に)	absolutely

Now go to the Activity Book for 練習.

Then do 評価 activities, including 読んでみよう, 書き取り, and 書いてみよう.

そういうわけにはいきませんし……。

第20幕
Act 20

聞(き)かずにはいられなくなって……。
I couldn't help but ask ...

過(す)ぎたるは及(およ)ばざるが如(ごと)し。
Too much of a good thing.

◆ 話す・聞く

Scene 20-1 お帰りになりました。
She went home.

Kanda-san is looking for Yagi-bucho in order to check on the status of the proposal he submitted. She has gone home early.

The script

神田	サーシャ
部長は？	お帰りになりました。
もう？珍しいですね。どこか悪いのかな。	ええ、熱っぽいし、体全体がだるいっておっしゃって……。
ああ、それは風邪の引きかけかもしれないですねえ。	ええ、それで……。
じゃあ、予算は？見ずに帰られちゃった？	いえ、ちゃんとご覧になりました。上に回してくださるそうです。

Kanda	Sasha
Where's the division chief?	She went home.
Already? That's unusual. Maybe something is wrong.	She said she felt feverish and sluggish all over . . .
Oh, it might be that she's coming down with a cold.	Right, so . . .
Well, what about the budget? Did she go home without looking at it?	No, she took a look. And said she would pass it along to the next level.

単語と表現

名詞

Verb stem + かけ	on the verge of X-ing
予算(よさん)	estimate, budget
数字(すうじ)	numeral, figure
依頼書(いらいしょ)	application, written request
手続(てつづ)き	paperwork process

動詞

お帰(かえ)りになる↑ (-U; お帰りになった)	go home (honorific)
おいでになる↑ (-U; おいでになった)	go (honorific)
ご覧(らん)になる↑ (-U; ご覧になった)	look (honorific)
Verb stem + かける (-RU; 〜かけた)	begin (but not finish)
渡(わた)す (-U; 渡した)	circulate, pass along
引(ひ)く (-U; 引いた)	pull, catch (a disease)

形容詞

熱(ねつ)っぽい	feverish
〜っぽい	-ish, -like (usually negative)
風邪(かぜ)っぽい	feel like a cold (is coming on)
だるい	sluggish, dull

表現

X 全体(ぜんたい)	whole, all over X
風邪(かぜ)を引(ひ)く	catch a cold
Verb 〜ず(に)	without X-ing, not X-ing

Behind the scenes

BTS 1 Honorific お + Verb stem + に + なる↑

In Act 13 you saw the honorific-passive polite form (for example 帰られる↑). An alternative honorific form consists of the polite prefix お〜 with a Verb stem followed by particle に and some form of なる. This new form is a bit more polite than the honorific passive, and is limited in the number of verbs that occur in the pattern.

先生、来週のワークショップにお出になるそうですね。	Professor, I heard that you're going to appear in next week's workshop.
バスをお降りになったら、そのまままっすぐお進みください。	When you get off the bus, continue on straight ahead.

BTS 2 Verb stem 〜かける

You have seen かける as a stand-alone Verb with a basic meaning of 'hang' or 'suspend,' but you have also seen that it has a number of English equivalents including 'wear (glasses),' 'put on top,' and 'pour.' When かける combines with the stem of some Verbs, it has yet another meaning: 'be about to' or 'begin to.'

悪い人だと知らなかったので、仕事を引き受けかけてしまいました。	I didn't know he was a bad guy and ended up starting to do some work for him.
起きかけてたんだけど、また寝ちゃった。	I started to get up but fell back asleep.
駅の前で部長を見かけてね、話しかけたんだけど、気がつかずにそのまま行っちゃった。	I thought I saw the division chief in front of the station, so I started talking to her, but she went on without noticing me.

BTS 3 Negative Verb form 〜ず(に)・ない(で)

In addition to the common negative form of Verbs (〜ない) there is an alternative form that ends in 〜ず. Replace 〜ない with 〜ず for all verbs except する which becomes せず and くる which becomes こず.

仕事関係の食事って言いながら、全然仕事せず・しないじゃない？	Even though she says it's a meal related to work, we don't do any work, right?

This negative form followed by に is used as a manner expression – it tells what didn't happen before what follows: 妹を待たずに、帰りました。 'I went home without waiting for my sister.' An alternative to the 〜ず form is the 〜ないで form: 妹を待たないで、帰りました。 There is very little difference between these two, except that the 〜ないで form can be used in negative requests (待たないでください 'Please don't wait') while the 〜ずに form cannot.

一人で全部食べてしまわずに・しまわないで、少しは僕のためにも残しておいてよね。	Please leave a little for me instead of eating it all yourself.
どうぞ、お待ちにならずに・ならないで、お先にお召し上がりください。	Please go ahead and eat without waiting.

The combination 〜ずにはいられない is equivalent to the English 'can't help but . . .'

言いたくはないけど、ひとこと文句を言わずにはいられませんでした。	I didn't want to say anything but I couldn't help but speak up to complain.
あまりおいしいのでで、お腹はいっぱいなのに、もう一つ、もう一つと食べずにはいられなくなりますよ。	It is so delicious that, even though you're full, you can't help but eat one more, one more.

Now go to the Activity Book for 練習 and 腕試し.

Scene 20-2 かえってよくないよ。
On the contrary, it's not good.

Brian went to a hot spring with members of the aikido club and has soaked in the bath several times.

The script

ブライアン	川村
あー、気持ちよかった。やっぱり温泉っていいですねえ。	あんまり一度に何度も入るとかえってよくないよ。今日はそのくらいにしておいたら？
あ、あ、あれですね。「過ぎたるは及ばざるが如し。」	お、よく知ってるね。

Brian	Kawakami
Ah, that felt good. *Onsen* are great, aren't they.	Still, it's not good to go in so many times at once. How about that's about it for today?
Hold on, hold on, what is it they say – "Too much of a good thing."	Oh, you're sharp!

単語と表現

名詞

ことわざ	proverb
格言(かくげん)	saying, proverb
恥(はじ)	shame, embarrassment
種類(しゅるい)	type, variety
忠告(ちゅうこく)(する)	advice

数詞

~歩

1歩 (いっぽ)	one step
2歩 (にほ)	two steps
3歩 (さんぽ)	three steps
4歩 (よんほ)	four steps
5歩 (ごほ)	five steps
何歩 (なんぽ)	how many steps

表現

かえって	on the contrary, rather
そのくらい	about that much
過ぎたるは及ばざるが如し。	Too much of a good thing.
千里の道も一歩から。	A journey of a thousand miles begins with a single step.
急がば回れ。	More haste, less speed. (lit. 'If you are in a hurry, go the long way.')
時は金なり。	Time is money.
聞くは一時の恥、聞かぬは一生の恥。	To ask may lead to shame for a moment, but not to ask leads to shame for a lifetime.
明日の百より今日の五十。	A bird in the hand is worth two in the bush.
類は友を呼ぶ。	Birds of a feather flock together.
好きこそものの上手なれ。	What one likes, one does well.
七転び八起き	Fall down seven times, get up eight.
目は口ほどに物を言い。	Eyes say as much as words.
可愛い子には旅をさせよ。	If you love your child, send them out into the world.
寝る子は育つ。	The child that sleeps well grows up well.
お	oh (expression of slight surprise)

Behind the scenes

BTS 4 ことわざ : Using proverbs

You have seen a Japanese proverb – ことわざ – begin each Act in this textbook. ことわざ can help you to understand Japanese culture and history. Many come from classical Chinese (一石二鳥), but others are native to Japan (一期一会 from the tea ceremony). Note that many take the form of 四字熟語.

When they are appropriately used, ことわざ can make your Japanese sound accomplished. You can also study grammar through ことわざ. Think about the use of particles and verb forms in 千里の道も一歩から, 類は友を呼ぶ, or 目は口ほどに物を言い. As you learn more about Japanese, you will realize that there is classical language in expressions such as 時は金なり and 聞くは一時の恥、聞かぬは一生の恥.

A: このチームには素晴らしい人がいっぱいいますね。 B: 類は友を呼ぶって言うでしょう？	A: There are a lot of amazing people on this team, aren't there! B: They say "birds of a feather flock together," don't they?
待たせますねえ。「時は金なり」って知らないのかなあ。	They make us wait, don't they. I wonder if they don't know "time is money."

Now go to the Activity Book for 練習 and 腕試し.

Scene 20-3 治してはくれないけど……。
It won't cure you, but ...

Sasha is showing signs of a cold. Kanda-san offers her a remedy.

The script

神田	サーシャ
試してみませんか、これ。	何ですか？
栄養ドリンク。	ええ？いいですよ。
飲むだけ飲んでみたら？騙されたと思って。	そうですか。じゃあ、いただきます。……お、意外とさっぱりした味ですね。
でしょ？治してはくれないけど、症状は抑えてくれますよ。	どうもご心配かけてすみません。

Kanda	Sasha
Want to try this?	What is it?
A nutritional drink.	What? It's okay.
Just try it. Trust me.	Really? All right, I'll have some. . . . Oh, it's surprisingly refreshing, isn't it.
Don't you think? It won't cure you, but it will lessen the symptoms.	I'm really sorry to make you worry.

単語と表現

名詞

栄養	nutrition
栄養ドリンク	nutritional drink
さっぱり	refreshing, clean

症状	symptoms
改善(する)	improvement
診断(する)	diagnosis
看護師	nurse
検査(する)	(medical) examination

動詞

試す (-U; 試した)	attempt, try out
騙す (-U; 騙した)	trick, cheat
治す (-U; 治した)	cure, heal
抑える (-RU; 抑えた)	curb, restrain
(X に)効く (-U; 効いた)	be effective for X
診る (-RU; 診た)	look over, assess

表現

騙されたと思って	trust me (lit. 'assume that you've been conned')
ご心配かけてすみません。	I'm sorry to make you worry.

Behind the scenes

BTS 5 Sentence + だけ

You saw できるだけ 'to the extent that one can' earlier. This is an example of a Sentence in combination with だけ where the meaning of だけ, depending on context, is 'just' or 'to the extent of.' 考えただけで, for example, means 'just thinking,' while できるだけ勉強したい。 means 'I want to study as much as possible.'

温泉？いいですねえ。考えただけで気持ちが良くなってきました。	Hot spring? That's nice. Just thinking about it, I feel better.

はい、どうぞ。今から１時間だけですよ！この袋(ふくろ)に詰(つ)められるだけ、全部(ぜんぶ)で２００円です。	Go ahead. It's only (valid) for one hour from now. As much as you can stuff in this bag, for all that, it's 200 yen.

In combination with the same verb in the 〜て form, typically followed by みる, this pattern means 'just try X-ing.'

今週中(ちゅう)にやれるだけやってみてください。	Please try and do as much as possible within this week.
覚(おぼ)えられるだけ覚えようと思って頑張(がんば)ったんだ。	I worked hard, hoping to memorize as much as I could.
できるだけのことはしてみますが、前(まえ)と同(おな)じように使(つか)えるようになるかどうか、お約束(やくそく)はできません。	I'll try doing my best, but whether you'll be able to use it the same way as before or not, I can't promise.

Now go to the Activity Book for 練習 and 腕試し.

Scene 20-4 肺が弱ってるとか。
I heard your lungs are weak.

Brian overheard a conversation about someone in a homestay family being ill.

The script

ブライアン	お母さん
お母さん、起きてて大丈夫ですか？	え？なんのこと？
あ、あの、何か、肺が弱ってるとか……。	肺が？何言ってんの、ブライアン君。それタマちゃんよ。
タマちゃん？猫の？	そう。私はピンピンしてますよ。お陰様で。
なぁんだ。てっきりお母さんのことかと思って。あ、すみません。タマちゃん、大丈夫ですか？	まあ、高齢だからね。

Brian	Mother
Mother, is it all right for you to be up?	What? What do you mean?
Oh, ummm, something, I heard your lungs are weak.	My lungs? What are you talking about, Brian? What (you heard) was about Tama-chan.
Tama-chan? The cat?	Right. I am healthy as a horse. Thanks for asking.
Oh, so THAT'S it! I thought it was you. Oh, I'm sorry. Is Tama-chan all right?	Well, she's elderly, so . . .

単語と表現

名詞

肺	lungs
血管	blood vessel, vein

脳（のう）	brain
筋肉（きんにく）	muscle
神経（しんけい）	nerves
骨（ほね）	bone
心臓（しんぞう）	heart
腎臓（じんぞう）	kidney
肝臓（かんぞう）	liver
胃（い）	stomach
食中毒（しょくちゅうどく）	food poisoning
精神（せいしん）	mind, spirit
タマ	[a common name for cats]
ピンピン	healthy, lively
丈夫(な)（じょうぶ）	strong
ドキドキ	thump-thump
どんどん	drumming
ごろごろ	grumbling (stomach), thundering
ぶらぶら	swinging, rambling, leisurely
はらはら	heart beating rapidly
だらだら	sluggishly, slowly
すらすら	smoothly, easily
ぺらぺら	fluent, frivolous
ふらふら	dizzy, wandering
にこにこ	smiling
がんがん	intense, pounding (headache)
ひりひり	stinging, prickling (pain)
ぺこぺこ	famished, hungry
からから	parched, clattering
回復(する)（かいふく）	recovery, improvement
高齢（こうれい）	old age

動詞

弱る (-U; 弱った)	get weak
痩せる (-RU; 痩せた)	get thin
太る (-U; 太った)	get fat
折れる (-RU; 折れた)	get broken, fold
折る (-U; 折った)	break X, fold X

表現

何のこと？	What do you mean? What is it?
なんだ・なあんだ。	Oh, so that's it!
てっきり	surely

拡張

If you have a chronic medical condition that you may need to discuss with a Japanese physician, check the internet to find how the condition can be described in Japanese and check with a competent Japanese speaker to ensure you have an accurate description.

Behind the scenes

BTS 6 Physical conditions

Physical conditions such as the common cold (風邪), stiff shoulders (肩こり), lack of sleep (寝不足), allergy (アレルギー), overeating or over drinking (食べ過ぎ、飲み過ぎ), and fatigue (疲れ) tend to be discussed quite openly along with a variety of remedies that Western medicine might consider unconventional. Depending on the community, however, hospitalization and other serious ailments are considered inappropriate subjects for casual conversation.

呑んで効く肩こりの薬って、知ってます？	Do you know medicine that you can take that works against stiff shoulders?
ただの疲れだと軽く思わず、早めに医者に診てもらった方がいいんじゃないですか？	Instead of thinking that it's just fatigue, it's better to have a doctor look at it promptly, isn't it?

Now go to the Activity Book for 練習 and 腕試し.

Scene 20-5 やればやるほど楽(たの)しくなってくる。
The more you do it the more fun it gets to be.

Takashi saw some people running and was reminded of Amy's experience running a marathon.

The script

孝	エイミー
マラソン続(つづ)けてる？	うん。やればやるほど楽(たの)しくなってくるんだ。
確(たし)かに、健康(けんこう)にもいいよね。毎日(まいにち)欠(か)かさず走(はし)ってるの？	いやいや。私(わたし)は1日おき。それもサボりがちの週(しゅう)もあるし。
ああ、毎日(まい)走(はし)らなければならないっていうわけでもないんだ。	まあね。

Takashi	Amy
Are you still working on your marathon?	Yeah. The more I do it, the more fun it is.
It must also be good for your health. Are you running without fail every day?	No, no. For me, every other day. I'm also likely to skip some weeks.
Aah, so it's not as if you have to run every day.	Well, you know.

単語と表現

名詞

ダンス	dance
トレーニング	training
運動(うんどう)(する)	(physical) exercise
ガーデニング	gardening
散歩(さんぽ)(する)	walk (for pleasure)
(お)稽古(けいこ)	practice, training

健康(な) (けんこう)	health
Verb stem + がち (な・の)	liable to, apt to

動詞

踊る (-U; 踊った) (おど)	dance
欠かす (-U; 欠かした) (か)	miss, fail
サボる (-U; サボった)	skip (school), skip out
植える (-RU; 植えた) (う)	plant, grow
(X に)飽きる (-RU; 飽きた) (あ)	get tired of X

形容詞

苦しい (くる)	painful, distressing

表現

気に入る (き, い)	like, be pleased with
やればやるほど	the more I do it, the more . . .
健康にいい (けんこう)	good for one's health
INTERVAL おき	after every other INTERVAL

拡張

Find out a way to discuss your hobby or your favorite activity in Japanese. What is it called? How do you express the time intervals of your participation?

Behind the scenes

BTS 7 〜れば……〜ほど

A special use of the provisional is in combination with a non-past Verb plus ほど: Provisional X + Non-past X + ほど. The meaning is essentially equivalent to English 'the more X, the more . . .'

説明(せつめい)しようとすればするほど、かえって誤解(ごかい)されてしまって。	The more we try to explain, the more we're misunderstood.
住(す)めば住むほど、住みやすくなる家(いえ)	a house that is easier to live in, the more you live in it
批判(ひはん)が多(おお)ければ多いほど、頑張(がんば)ろうという気(き)になるんです。	The greater the criticism, the more I feel I want to keep at it.
複雑(ふくざつ)であればあるほど、時間もかかりますよね。	The more complex it is, the more time it takes, right?

Now go to the Activity Book for 練習 and 腕試し.

Scene 20-6 ブライアンの話(思い違い)
Brian's story (a misunderstanding)

Sakamoto-sensei asked about a miscommunication experience, and Brian recalled his recent misunderstanding regarding his homestay mother's health.

The script

ブライアン	坂本先生
この間家の人が、「肺が弱っている」って話しているのを聞いて、	あら。
てっきりお母さんのことだと思っちゃったんですよ。	まあ、そう。
で、心配だけど聞いたら失礼かと思って、2、3日悩んだんですけど、	そりゃそうだわねぇ。
でも、やっぱり聞かずにはいられなくなって、本人に聞いたんです。	そうしたら？
そしたらぁ、家で飼ってる猫のタマちゃんの話だったんです。	はは、そうだったんですか。猫ちゃんはかわいそうだけど、お母さんじゃなくてよかったですね。
ええ、それにしても、とんだ思い違いで、恥ずかしかったです。	まあ、勘違いはよくあることだから。

Brian	Sakamoto-sensei
The other day I heard a family member say that someone in the family has weak lungs . . .	Oh!
I was sure they were talking about the mother.	Right.
And so I worried and was beside myself for two or three days, thinking that it would be rude to ask.	Of course.

But in the end I couldn't help but ask, and so I did.	And then what (did she say)?
Then she told me that they were talking about their pet cat, Tama-chan!	Oh, so that was it. I feel sorry for the cat, but it's a good thing it's not the mom, right?
Yeah, but even so, it was an incredible misunderstanding on my part. I was embarrassed.	Look, we often get the wrong idea about things, so . . .

単語と表現

名詞

思い違い(する)	misunderstanding, false impression
勘違い(する)	mistaken idea, wrong guess
誤解(する)	misunderstanding
本人	the person in question, said person
知人	acquaintance
他人	another person, outsider
手術(する)	surgery
ワンちゃん	doggy
うっかり(する)	inadvertently, carelessly
安心(する)	relief, peace of mind

動詞

生まれる (-RU; 生まれた)	be born
産む (-U; 産んだ)	give birth to
驚く (-U; 驚いた)	be surprised

形容詞

恥ずかしい	embarrassing

表現

とんだ X	unthinkable X, awful X

Behind the scenes

BTS 8 Sentence Particle わ

The use of Sentence Particle わ depends a great deal on dialect/region as well as intonation. In Tokyo and with rising intonation (or in combination with other particles such as わね), わ is frequently referred to as a feminine particle – it is much more common in the speech of middle-aged and older women. On the other hand, both men and women use わ with falling intonation, especially in situations where something unexpected happens. If someone has been working on a puzzle for some time and suddenly something happens and the puzzle is suddenly solved, the response is likely to be something like あ、できたわ。 'Oh, it got done.' In the Kansai region, わ is used by both men and women for emphasis, and is a bit softer than よ.

あれ？ここ３丁目だよね？あ、違うわ。ごめん。	Huh? This is 3-chome, isn't it? Oh, it's not. Sorry.
さ、始めよう！遠慮しないで食べて。あ、お箸でてなかったわ。はい、これ。	Okay, let's begin! Don't hold back – eat! Oops, chopsticks aren't out. Here they are.

BTS 9 Contractions

You have seen numerous contractions that are typical of spoken language: 〜てしまう becomes 〜ちゃう, わからない becomes わかんない, なにか becomes なんか and です is a contraction of であります. In this Scene, Sakamoto-sensei uses そりゃそうだ where そりゃ is a contraction of それは. Needless to say, you will also hear こりゃ (これは), and ありゃ (あれは). Similarly, negative provisional (〜なければ) forms contract to 〜なきゃ and negative 〜なくては contracts to 〜なくちゃ. Keep in mind that these contractions are most typical of spoken language but can also be seen in informal writing among friends.

さ、宿題やんなきゃ！	Okay, we need to do homework!
そんな大事なこと、忘れちゃっちゃだめだよ。	You can't completely forget such an important thing!
ありゃ問題になるよ。	That's gonna become an issue, for sure.

BTS 10 More on storytelling

In this Scene, Sakamoto-sensei uses several strategies to encourage Brian to relate his anecdote (失敗談<ruby>しっぱいだん</ruby>).

(a) Recognition and a moderate level of surprise

あら is used when something comes to one's attention, often when it's something unexpected. It is more commonly used by female speakers. へえ is more gender-neutral. Likewise, ああ is more gender-neutral than まあ when indicating a moderate level of surprise.

(b) Approval

Sakamoto-sensei acknowledges that Brian's concern was justified. A more gender-neutral version would be そりゃそうだねえ。

(c) Interest in what happens next
(d) Comprehension and reaction
(e) Empathy

Now go to the Activity Book for 練習 and 腕試し.

Then do 評価 activities.

◆ 読み書き

シーン 20-7R 起承転結(きしょうてんけつ)
Introduction, development, twist, conclusion

Here are two four-frame comic strips that Brian's friend drew featuring Go the dog and Nyau the cat.

テキスト Text

+火山(かざん)	'volcano'
#フシギ(不思議(ふしぎ))	'mystery'

Volcano Museum	Fall seven times, stand up eight
The mystery of an astonishing volcano, please look from here.	A little more . . .
Wow.	Two more cards!
Press that button for an explanation.	I'm home. Rattle Scatter Oh no.
Boom! Heeheehee.	I'm sorry. Please don't be so disappointed. Don't give up. Fall seven times, stand up eight.

Between the lines

BTL 1 起承転結(きしょうてんけつ)

Japanese writers often compose their narratives and arguments following a structure called 起承転結(きしょうてんけつ). The 起(き) phase introduces relevant background information. The 承(しょう) phase provides a development that leads towards a twist in the story. The 転(てん) phase provides the twist or unexpected development – this is the climax of the story. Finally, the 結(けつ) phase ties up everything together. These four elements do not have to be equal in length in a text, so they may not line up with each cell in the 4コマ漫画(まんが) 'four-frame manga' just shown. An author may choose to spend more time in the 起 phase to provide additional background information – risking the possibility of audience boredom. Others may choose to end a story in the 転 phase without presenting a definitive conclusion – leaving the interpretation up to the audience. Familiarizing yourself with these elements will not only help you appreciate stories told in Japanese, but will also help you tell your own stories in Japanese more effectively.

BTL 2 Onomatopoeia in manga

You find a wide variety of onomatopoeic words in Japanese manga. They are written in styles and fonts that allow writers to express sounds and feelings. Were you able to tell the meaning of the following onomatopoeic words from the four-frame manga just shown without looking at the translations?

| ドカーン | boom | バラバラ | scatter |
| ガラガラ | rattle | ガーン | oh no (shocking feeling) |

BTL 3 Creative sentence endings: キャラ語尾(ごび)

Japanese speakers make use of creative sentence endings for unique or stereotypical effects. For example, onomatopoeic sounds such as ニャン and ワン may be added to the sentence ending of characters with cat-like or dog-like characteristics. Dialectal variations of です such as 〜だべ (Kanto and Tohoku dialect), 〜どす (Kyoto dialect), and 〜やで (Kansai dialect) may be added to indicate where characters are from. As you read manga or watch anime, look for creative sentence endings that highlight the unique background of characters.

Other examples include:

〜じゃ	old male characters	〜ザマス	mother of rich people
〜アル	Chinese speakers	〜たまえ	adds a sense of arrogance
〜ござる	samurai and ninja characters		

文字と例 Kanji with examples

323. 体 からだ　タイ　　　　　body　　　体

1. 体(からだ) — body
2. 体がだるくて動きたくない。 — My body is sluggish and I don't want to move.
3. お体にお気を付けてお過ごしください。 — Please take care of yourself.

4.		お体を大切になさってください。	Please take care of yourself
5.		疲れた体をリラックス！	Relax your tired body!
6.		全体(ぜんたい)	whole, entirety
7.		全体的にもう少し明るくできますか。	Can you make it brighter as a whole?

324. 熱　あつ(い)　ネツ　hot (other than temperature), intense　熱

1.		体(からだ)が熱(あつ)い。	I feel hot.
2.		お茶、熱いですから召し上がる時はお気を付けて。	The tea is hot so please be careful when you drink it.
3.	#	鉄(てつ)は熱(あつ)いうちに打(う)て。	Strike while the iron is hot.
4.		熱(ねつ)があるみたいです。	I seem to have a fever.
5.		まずは熱を下げる必要があります。	First of all, we need to lower the fever.
6.		熱は下がったけど、まだ治りかけです。	My fever went down, but I'm still getting over the cold.
7.		実は熱が下がらずに困っています。	Actually, my fever is not going down and I'm troubled.

325. 死　し(ぬ)　シ　die, activity halts, death　死

1.	母の死(し)	mother's death
2.	ペットが死(し)んでしまった。	My pet died.
3.	このステージ死(し)なずにクリアできる？	Can you clear this (video game) stage without dying?
4.	スマホが死んじゃった〜。	My smartphone is dead.
5.	あの仕事、死ぬほど大変だったので、辞めてしまいました。	The job was so hard I (thought I'd) die, so I quit.
6.	死にかけたことってありますか。	Have you had a near-death experience?

7.	#	九死に一生を得る。		A narrow escape from death.
8.	#	必死(な)		desperate

326. 引 ひ(く)　　　　pull, draw (a number), subtract　　　引

1.		引く	pull
2.		次は私に引かせてください。	Please let me draw next.
3.		お引きになられた番号をお持ちのまま、お待ちください。	Please wait, holding onto the number you drew.
4.		あんなに寒かったのに、よくカゼを引かないでいられましたね。	It was so cold, but you managed not to get sick.
5.		これを引くべきかどうか考えているところです。	I'm just thinking about whether I should draw this one or not.
6.	+	引き算	subtraction
7.		１００から５を引いてください。	Please subtract 5 from 100.
8.	+	引き出す	draw, pull out
9.	+	お引き出し	withdrawal
10.		昨日銀行からお金を引き出したんだけど、どこに行ったんだろう。	I withdrew money from the bank yesterday, but I wonder where it went.
11.		引き出し	drawer
12.		よかった、引き出しにしまってあった。	Thank goodness, it was put away in the drawer.
13.	#	引くに引けない	can't turn back now

327. 押 お(す)　　　　push　　　押

1.	ボタンを押す	push a button
2.	他の人を押さないで歩いてください。	Please walk without pushing others.

3.	ドアを押したり引いたりしてみたけど、開かなかった。	I tried things like pushing and pulling the door, but it didn't open.
4.	コントロールキーを押したまま、シフトボタンを押してください。	Please press the shift button while you press the control key.
5.	ちょっと危ないけど、みんなで一緒に押せる？	It's a little dangerous, but can we all push it together?
6.	音楽を聞きたい場合はこのボタンを押してください。	In case you want to listen to music, please push this button.

328. 転　ころ(ぶ)　テン　fall, roll

1.	転ぶ	fall down
2.	道で人が転んだ。	A person fell down on the street.
3.	とりあえず、転ばずにあそこまで行けるようにがんばろう。	For now, let's do our best to make it over there without falling down.
4.	自転車	bicycle
5.	運転(する)	driving
6. +	飲酒運転	driving while intoxicated
7. +	自動運転	automated driving
8.	飲酒運転はしてはいけません。	You must not drive while intoxicated.
9. +	転送(する)	transfer
10.	このメール、他の人にも転送してあげてください。	Please do others a favor and forward this email.

329. 起　お(きる)　キ　arise, wake up, occur

1.	予定通りに7時に起きてください。	Please wake up at seven as scheduled.
2.	子どもを起こさないように注意してください。	Be careful not to wake up the child.
3.	朝に弱くてなかなか起きられず、困っています。	I'm not a morning person and I can't quite wake up, so I'm troubled.

4.	七転び八起き	fall seven times, stand up eight
5.	七転び八起き。あきらめずにがんばろう。	Fall seven times, stand up eight. Let's do our best without giving up.
6. +	Xが起こる	X occurs
7.	何かが起こってからじゃ遅いんですよ。	It will be too late if something happens.
8. #	起承転結	introduction, development, twist, conclusion
9. #	起死回生	miraculous recovery

330. 説 セツ — explain, preach, theory

1.	説明(する)	explain, explanation
2.	説明せずにいられないんです。	It's that I can't help but explain.
3.	この映画、説明がないと訳が分からないよ。	I can't follow this movie without an explanation.
4.	今説明するわけにもいかないので、また後ほど。	I can't explain it now, so at a later time.
5. +	小説	novel, fiction
6.	この小説って話がちょっとややこしいんだよね。	The story of this novel is a bit complicated, isn't it?
7. +	説	theory
8.	どちらの説も信じられないなあ。	I can't believe either theory.

331. 覧 ラン — look, view

1.	ご覧になってください。	Please look.
2.	映画の始めから終わりまでご覧ください。	Please watch the movie from the beginning to the end.
3.	この絵はもうご覧になりましたか。	Have you seen this picture?

4.	もう一度ご覧になってお確かめになってください。	Please check by looking at it again.
5.	反対の方もご覧ください。	Please take a look at the opposite side.
6.	ご覧になった絵の他にもいろいろございますので、お楽しみください。	There are various things other than the picture you looked at, so please enjoy them.

Now go to the Activity Book for 練習.

シーン 20-8R 寝耳に水 An astonishing surprise

Here is one of the slides that Brian prepared for his presentation on *kotowaza*.

テキスト Text

寝耳に水

読み方：ねみみにみず
意味：思ってなかった知らせにびっくりすること
由来：
- 水の音が聞こえる説
- 寝ている時に耳に水が入る説

例文：
- ジャイアンツのあのプレーヤー、試合で見なくなったから心配してたんだけど、もう辞めてたなんて、寝耳に水ですよ。
- 試験が明日だったなんて、寝耳に水だけど、今からやれるだけやってみるよ。

#由来(する)　　　　　　　　　origin, etymology,

Nemimi ni mizu

Reading: Nemimi ni mizu
Meaning: an astonishing surprise

Etymology:
- Theory – Hearing water sounds
- Theory – Water dripping in the ear while sleeping

Example sentences :
- I was worried about that player from the Giants because I didn't see him in the game. His quitting (the team) was a great surprise.
- The exam being tomorrow was news to me, but I'll do as much as I can now.

Between the lines

BTL 4 名詞（めいし）止（と）め Ending with noun

In written style, Nouns and Noun phrases are used frequently in order to concisely present points – omitting formality and politeness markings. In that sense, they are a depersonalized way of presenting information. A Noun with a Sentence modifier (e.g., 心配（しんぱい）な天気（てんき）) or a Sentence ending with a Noun without a form of です (e.g., 天気が心配) is called 名（めい）詞（し）止（と）め. You will see these in advertising, messaging, listing, and in slide presentations. The text for this Scene presents two possible theories on the origin of the expression 寝（ね）耳（みみ）に水（みず） in the format of 名詞止め.

Compound Nouns are also common in titles, headings, and captions. For example, in １０時開（かい）始（し）, the last two kanji (開始) comprise a compound, indicating when an activity is to begin. The relationship between the activity (開始) and the Noun that precedes it (１０時) becomes clear from convention and the context. Thus, Phrase Particles that are required in a Sentence １０時に始（はじ）まります are omitted in such compounds.

Japanese presentation slides usually are full of information. 名詞止め forms are a practical way to concisely convey a large volume of information.

BTL 5 Identifying and describing kanji: 部首（ぶしゅ）

There are many words in Japanese that sound identical but are written using different kanji. For example, both 河村（かわむら） and 川村（かわむら） are common family names. The different kanji used can be described in order to distinguish the two. The first kanji includes a component or a radical 氵（さんずい） which occurs in many kanji that are associated with water, including 海（うみ） 'ocean,' 汁（しる） 'soup,' 池（いけ） 'pond,' and 河（かわ） 'river.' One might hear さんずいのカワです 'It's *kawa* with the *sanzui* radical' or 三本川（さんぼんかわ）のカワです 'It's *kawa* with three strokes ('shaped like a stream')' to identify the correct kanji for a particular name.

The recurring component parts with which kanji are often classified and identified are called 部首（ぶしゅ） 'major radicals.' In a kanji dictionary (paper or electronic), radicals are often used to narrow down the search. All kanji that share the same major radical (e.g., the *sanzui*) are presented in the order of the number of strokes. Thus the four kanji with the 氵 radical are listed in the following order: 汁 (5 strokes), 池 (6 strokes), 河 (8 strokes), and 海 (9 strokes).

Here are a few more common major radicals.

言	ゴンベン	語, 説, 訓, 評, 計
亻	ニンベン	他, 似, 休, 体, 仕

宀	ウかんむり	安, 宅, 守, 家, 室
囗	くにがまえ	国, 四, 回, 園
辶	シンニョウ	道, 近, 送, 迎

Other (non-major) radicals that occur in a character may suggest the *on*-reading of the kanji. For example, 姉, 市, and 柿 all share the シ reading, and 寺, 時, 持, and 鰤 all share ジ as their *on*-reading. While the major radicals are useful when searching for a kanji or describing kanji, the non-major radicals are often useful in guessing the *on*-reading of a kanji in a compound.

文字と例 Kanji with examples

332. 試 シ　　　　　try, attempt　　試

   1. 試合(する)　　　　　match
   2. 次の試合、やれるだけがんばってみるから見てね。　　I'll do as much as I can for the next match, so please watch it.
   3. 雨が降っておりますが、試合は予定通り行われます。　　It is raining, but the match will go on as scheduled.
   4. 合気道の試合は8時開始です。　　The aikido match will start at eight.
   5. 試合を始める事に反対している人がいるんです。　　There are people who oppose the idea of starting the match.
   6. # 試食・試飲　　tasting

333. 数 かず　スウ　　　number, count　　数

   1. 数が多い。　　There are many numbers.
   2. 終わりの数から始まりの数を引いてください。　　Please subtract the first number from the last number.
   3. 数字　　number
   4. もう一度言っていただけますか。私、数字に弱いので……。　　Could I have you repeat it? I'm not good with numbers . . .
   5. 数学　　mathematics
   6. 数学的に考えないと分からない問題　　a problem that cannot be understood unless you think mathematically
   7. + 理数系　　science and mathematics type
   8. + 日数　　number of days

9.		仕事に入る日数は後で話し合って決めましょう。		Let's decide how many days you are working by discussing it with each other later.
10.	#	お手数おかけします。		I'm sorry for troubling you.

334. 寝　ね(る)　シン　　sleep　　寝

1.		部屋で寝る	sleep in a room
2.		遅くまで仕事だったから少し寝かしてもらっていいですか？	I was working late, so can you allow me to sleep a little?
3.		これから試合が始まるっていうのに、寝ている場合じゃないよ。	The match is starting now, it's not time to be sleeping.
4.	+	寝過ごす	sleep through
5.		電車で寝過ごしてしまい、家に帰れなくなった。	I slept through on the train, so I couldn't go home.
6.	#	寝台	bed

335. 足　あし　た(りる)　ソク　　foot, leg, be sufficient　　足

1.		足が短い	my legs are short
2.	+	手足	arms and legs
3.		足りる	suffice
4.		時間が足りない。	There is not enough time.
5.		不足(する)	lack, insufficiency
6.		寝不足が引き起こす問題	problems triggered by lack of sleep
7.		やれるだけやってみたけど、まだまだ練習不足。	We tried as much as we could, but we are still lacking practice.
8.	#	一足	one sock/shoe
9.	#	遠足	field trip

336. 耳　みみ　ジ　　ear　　耳

1.		耳が聞こえない	cannot hear
2.	+	耳が遠い	poor hearing
3.		耳が遠くて聞こえず、意味が全く分かりませんでした。	I couldn't hear due to my poor hearing, so I couldn't understand it at all.

4.	#	空耳(そらみみ)	mishearing
5.	#	聞く耳持たない(きくみみもたない)	have no ears to listen
6.	#	馬の耳に念仏(うまのみみにねんぶつ)	preaching to deaf ears (lit. 'Buddha in a horse's ear')
7.	#	中耳炎(ちゅうじえん)	middle ear infection

337. 首 くび シュ　　neck

1.		首が長い(くびがながい)	his neck is long
2.		首が上がらず、動かしにくいときってどうすれば治りますか。	What should I do to get better when I can't lift my head (lit. 'my neck can't be lifted') and it's hard to move?
3.		首から下が動かなくなってしまう場合もあります。	There are cases in which your body from neck to toe becomes immobile.
4.	+	部首(ぶしゅ)	(major) radical of a kanji
5.	¥	首相(しゅしょう)	prime minister
6.	#	百人一首(ひゃくにんいっしゅ)	the Hundred Poems by One Hundred Poets
7.	#	借金で首が回らない(しゃっきんでくびがまわらない)	being up to one's neck (in debt)
8.	#	首を長くしてお待ちしています。(くびをながくして)	We are really looking forward to it. (lit. 'We are stretching our necks out in anticipation.')

338. 声 こえ セイ　　voice

1.		声が大きい(こえがおおきい)	her voice is loud
2.		声が出ないわけではないのですが、話すのがちょっと大変なんです。	It's not that I can't use my voice, but it's a little difficult to speak.
3.		死ななかったからよかったようなものの、びっくりしてしばらく声が出せなくなりました。	Good thing I didn't die, but I was surprised and couldn't use my voice for a while.
4.		熱があって声も出ないくせに、カラオケ行くの？	Even though you have a fever and can't even use your voice, you're still going to *karaoke*?
5.		男としては声が高い方ですね。	My voice is relatively high for a man.
6.	#	鶴の一声(つるのひとこえ)	a word from the throne
7.	#	音声(おんせい)	sound

339.	心	こころ　シン		heart (mind)	心
	1.	人の心		a person's heart	
	2.	心温まるストーリー		a heart-warming story	
	3.	心からのありがとうの気持ちを伝えたいです。		I want to convey my feelings of gratitude from my heart.	
	4.	忙しくて実は心も体もボロボロです。		I'm so busy and actually I'm physically and emotionally worn out.	
	5.	何か心に残ったことはありますか。		Do you have anything that is memorable (lit. 'remained in your heart')?	
	6.	# 一心に		wholeheartedly	
	7.	# 以心伝心		be in tune with each other	
340.	配	くば(る)　ハイ		hand out	配
	1.	心配(する)		worry	
	2.	どうぞご心配なさらずに。		Please don't worry.	
	3.	うちの父が心配しているわけないよ。		There is no way my dad is worried.	
	4.	工事が予定通りに行くか心配です。		I'm worried that the construction will proceed as scheduled.	
	5.	心配なのは返事が来るかどうかです。		What I'm worried about is whether I get a response or not.	
	6.	心配する必要はありませんので、どうぞ気になさらないでください。		There is no need for you to worry, so please don't mind it.	
	7.	+ 配信(する)		deliver information	
	8.	新しい動画、配信中です。		The new movie is now streaming.	
	9.	# 配る		distribute, hand out (something)	

Now go to the Activity Book for 練習.

シーン 20-9R ミステリートマト The mystery tomato

Here is the first page of a manga that Brian's friend, whose username is Kei Chizuno, drafted.

テキスト Text

NihonGO & Nyau! The first episode of The Mystery Tomato (by) Kei Chizuno
My name is Go. My hobby is gardening and cooking. It's quite difficult to grow vegetables, but one interesting aspect of gardening is that it gets fun as I do it more and more.
Let's see which one of us can grow tastier ones. It's a match!
Mystery tomatoes
So, I tried to grow the tomatoes that Nyau gave me, but . . .

When I went to the park . . .	These tomatoes grew on their own and fell off on their own, then . . .
Yours speak, too, Nyau?	
Tomatoes . . . or pumpkins?	Mr. Dog, we would like you to take us to Fukuzawa Park.
My name is Tomato, nice to meet you.	
What is Tomato Exam?	Ta-Da!
Fukuzawa Park	Nice to meet you.
Tomato Exam Site	Nice to meet you.
You came . . . heeheehee . . .	Mr. Dog . . .
	What a surprise!
	Ninja-style tomatoes?
	Cool voice.

Between the lines

BTL 6 Choosing words to refer to yourself

Besides *watashi*, Japanese speakers use a wide variety of Nouns to refer to themselves. Different words have different connotations that may be associated with gender, status, age, and dialect. Pay attention to which words other Japanese speakers use. As necessary, ask for advice about how you should refer to yourself in different settings.

僕 (ぼく)	Commonly used by male speakers in casual settings; has a soft, and polite touch	うち	Commonly used by female speakers
俺・俺様 (おれ・おれさま)	Commonly used by male speakers in casual settings to highlight their masculinity	あたし	Commonly used by female speakers, less formal than わたし
わし・わい	Associated with older male speakers	自分	Commonly used by male athletes
おいら・おら	Associated with people from rural area		

BTL 7 Usernames

Japanese people commonly take usernames or handles on social media to avoid revealing their real names. They create their usernames based on their own names or key words associated with their background or what they are intending to do. For instance, 神田(かんだ)さん might make use of the fact that he is グルメ and creatively combine his given name (健太(けんた)) and family name (神田) to come up with グルメかんた as his username. When creating your own username, be sure to check with others to make sure that it is not inappropriate or offensive. It might be interesting to ask how your Japanese friends came up with their usernames on social media or to look up how the writers of your favorite book, comic, or anime series made theirs.

BTL 8 Reading manga and watching anime

Many Japanese people, including small children, read manga and watch anime. Small children cannot read or understand everything, but they still enjoy reading manga and watching anime. Perhaps this is because they develop the ability to make inferences based on visual components other than written language and are not necessarily worried about understanding everything. As mentioned previously, proficient readers do the same thing by reading selectively. You can do the same as you read manga or watch anime in Japanese. While there is a tendency for language students to try to understand everything, it is good practice to start reading and watching something in Japanese for enjoyment without worrying about understanding everything. There are many iconic characters in manga and anime series that are mentioned in daily conversations, so it is good idea to familiarize yourselves with some aspects of manga and anime culture. Be aware that different cultures have different standards for depicting sensitive elements such as violence and sexuality and there are manga and anime series with mature content.

文字と例 Kanji with examples

341. 育　そだ(てる)　そだ(つ)　イク　　grow, nurture　　育

1.	動物を育(そだ)てる	raise an animal
2.	野菜は大切に育てれば育てるほどおいしくなりますよ。	Vegetables become tastier the more you grow them with care.
3.	木が育(そだ)つ	a tree grows
4.	寝る子は育つ	a well-slept child is a well-kept child
5.	教育(きょういく)	education
6.	英語教育はいつから始めるべきなのでしょうか。	When should we start teaching English?
7.	# 体育(たいいく)	physical education

342. 難　むずか(しい)　ナン　difficult　難

1. 難しい問題 — a difficult problem
2. ありゃ難しいわ。 — That is difficult.
3. 考えれば考えるほど難しい。 — It's difficult, the more I think about it.
4. 実は難しければ難しいほどチャレンジがあって楽しい気がします。 — Actually, the more difficult it is, the more challenge and enjoyment I feel.
5. こんなに難しい問題わかるわけないよ。 — There is no way I understand such a difficult question.
6. 1年生のくせにこんな難しい漢字書けるの？ — You are a first grader and you can write these types of difficult *kanji*?
7. # 難問 — difficult question

343. 勝　か(つ)　ショウ(See kanji #344.)　win　勝

1. 試合に・で勝つ — win a game
2. 合気道を始めてまだ勝ったことがない。 — I haven't won a match since I started aikido.
3. 勝ったからいいようなものの、今日の試合のプレーは君らしくなかったし、危なかった。 — Good thing you won, but today's play in the game was not like you and it was a close one.
4. (自分)勝手(な) — selfish
5. 個人で勝手にやって、しかられてしまいました。 — I did it by myself and I was scolded.
6. 自分勝手な事言ってないで、手伝ってくれる？ — Don't be saying selfish things, please help.

344. 負　ま(ける)　フ　lose　負

1. 友人に負ける — lose to a friend
2. この試合で負けるわけにはいかない。 — I can't lose this match.
3. もう終わったね。こりゃ負けるしかないわ。 — That's it. We have no choice but to lose.
4. 負ける予定ではなかったけど負けちゃったのだから仕方がない。 — I wasn't planning for them to lose, but they lost and there is nothing I can do.

5.	「雨ニモマケズ風ニモマケズ」ってあるように、負けずにがんばりたい。[1]	As (the poem) says, "not losing to the rain and not losing to the wind," I want to do my best without giving up.
6.	+ 勝負(する)	match
7.	勝負に負けるわけないと思っていたのに、負けちゃった……。	I thought they it's not possible for them to lose the match, but they did…

345. 験 ケン — evidence, sign

1.	試験(する)	exam, test
2.	試験はいつ取るつもりですか。	When are you planning to take the test?
3.	たとえ今回の試験があまりよくなかったとしても、七転び八起きで次はもっとがんばります。	Even if the exam this time was not good, I'll work harder next time and "fall seven times, stand up eight."
4.	試験の予定はまだ決まってないらしいですよ。	I heard that the exam schedule has not been decided yet.
5.	実験(する)	experiment
6.	この実験するのにどのぐらいのお金がかかるか知ってる？	Do you know how much money it costs to do this experiment?
7.	実験を止めるって言いだしたのはだれだったっけ？	Who was it again that started saying that they are done with the experiment?
8.	+ 体験(する)	(personal) experience
9.	他の人にあんな体験をさせたくない。	I don't want to make other people go through such an experience.

346. 落 お(ちる) お(とす) ラク — fall (from a higher location)

1.	試験に落ちる	fail an exam
2.	落ちるところだったよ。危ない危ない。	It was about to fall. That was close!
3.	あそこでセルフィーやろうとしたら、落ちそうになって死にかけたよ。	I attempted to take a selfie there, but I almost fell and died.
4.	スマホを落とす	drop a smartphone

---

1 *"Ame ni mo makezu" (1931) by Miyazawa, Kenji (1896–1933)*

	5.		そんなに気を落とさないで次にがんばりましょう。		Don't despair so much and let's do our best next time.
	6.	#	落合(おちあい)		[family name]
	7.	#	下落(げらく)(する)		fall, decline

347. 公　コウ　　public　　公

	1.	+	公立(こうりつ)		public
	2.		公立学校		public school
	3.	#	公私(こうし)		public and private

348. 園　その　エン　　garden　　園

1.		公園(こうえん)		park
2.		お疲れのようですので、公園で少しお休みになったらどうでしょう。		You seem tired, so how about you take a break at the park?
3.		さっき確かめたんだけど、あの公園の工事ってまだ終わってないよ。		I just checked it a while ago, but the construction in that park is still not completed.
4.		公園の中では自転車に乗っちゃいけないよ。		You are not allowed to ride a bicycle inside the park.
5.		趣味は公園を歩くことです。		My hobby is to walk in the park.
6.	+	園村(そのむら)		[family name]
7.		園村さん、部長に会社辞めさせられたらしいよ。		I heard that Sonomura-san was forced to quit his job by the division manager.
8.	#	エデンの園(その)		Garden of Eden

349. 犬　いぬ　ケン　　dog　　犬

1.	犬(いぬ)		dog
2.	犬を連れてくる必要はありますか。		Is there a need to bring my dog?
3.	あの公園(こうえん)でよく見る犬ってだれの犬なの？		The dog that we see often at the park, whose dog is it?
4.	だれかの犬がここに連れてこられたんだけど……。		Somebody's dog was brought here, but . . .

5.		あの犬に水を飲ませてあげてくれる？	Could you do me a favor and let that dog drink some water?
6.	+	子犬(こいぬ)	puppy
7.		公園で見た子犬を家に連れて帰ったら母に反対された。	My mom was against it when I brought home the puppy I saw at the park.
8.	#	秋田犬(あきたけん)	Akita (breed) dog

Now go to the Activity Book for 練習.

Then do 評価 activities, including 読んでみよう, 書き取り, and 書いてみよう.

第 21 幕
Act 21

典型的な夜型です。
I'm a typical night owl.

早起きは三文の徳。
The early bird catches the worm.

◆ 話す・聞く

Scene 21-1 つまり……っていうこと。
In other words, it means . . .

Amy couldn't quite understand a description someone used for a character in an anime that she was watching.

The script

エイミー	孝
「乙女チック」って何？	「乙女」、つまり優しい女の子っぽいっていうこと。まあ、ステレオタイプだけどね。
いや、「乙女」はわかるけど、どうしてチックなの？	あ、それはロマンチックの「チック」じゃない？「マンガチック」とかもあるしさ。
オトメtic、ああ、何々チックか……。じゃあ、「タカシチック」っていうのもあり？	え？なにそれ。どういう意味？
論文苦手っていう意味。	え、まじウケる。でも、ええー！？それって「トモハラ」じゃない？

Amy	Takashi
What's *otomechikku*?	It means 'little girl,' in other words like a little girl. Well, it is a stereotype.
No, I understand *otome* but why *chikku*?	Oh, that; It's the -tic of romantic, right? There's also *mangachikku*.

Otome-tic, Oh, I see. So then . . . there's also *Takashi-chikku*?	What? What do you mean?
It means bad at thesis (writing).	No kidding. But, what? No! That is, isn't that 'friend harassment'?

単語と表現

名詞

乙女 (おとめ)	little girl, young lady
乙女チック (おとめ)	girlish
ロマンチック	romantic
マンガ	manga, comic
マンガチック	manga-tic, cartoonish
ステレオタイプ	stereotype
セクハラ	sexual harassment
マタハラ	harassment of pregnant women (*mata* from "maternity")
パワハラ	harassment of underlings (those over whom one has power)
あり	there is/are (from ある)

動詞

ウケる (-RU; ウケた)	can work as a joke (slang)

表現

X、つまりYっていうこと	X, in other words Y
何々 (なになに)	so-and-so, such-and such
○○・マルマル	[placeholder when content is unclear], certain, unnamed

Behind the scenes

BTS 1 Being creative with language

Word play, including puns, is a time-honored tradition in Japanese. In this Scene, you see two examples of creative word play. One is the suffix チック, the appropriation of *-tic* from English (romantic, pedantic, antiseptic) appended to Japanese words. Another is ハラ (from harassment) which has been borrowed into Japanese as a combination of harassment, discrimination, and bullying. One website listed 35 different combinations that include ハラ. Among them are the ones you see listed in 名詞 previously, along with アルハラ 'alcohol harassment,' カラハラ 'karaoke harassment,' スモハラ 'smoker harassment,' フォトハラ 'photo harassment,' and ジェンハラ 'gender harassment.' In this Scene, Takashi invents a new kind of ハラ as a joke: トモハラ 'friend harassment.'

Now go to the Activity Book for 練習 and 腕試し.

Scene 21-2 私(わたし)なりの健康管理(けんこうかんり)です。
It's my way of health management

Yagi-bucho notices that Sasha packs appetizing meals for lunch.

 The script

八木	サーシャ
お弁当(べんとう)、いつも美味(お い)しそうですね。	あ、どうも。私(わたし)なりの健康管理(けんこうかんり)です。
健康管理(けんこうかんり)というと？	まあ、病気(びょうき)になって会社(かいしゃ)の人(ひと)に迷惑(めいわく)かけたくないですし。
感心(かんしん)ですね。	あ、いえいえ。どんなに忙(いそが)しくても、おにぎり1個だけとかはやめようと思って。
それどころか、私(わたし)なんか、全(まった)く抜(ぬ)いちゃうこともありますからね。	あ、それは最悪(さいあく)なパターンですよね。

Yagi	Sasha
Your lunches always look so delicious.	Oh, thanks. It's my way of health management.
Health management? Meaning?	Well, I don't want to become a burden to office people by getting sick.
That's impressive.	No, but even when I'm super busy, I thought I shouldn't go with just one *onigiri* for lunch.
In fact, in my case, there are times when I skip it altogether, you know.	Oh, that's the worst, isn't it.

単語と表現

名詞

Xなり(に)	X for instance (though there may be other options)
管理(する)	manage, control
健康管理	health management
感心(する)	admiration, being impressed
おにぎり	*onigiri* (rice formed into a triangular or round shape and often wrapped in nori ('seaweed'))
最悪(な・の)	the worst
最善	the best
最新	newest
最高	greatest (often used as an exclamation of approval)
最低	lowest, worst
最大	biggest, largest
最小	smallest, least

動詞

抜く (-U; 抜いた)	omit, extract
飛ばす (-U; 飛ばした)	skip X

表現

XなりのY	Y in X's own way
(X)というと？	What do you mean (by X)?
それどころか	on the contrary, in fact

Behind the scenes

BTS 2 X なりに；X なりの Y

The phrase Noun + なり(に) refers to a way or style particular to that Noun in the sense of being minimally proficient: 私なりの教え方 'my own (best) way of teaching.' By extension, the phrase それなり(に) refers to the degree (minimally) expected of who or what それ refers to. If a company has made a nearly impossible request of a reputable consultant, the company spokesperson might say それなりのお礼はさせていただきます。 'Allow me to compensate you commensurate with your work.' Sentence + なり works the same way.

母親には母親なりの苦労があるんですよ。	Mothers have their own challenges, you know.
私もできないなりに頑張ってます。	I'm doing my best, even though I'm not good at it.
大きな違いはないかもしれませんけど、こちらもそれなりの努力はしたつもりです。	There may be no big difference, but as far as I'm concerned, I believe I have put in effort that is comparable to your expectations.

BTS 3 X というと

When というと is preceded by a Phrase or Sentence, it indicates a hypothetical: 'if one were to say/talk about . . .' or 'if it were the case that . . .' If something follows, it is linked in one's imagination with what precedes というと. In this use, というと is very close to といえば.

２万円というと、すごくおいしいレストランで食べられるんじゃないですか。	For ¥20,000, you should be able to eat at a fabulous restaurant, shouldn't you?
一番大切なことというと？	(What do you mean by) the most important thing?
健康管理というと筋トレ、筋トレというと山田コーチ、山田コーチというと……	Health maintenance means weight training, weight training means Coach Yamada, Coach Yamada means . . .

The question というと？ (with or without a preceding phrase) is a request for clarification: 'What do you mean?'

え？乙女（おとめ）？乙女というと？ここにはいませんよね。	What? "Girl?" What do you mean by "girl?" There are certainly none here.
部長（ぶちょう）：この企画（きかく）は残念（ざんねん）ながら……。	Division Chief: Too bad about this project.
社長（しゃちょう）：というと？	Section Chief: What do you mean?
部長：はい、しないことになったんです。	Division Chief: It's been decided not to do it.

Now go to the Activity Book for 練習 and 腕試し.

Scene 21-3 誰にでも当てはまるとは限らないんじゃないですか？ Isn't it the case that it doesn't apply to everyone?

Brian is out for a light dinner with people from the aikido dojo after training.

 The script

ブライアン	鈴木
昔からよく「早寝早起き」とか「早起きは三文の徳」って言われますよね。	ええ。
でも、あれって本当ですかね。	まあ、必ずしもそうではないかもしれませんね。
ええ、誰にでも当てはまるとは限らないんじゃないですか？	ブライアンさんは早起き苦手な方ですか？
まあ、典型的な夜型です。	

Brian	Suzuki
It's often said "early to bed and early to rise," and "the early bird catches the worm," isn't it.	Yes.
But is that true?	Well, maybe not always.
But isn't it the case that it doesn't apply to everyone?	For sure, it depends on the person. Oh, you aren't so good at getting up early, are you?
Well, I'm a typical night owl.	

単語と表現

名詞

昔 (むかし)	long ago
早寝 (はやね)	go to bed early
早起き (はやおき)	get up early
三文 (さんもん)	three *mon* (coins) (old unit of currency)
徳 (とく)	virtue, benevolence
経済的(な) (けいざいてき)	economical
典型的(な) (てんけいてき)	typical
典型 (てんけい)	pattern, model
科学的(な) (かがくてき)	scientific
科学 (かがく)	science
例外的(な) (れいがいてき)	exceptional
例外 (れいがい)	exception
一般的(な) (いっぱんてき)	generally
一般 (いっぱん)	general, average
常識的(な) (じょうしきてき)	common, sensical
常識 (じょうしき)	common sense

動詞

当てはまる (-U; 当てはまった)	apply (a rule)
限る (-U; 限った)	limit, restrict

形容詞

正しい (ただしい)	correct

表現

早寝早起き (はやねはやおき)	early to bed and early to rise
必ずしも (かならずしも) + negative	not always, not necessarily
Sentence とは限(かぎ)らない	is not limited to X
Noun に当(あ)てはまる	apply to Noun

Behind the scenes

BTS 4 Passive for general description

You saw the passive used to indicate that someone or something (the subject) is not in control of the action. 友達に招待された。 'I was invited by a friend.' There is another use of the passive for generalizations where the subject is unspecified or absent – for example, ……と言われている 'it is said,' or ……と書かれていた. 'it was written.'

これはもう決められたことですから……。	This is a matter that has already been decided, so . . .
みんなに見られながら話すのはちょっと恥ずかしいけど、頑張ります。	To talk while being watched by everybody is a bit embarrassing, but I'll do my best.

BTS 5 必(かなら)ずしも + negative

You saw 必ず 'without fail, always' in Act 8. The extended form 必ずしも in combination with a negative means 'not always.' You will see it frequently with phrases such as 〜とは限(かぎ)らない, 〜わけじゃない, and 〜ということじゃない.

安くてもすぐ壊れるものは、必ずしも経済的とは言えません。	You can't always say that things that are cheap and break right away are economical.
必ずしも常識という訳ではありませんが、一般的にはこのようなことはあまりしませんね。	It's not that it's always common sense, but we don't normally do this sort of thing.

Now go to the Activity Book for 練習 and 腕試し.

Scene 21-4 答え合わせしていきましょう。
Let's check our answers.

Brian teaches English to a middle school student at a neighbor's house. He just gave her a short quiz.

The script

ブライアン	中学生
はい、時間です。じゃあ、一つずつ、答え合わせしていきましょう。1番は？	C
はい、正解！いいぞ！その調子。じゃ、正解には丸つけて。2番は？	AかBですよね？Dはあり得ないでしょ？
残念。その「あり得ない」Dが正解。	(小さな声で)やば。

Brian	Student
Okay, time's up. So let's check the answers, going one by one. Number 1?	C
Yes, correct! Way to go! Put a circle around the correct ones. Number 2?	It's A or B, right? It surely can't be D.
Too bad. It's "it can't be" D.	[in a small voice] Crap.

単語と表現

名詞

答え合わせ(する)	check answers
採点(する)	scoring, grading
満点	full score

正解	correct (answer or solution)
不正解	incorrect
誤り	mistake, error
間違い	mistake, blunder
丸・まる	circle (used to indicate an item is correct)
ばつ	x-mark, wrong
ぺけ	x-mark, wrong

動詞

比べる (-RU; 比べた)	compare
間違う (-U; 間違った)	make a mistake
足す (-U; 足した)	add (numbers)
掛ける (-RU; 掛けた)	multiply (numbers)

助詞

ぞ	[particle adding force or emphasis]

表現

Noun に丸(を)つける	put a circle around Noun
時間です。	Time's up.
いいぞ！	Way to go! Nice going!

Behind the scenes

BTS 6 Verb 〜ていく

You saw Verb 〜ていく earlier meaning 'do and then go somewhere': 勉強していく 'study and then go, go after studying.' This pattern can also mean 'a little at a time' or 'continually,' as in the following:

大変（たいへん）ですが、少（すこ）しずつ片付（かたづ）けていきましょう。	It's tough but let's clean up a little at a time.
気（き）をつけて見（み）ていってたら、違（ちが）うところに気がつきました。	When I continued to look at it carefully, I noticed something different.

BTS 7 Sentence particle ぞ

Sentence Particle ぞ is similar to よ in the sense that it is assertive and indicates new information. It is much blunter than よ and is sometimes called "masculine," even though women use it in casual conversation.

わあ、美味（お い）しそう！よ～し、食（た）べるぞ！	Wow, looks delicious! I'm gonna have some!
１５分休（やす）んだね。じゃ、行くぞ。	We've rested for 15 minutes. Okay, let's get a move on.

BTS 8 その [Modifier] + noun (discourse strategy)

You have already seen that こ・そ・あ・ど forms may refer to something that has already been mentioned. In some instances, the Noun that has already been described may be brought up again with the description as a sentence modifier. In this Scene, Brian picks up from his student's comment that "D is impossible" and refers to そのD with the sentence modifier あり得（え）ない.

カレーってあまり好（す）きじゃないだよね。その好きじゃないカレーを全部（ぜんぶ）食（た）べちゃった。そのくらいお腹（なか）が空（す）いてたんだ。	I don't like curry very much, right? That curry that I don't like very much – well, I just ate all of it. That's how hungry I was.

Now go to the Activity Book for 練習 and 腕試し.

Scene 21-5 エイミーの話（難しいこと）
Amy's story

Amy tells her Japanese teacher and her assistant about creative phrasing in Japanese.

The script

エイミー	林	日本語の先生
日本語には、外来語っぽいけど外来語じゃない言葉がありますよね。		うん、シャーペンとか。
	略語になるとさらに分かりづらい。	そうでしょうね。モンペアなんてわかんないでしょう。
「何々チック」っていうのもそうですし。		色々組み合わせますからね。
それで、論文がなかなか書けない友達がいてぇ、	ああ、タカシくん。	
そうそう。それで、論文苦手っていう意味で「タカシチック」っていうのを作ったら、	おお、クリエイティブ。	（笑い）
それは「トモハラ」だって言われちゃいました。		はあ、それもうまい。（笑い）
え？先生、感心してます？		

Amy	Hayashi	Japanese Professor
There are words in Japanese that sound like borrowed words but aren't, right?		Yeah, like *shaapen* and that sort of thing.
	When they get contracted they're even harder to understand.	That must be true. You probably don't understand *monpea*.

Such-and-such-*chikku* is also like that.		Because they combine in various ways, don't they.
So I have this friend who just can't write his thesis …	Aah, Takashi.	
Right, right. So when I made up one called *Takashi-chikku* meaning 'bad at thesis' …	Aah, creative.	(laughs)
I got told, "That's *tomohara*."		Ohh, that's also clever. (laughs)
What? Professor, you're impressed?		

 ## 単語と表現

名詞

外来語(がいらいご)	borrowed vocabulary
略語(りゃくご)	contraction
可能(かのう)(な)	possibility
不可能(ふかのう)(な)	impossibility
得手(えて)(な)	strong point, strength
不得手(ふえて)(な)	weak point, weakness
公平(こうへい)(な)	objectivity, fairness
不公平(ふこうへい)(な)	partiality, unfairness
モンペア	monster parent (from モンスターペアレント)
クリエイティブ(な)	creative

動詞

組(く)み合(あ)わせる (-RU; 組み合わせた)	combine, join together

形容詞

Verb stem + づらい	difficult to X
苦(くる)しい	painful, stressful

表現

さらに・更(さら)に	even more, moreover

Behind the scenes

BTS 9 Constructing a narration with multiple participants

This Scene presents another example of narration. Notice how the listeners help construct the narration by adding examples and commentary to strengthen Amy's argument and identify shared information.

A: うちのスタッフって優秀(ゆうしゅう)ですよね。 B: ええ、山下(やました)さんとか、中川(なかがわ)さんとか、すごいですよね。	A: Our staff is excellent, isn't it? B: Yes, Ms. Yamashita and Mr. Nakagawa, for example, are amazing.
A: うちのスタッフって優秀ですよね。 B: 上に「超(ちょう)」がつく優秀です。	A: Our staff is excellent, isn't it? B: They are excellent with "extremely" in front of the word.

Now go to the Activity Book for 練習 and 腕試し.

Scene 21-6 孝の話 (ことば遊び)
Takashi's story (language play)

Takashi recounts the same scene with Amy to another club member.

The script

孝	クラブのメンバー
この間エイミーさんに「乙女チック」って何？って聞かれてさ。	「乙女」ねえ。(新型イントネーションで)ちょっと古くない？ほとんど死語。
いや「乙女」はいいけど、「チック」がわからないって。	ああ、それはわかりにくいかも。
で、ロマンチックのチックだって言ったらエイミーさん調子に乗って……。	うん。
僕が論文苦手なの知ってるじゃない。だからそれを「タカシチック」だって。	はは、エイミーも結構言うね。
だから、それは「トモハラ」だって言ってやったよ。	トモハラ？何それ。あ、友達ハラスメント？
その通り。	

Takashi	Club member
The other day, I got asked by Amy, "What's *otome-chikku*?"	*Otome*. Isn't that a little old-fashioned? It's almost obsolete.
No, *otome* is fine but she said she didn't understand *chikku*.	Ohh, that may be a little hard to understand.
So when I said it was the *chikku* of *romanchikku* she got carried away.	Yeah.
She knows I'm struggling with my thesis, right? So she called that *Takashi-chikku*.	Haha, good for Amy.
So, of course I said back to her that that was *tomohara*.	*Tomohara*? What's that? Oh, friend harassment?
Exactly.	

単語と表現

名詞

死語(しご)	obsolete word, extinct language
憤慨(ふんがい)(する)	indignation
絶滅(ぜつめつ)(する)	extinction

表現

調子(ちょうし)に乗(の)る	get caught up, get carried away
だから	so of course, so
言ってやった	said back to, (did the favor of) telling

Behind the scenes

BTS 10 言ってやった

You saw やる among verbs of giving to an out-group when an out-group is subordinate (animals, plants, or children). In this sense, やる can have a negative tone if it is used with peers. It can also be used when there is no one who obviously benefits from the action.

今度(こんど)こそ１００点(てん)取(と)ってやる。	This time for sure I'm going to get a hundred points.
いつもいじめるクラスメートを見返(みかえ)してやる。	I'm going to stare back at the classmate who always teases me.

BTS 11 Empathy-seeking intonation: 古(ふる)くない？

Listen carefully to the first thing that the club member says in this Scene: 「乙女(おとめ)」ねえ。ちょっと古くない？ 'Otome. Isn't that a little old-fashioned?' Ordinarily, the accent of 古くない？ would be hu⌐ruku ⌐na⌐i? or hu ⌐ru⌐ku ⌐na⌐i? But in this case the speaker says hu⌐ruku nai? (rising on the second syllable and staying high throughout). This intonation pattern is common among young people; some older speakers frown upon it.

BTS 12 だから as a discourse connector

You have seen だから following a Sentence to show reason or cause: これ、外来語(がいらいご)ですね。だから、カタカナで書(か)くんじゃないですか？ 'This is a borrowed word, isn't it? So isn't it true that one writes it in katakana?' At the beginning of an utterance, だから means 'so' or 'therefore' but often shows impatience at having to state what is obvious (to the speaker, at least).

A: きれいに書(か)いてね。 B: だからわかってるよ。子供(こども)じゃないんだから。	A: Write neatly, okay? B: So I know! I'm not a child, you know.
こんなに残(のこ)してる。だから食(た)べられるだけ取(と)ってって言ったでしょう？	You are leaving this much (on the plate). So I told you to take only as much as you could eat, didn't I?

Now go to the Activity Book for 練習 and 腕試し.

Then do 評価 activities.

典型的(てんけいてき)な夜型(よるがた)です。

◆ 読み書き

シーン 21-7R 自分(じぶん)なりに考(かんが)えよう。
Let's think for ourselves.

Brian is looking for an interesting news story in the Daily Fukuzawa, a local online newspaper.

テキスト Text

| デイリー福沢オンライン | 検索：パワハラ問題 |

トップニュース　写真・動画　お天気　政治・経済　スポーツ　カルチャー　オピニオン

- 子育てでできる自分なりの「グローバル教育」　福沢大学　坂本教授
- 【キラキラネーム】による最悪な思い出
- 外国人の声　フクザワというとどんなイメージ？
- 今日のお天気　最高気温と最低気温がほぼ同じ
- 「手作り料理＝おいしい」と思えるそのワケとは？
- 福沢大学受験生の数　過去最高の5000人強
- ジャイアンツ、5連勝！　平井がサヨナラホームラン
- 今年度のアプリの売り上げ・DL数「トップ１０」

自分で作る料理はうまい？

#検索(する) search

Daily Fukuzawa Online		Search : Problems with Power Harassment
Top News	Photos・Videos　Weather　Economics・Politics	Sports　Culture　Opinion

- "Global education" in your parenting style (by) Fukuzawa University Prof. Sakamoto

Food cooked by yourself is tasty?	• Worst memories caused by [unconventional baby names] • Voices of foreigners – What do you imagine when you hear "Fukuzawa"? • Today's weather – high and low temperatures almost the same • Why do people think "homemade cooking = delicious"? • Number of Fukuzawa University college exam test takers hits an all-time high of 5,000 plus • Five consecutive wins for the Giants! Hirai's game-ending homerun • This year's top 10 apps – sales and number of downloads

Between the lines

BTL 1 Including 平仮名 and カタカナ as part of search words

Your search results often come up with Chinese websites when you enter only kanji characters in the search bar. You can solve this problem by including a hiragana or katakana character in the search bar. For example, instead of just typing 日本料理, you may want to try 日本の料理 or 日本料理レシピ to get Japanese websites in the result.

BTL 2 Using online resources to study Japanese

Learners often use online resources to study foreign languages, including Japanese. When you are looking up a word, instead of just looking up an English equivalent or relying on a single resource, it is good to use multiple resources to see how the word is used. For instance, you may check what types of words and particles are associated with certain vocabulary by simply typing in the target vocabulary online and scrolling through the search results. If you want to say 'I received a gift' but are not sure whether it is appropriate to use 受ける or もらう, you may try looking up プレゼントを受ける and プレゼントをもらう to see which one seems more fitting in your own situation. Similarly, if you are not sure about how certain loanwords are realized in katakana, it is good to use online resources to see how they are commonly written.

BTL 3 Composing catchy headlines and titles in Japanese

People use catchy headlines and titles to grab readers' attention. Headlines should be concise and make use of words that speak to the intended audience. If you are struggling to come up with a headline or title, type in key words to see what kind of headlines and titles come up in popular websites. You should not copy them as is, but study them to create your own. As you study different headlines and titles, pay attention to how they summarize the content, make use of specific examples and numbers, and benefit the readers. Some examples of key phrases include これは気になる！○○の本当の使い方, ○○したい人におススメの○○, and ○○だった人が○○できる!? You can also create impact by purposefully using titles that contradict common sense (e.g., 日本語は勉強しちゃダメ！？) or combining things that are not commonly associated with each other (e.g., ネコとお料理).

BTL 4 キラキラネーム

キラキラ 'shining, glittering' names are given names that make use of 当て字 to assign unusual readings to kanji characters. Some examples:

七音 (どれみ)　using the two kanji meaning 'seven musical notes' for the female name ドレミ (a reference to the names of the notes in a musical octave)

五月 (めい)　using the two kanji meaning 'the fifth month' for the female name めい (which is homonymous with the month of May)

天 (しえる)　using the kanji meaning 'heaven' for the female name しえる (which is homonymous with the French word *ciel* 'sky')

心人 (はあと)　using kanji for 'heart' and 'person' for the male name はあと

月 (らいと)　using the kanji for 'moon' for the male name らいと 'light'

While these names are unique and catchy, they can be difficult to read and some people find them inappropriate and/or embarrassing.

文字と例 Kanji with examples

350. 受　う(ける)　う(かる)　ジュ　receive, accept　受

1.	受ける	receive (service)
2.	実は明日までに受けないといけない試験があるんです。	Actually, I have a test that I need to take by tomorrow, so . . .
3.	引き受ける	undertake X
4.	この仕事、引け受けなければよかった。	I wish I hadn't accepted this job.

5.		受け取る	receive (by hand)
6.		手紙を受け取りに参りました。	I came to get a letter.
7.	+	受付	reception, receptionist
8.		野田様というお客様が受付の前で待っていらっしゃいますよ。	There is a guest named Noda waiting in front of the information desk.
9.	+	Xに受かる	pass X
10.		大学受験には死んでも受かりたい。	I want to pass the college entrance exam even if I die trying.
11.	+	受験(する)	examination
12.		受験というと？	What about the examination?

351. 最　もっと(も)　サイ　the most

1.		最近	lately
2.		あの学生、最近元気がないようだけど、受験落ちちゃったのかな。	That student seems like he is not doing well; I wonder if he failed his college entrance exam.
3.		最高(な)	highest, supreme
4.		今日の最高気温は３０度まで上がるらしいですよ。	I heard that today's maximum temperature will go as high as 30 degrees.
5.		最新	newest
6.		最新の動画配信中！	The newest movie is not available!
7.		最大	biggest
8.		最小	lowest
9.		最後	last
10.	#	最も	most

352. 初　はじ(め)　はつ　ショ　first time, new

1.		初めまして	how do you do (often written in *hiragana*)
2.		初めて	first time
3.		初めての方はこちらからご覧ください。	If this is your first time, please look from here.
4.	#	初雪	first snow (of the year)

5.		最初(さいしょ)		beginning, at first
6.		この小説、最初から最後まで読ませてくださってありがとうございました。		Thank you for letting me read this novel from beginning to end.
7.	#	初心(しょしん)		beginner's spirit
8.	#	初心者(しょしんしゃ)		beginner
9.	¥	初段(しょだん)		first rank black belt in martial arts, calligraphy, etc.

353. 低　ひく(い)　テイ　　low, base　　低

1.		低い(ひくい)	low
2.	¥	背が低い(せがひくい)	short
3.		明日山に行くのって気温が低すぎて危なくないですか。	About going to the mountain tomorrow, isn't the temperature too low and dangerous?
4.		最低(さいてい)(な)	lowest
5.		最低の人	worst person (on a test, for example), horrible/worst person (character attribute)
6.		最低な人	horrible/worst person (character attribute)
7.		今朝の最低気温は０度以下でした。	Today's lowest temperature was below zero degrees.

354. 悪　わる(い)　アク　　bad, evil　　悪

1.	悪い(わるい)	bad
2.	気持ちが悪くなったらすぐに教えてください。	Please tell me immediately if you feel sick.
3.	すみません、来週は都合が悪くて……。	I'm sorry, next week will not work for my schedule . . .
4.	センパイでも言っていいことと悪いことがあると思います。	I think even for *senpai*, there are things that are okay to say and things that are not okay to say.
5.	悪いとは分かってるんだけど、つい……。	I know it's bad, but I can't help it . . .
6.	最悪(さいあく)(な)	worst
7.	最悪死んでしまう場合もありますので、ご注意ください。	People die in the worst case so please be careful.

355.	平 ひら ヘイ		plane, level, flat 平
1.		公平(な)	fair
2.		不公平(な)	unfair
3.		この間の試験、ちょっと不公平だと思いませんか？	Don't you think the test we took the other day was a little unfair?
4.	+	平和(な)	peaceful
5.		もっと平和になりますように……。	Wishing that it will be more peaceful . . .
6.	+	平日	weekday
7.		平日は学校とバイトでかなり忙しい。	I'm quite busy on weekdays with school and part-time work.
8.	+	洋平	[male first name]
9.	¥	平成	Heisei era (1989–2019)
10.	¥	平均	average
11.	#	太平洋	Pacific Ocean
12.	+	平井	[family name]
13.		平井さんも自分なりの趣味を始めるべきですよ。	Hirai-san, you too should start your own hobby.
14.	¥	平仮名	hiragana

356.	経 ケイ		pass, experience, sutra 経
1.	+	経験(する)	experience
2.		絵の経験0の自分でもできました。	Even I, with no experience of drawing, could do it.
3.		すみません、少し経験不足なもので……。	I'm sorry, I'm a little inexperienced, so . . .
4.		音楽経験がないと難しいかもしれません。	It might be difficult without having music experience.
5.	¥	神経	nerve

357.	済 す(ます) す(む) サイ		settle, complete, finish 済
1.		経済	economics, economy

2.		最近経済が少し悪くなってきたように思えます。	It seems to me the economy has gotten worse recently.
3.		経済学	economics
4.		経済的(な)	economical
5.		済(す)ませる	finish X, get through X
6.		仕事を早く済ませて家に帰りたい。	I want to finish work early and go home.
7.	+	済(す)む	finish, come to an end
8.		これはジョークでは済まないですよ。	Jokes won't settle this.
9.		予定通りに工事は済んだみたいだね。	It seems that the construction was completed on schedule.

358. 政 セイ — rule, government 政

1.	+	政治(せいじ)	politics
2.		政治家(せいじか)	politician
3.		政治家は政治家なりにがんばっているのであるが……。	Politicians are doing their best in their own way as politicians, but . . .
4.		明日の政治のクラスに出席しなければならなくなった。	I came to (the decision) that I must attend tomorrow's politics class.
5.		心配しているのはこれからの政治……。	What I'm worried about is the politics of the future.
6.		あの政治家があきらめるわけないよ。	There is no way that politician will give up.

Now go to the Activity Book for 練習.

シーン 21-8R 「勉強は朝するべきではない」
"Study should not be done in the morning"

Brian received feedback from Sakamoto-sensei on the second draft of his opinion paper.

テキスト Text

勉強は朝するべきじゃない

ブライアン・ワン

勉強は朝する方がいいとよく言われている。たしかに朝はリフレッシュした気持ちで勉強できると考える人も多いだ。だが、夜型の人にとって、朝早く起きることは問題だ難しい。

なぜなら、夜型の人にはあその人に合った違うのライフスタイルがあるからだ。ある調べたこと研究によると夜型の人はがんばっても、朝型のスケジュールに合わせようとすると、ストレスを感じ、死亡リスクが上がる答えがあるとも言われている。だから必ずしも勉強は朝するべきではやないと言える。

よって僕私は、「朝方型の人は朝に、夜型の人は夜に」という風に、人それぞれ自分に合った時間に勉強した方がいいと考える。

+ だが　　　　however, nevertheless
# 死亡(する)　die
+ それぞれ　　each

Study should not be done in the morning
Brian Wang
It is commonly said that it is better to study in the morning, but is that really true?
It's true that there are many people who think that they can study with a refreshed feeling in the morning.
However, it is difficult for night owls to wake up early in the morning.

This is because night people have their own lifestyles that suit them. According to research, a night person cannot become a morning person even if they try hard. It is also said that if nocturnal people try to follow morning people's schedules, they feel stress and the risk of death increases. Thus, it can be said that study should not necessarily be done in the morning.

In conclusion, I think that people should study at times that suit them – in the morning for morning people and at night for night people.

Between the lines

BTL 5 How to use 原稿用紙

Here are some rules when you use 原稿用紙 for your writing:

- Line 1, title: Leave two or three spaces before the title and some spaces after it.
- Line 2, name: Align your name to the end of the line, leaving one space after it.
- Body: Begin each paragraph with a space.
- Punctuation marks: Use one space for all punctuation marks such as 、 and 。.
- Quotation marks: Use one space for the beginning of the quote (「) and the end of the quote (」).
- Line breaks: Avoid beginning a line with punctuation or quotation marks. Instead you can either put the marks outside the last box in the line, or leave one box empty and move to the next line.

BTL 6 Compositions and papers: 作文、小論文

You will almost surely have many opportunities to write 作文 'compositions' and 小論文 'short formal papers' in the course of your Japanese study. 作文 include essays, blogs, opinion pieces, reports, book reviews, and the like that are not under the same formal constraints as 小論文, which are expected to follow a set structure in terms of argument. In either case, it is a good practice to read similar genres of writing to look for models that you want to follow.

It is also important that you follow a conventional format so that your readers are able to follow your writing easily. For instance, Brian's opinion paper consists of five short paragraphs: the first asks a question (〜だろうか); the second acknowledges an opposing view (たしかに〜); the third states his opinion (だが〜); the fourth provides his explanation (なぜなら〜); and the fifth summarizes his opinion (よって私は〜).

When writing 作文, don't forget the technique of 起承転結 that you saw in Act 20.

In terms of formality and politeness, end your sentences using a consistent style. Note that Sakamoto-sensei corrects Brian's use of です and 〜ます because most of his paper is written in an informal (and therefore impersonal) style.

Be on the lookout, too, for useful transition words to develop your technique; these can improve your versatility and bring your writing alive. As you study other people's writing, pay attention to how ideas are connected by transition words. Take note of unfamiliar transition words and try to use them in your own writing.

Needless to say, always proofread your paper, and if possible, have someone else read it for you.

BTL 7 More on written style

There are several groups of words that are more typical of written style (though you may hear them in spoken discourse in more formal settings).

Transition words such as だが, たしかに(確かに), and よって in this Scene are commonly used in opinion essays. Other transition words that are more typical of written style include しかし, とは言え 'that being said,' さらに 'furthermore,' and 従って 'therefore.'

Compounds are common for time expressions, including those with 明 to indicate the next day (明日 'tomorrow,' 明晩 'tomorrow night') and 昨 to indicate the preceding day or recent point in time (昨日 'yesterday; recently,' 昨晩・昨夜 'last night,' 昨年 'last year,' 昨今 'lately').

A question is often used to conclude an opinion essay. This may seem to be a weak way to wrap up from an English reader/writer's perspective, but in Japanese it is considered to be a good way to bring the argument to a successful close. Here are a few examples.

本当だろうか。	Is it true?
いいのではないだろうか。	Isn't it good?
本当だと言えるだろうか。	Can one say that it's true?
いいとは考えられないか。	Can't one think that this is a good thing?
本当だと言える。	One can say that it's true.

文字と例 Kanji with examples

359.	夜 よ よる ヤ		night	夜
	1.	夜	night	
	2.	首がいたくて夜寝られなかったんだ。	My neck hurt and I couldn't sleep at night.	
	3.	夜になっても必ずしも見えるわけではない。	Even if it's at nighttime, we cannot necessarily see it.	

4.	+	月夜(つきよ)		moonlit night
5.	+	夜中(よなか)		in the middle of the night
6.		夜中に外で変な音がしたんだけど、なんだったんだろう。		I heard a strange sound outside in the middle of the night; I wonder what it was.
7.	+	今夜(こんや)		tonight
8.		今夜は寝ないで勉強するぞ！		I'm going to study without sleeping tonight!
9.	+	昨夜(さくや)		previous night
10.	¥	徹夜(てつや)(する)		pull an all-nighter

360. 型　かた　ケイ　　type, pattern, model　　型

1.		夜型(よるがた)	night person, night owl
2.		朝型の人	morning person
3.		あなたは朝型？夜型？	Are you a morning person or a night person?
4.		朝型か夜型かって言われるとどっち？	Between morning type and night type, which one are you?
5.		朝型の人って早寝早起きができてうらやましいですね。	I'm jealous that a morning person can sleep and wake up early.
6.		夜型は夜型なりのペースがあるんだ。	I tell you that a night person has his own pace.
7.	+	小型家電(こがたかでん)	small appliances
8.	+	大型家電(おおがたかでん)	large appliances
9.		大型家電はあの店に行かないと売ってないよ。	You won't find big appliances anywhere else but that store.
10.	¥	典型的(てんけいてき)(な)	typical

361. 論　ロン　　theory　　論

1.		論文(ろんぶん)	thesis
2.	+	小論文(しょうろんぶん)	short formal paper
3.		さあ、今日も論文書くぞ！	Well today, too, I'm going to write my thesis.

4.		この論文あと３０ページ読まないといけなくて……。	I have to read 30 more pages of this thesis.
5.		論文が予定通りに書けずに困っています。	I'm troubled that I can't write essays as scheduled.

362. 答　こた(え)　こた(える)　トウ　　answer, solution, response　　答

1.	答え	answer
2.	１２ですね。はい、その答えで合ってます。	It's 12, right? Yes, that answer is correct.
3.	必ずしも答えが合っているわけじゃないから気を付けてね。	Please be careful that answers are not necessarily correct.
4.	答え合わせ	checking answers
5.	答える	respond
6.	聞かれたことだけに答えるようにしてください。	Please answer only what you are asked.
7. #	答案	examination paper, answer

363. 調　しら(べる)　チョウ　　search　　調

1.	調べる	search
2.	調べさせてほしいことがあるのですが……。	I have something that I want you to let me search for, but...
3.	もう少し調べてみる必要がありますね。	We need to try to search further.
4.	調子	condition
5.	調子に乗る	get carried away, show off
6.	体調	physical condition
7.	今日は体調が悪いので早めに帰らせていただきます。	I'm not feeling well today so I'm going home early.
8.	空調	air conditioning
9.	空調の調子が悪くて、部屋が暑い。	The air conditioning is malfunctioning, so the room is hot.
10. ¥	調査(する)	investigate

21-8R 典型的な夜型です。

364. 正 ただ(しい) ショウ セイ correct   正

1.		正しい	correct
2.		正しい答えってどこに書かれているんですか。	Where are the correct answers written?
3.		僕としては正しいと思ってたんですけど……。	As for me, I thought it was correct, but . . .
4.	+	正社員	full-time employee
5.		正社員になった時のメリットとデメリット	merits and demerits of becoming a full-time employee
6.	¥	正解	correct answer
7.	¥	正確(な)	accurate
8.		正直(な)	honest, frank
9.		どうして正直に答えられないんですか。	Why can't you answer honestly?
10.		大正	Taisho era (1912–1926)
11.		お正月	New Year's Day/Month

365. 違 ちが(う) イ   differ, different, incorrect   違

1.		違う	different from X
2.		だって、違ってたんだもん。	It's because it was wrong.
3.		写真と違わないぐらいきれいだね。	It's beautiful, not any different from the photo.
4.	+	違い	difference
5.		あの二人の違いが分かりません。	I don't see any difference between those two.
6.		思い違い	misconception
7.		ただの思い違いでした。	It was just my misunderstanding.
8.		間違い	mistake
9.		正しければ○、間違いは✗を付けてください。	Circle it if it's correct, put an X for wrong answers.

10.	間違(まちが)える	make a mistake
11.	彼、あの問題の答え間違ってたくせに。	Even though he got that problem's answer wrong.
12.	外国語っていうものは間違えば間違うほどうまくなるものですよ。	You get better at a foreign language the more mistakes you make.
13.	正しかったからよかったようなものの、もし間違っていたらどうしたんですか？	Good thing it was correct, but what would you have done if it was wrong?
14. #	違反(いはん)(する)	illegal

366. 研 ケン — enhance — 研

| 1. ¥ | 研修(けんしゅう)(する) | training |

367. 究 キュウ — study, master — 究

1.	研究(けんきゅう)(する)	research
2.	研究で分かったことが必ずしも正しいわけじゃない。	Things you find out through research are not necessarily correct.
3.	自分なりのペースで研究してます。	I'm doing research at my own pace.
4.	動物実験をする研究には反対です。	I'm opposed to research that uses animal experiments.
5. +	研究費(けんきゅうひ)	cost of research
6.	研究費が高くなることなんて最初から分かっていたはずなのに……。	I expected that the cost of research would be expensive from the beginning, but...
7.	研究所(けんきゅうじょ)	research institute
8. +	研究室(けんきゅうしつ)	research office, university faculty office

Now go to the Activity Book for 練習.

シーン 21-9R　SF 映画の歴史が変わる。
Changes in the history of sci-fi movies

Sasha and Eri are checking the reviews for the following movies.

テキスト Text

笑いと感動の全米大ヒット No. 1
SF 映画の歴史が変わる
ジェフリー・ライオン最新作

日本中の読者を泣かせた
神田まみのロングセラー小説
ついに映画化！

	レビュー・感想
☆☆☆☆☆	自分もあきらめずにやってやるぞ！という気持ちにさせてもらいました。
☆☆☆☆	笑いながら感動してしまいました。
☆☆	授業のシーンがちょっとつまんなかった。

	レビュー・感想
☆☆☆☆	思ってた通り、悪くない。
☆☆	最後が「え、だから？」って感じの終わり方で残念
☆☆☆	小説読まないと分かりづらくない？

+全米（ぜんべい）	all of America
+最新作（さいしんさく）	the most recent production

Cosmos Heroes	Moonlit Wolves
Funny and Exciting No. 1 in the U.S. Changes the history of sci-fi movies Newest production of Jeffery Lyon	It made readers cry across Japan A long selling novel by Mami Kanda is finally cinematized
Review・Impressions ☆☆☆☆☆ It gave me the feeling that I, too, will do it without giving up! ☆☆☆☆ It touched me with laughter. ☆☆ The class scene was boring.	Review・Impressions ☆☆☆☆ As expected, not bad. ☆☆ The ending was disappointing. I was like "so what?" ☆☆☆ Isn't it difficult to understand without reading the novel?

文字と例 Kanji with examples

368. 歴 レキ　　history　　歴

1. +学歴（がくれき）　　educational background
2. 学歴が高い人が多くていづらい……。　　It's hard to be here because there are many people who are highly educated.
3. たとえ学歴が低くても勝てるチャンスはあるよ。　　We have a chance to win even if we are less educated.
4. 学歴低いから難しいって言われてたけど、仕事ゲットしてやったぞ！　　I got the job despite being told that it would be difficult with my lack of education.
5. 日本の英語教育の問題の一つは、学歴があるのに英語がまだ話せない人が多いことです。　　One of the problems of English education in Japan is that there are many people with higher education who still cannot speak English.

369. 史 シ　　history　　史

1. 歴史（れきし）　　history
2. 歴史的な場所って聞いたけど、なんか新しくない？　　I heard it's a historical place, but isn't it a bit new?
3. だから歴史にはくわしくないって言ったでしょう！　　That's why I told you that I'm not an expert on history.

21-9R 典型的な校型です。

	4.		歴史的な説明をされても分かりづらいなあ。	Despite being given a historical explanation, it's difficult to understand.
	5.	+	日本史(にほんし)	Japanese history

370. 授 ジュ — give, award, teach 授

1.	教授(きょうじゅ)	professor
2.	教授と話せるようにできるだけがんばってみるよ。	I'll try my best to talk to the professor.
3.	教授は教授なりに何か考えがあるんだよ。	The professor probably has some kind of idea himself.

371. 業 ギョウ — work, a deed 業

1.	授業(じゅぎょう)	class
2.	歴史(れきし)の授業ってつまんないとよく思われてるけど、僕は好きだよ。	History class is often considered boring, but I like it.
3.	明日は数学と歴史と英語の授業があるからちゃんと勉強しておかないと……。	Tomorrow I have classes in math, history, and English, so I had better study for them in advance...
4.	学校の人に授業料が高過ぎって言ってやったよ。	I told someone working for school that tuition is too expensive.
5. +	残業(ざんぎょう)(する)	overtime work
6.	残業したくないけど、まだ仕事がたくさん残っていて……。	I don't want to work overtime, but I still have a lot of work remaining...
7. ¥	営業部(えいぎょうぶ)	operations division

372. 感 カン — feel 感

1.	感動(かんどう)(する)	be touched by
2.	感動的な話	a touching story
3.	この感動をみんなに伝えたい。	I want to convey my excitement to everyone.
4.	あんな勝負を見て、感動せずにはいられないよ。	Seeing that kind of match, I can't help but be impressed.

5.		感心(かんしん)(する)	be impressed by (with admiration)
6.		そんなことに感心している場合じゃないよ。	It's not time to be impressed with that kind of thing.
7.	+	感(かん)じる	feel X
8.		後ろから何かを感じるんだけど……。	I feel something from behind us...
9.	+	Xって感(かん)じ	like X
10.		気持ち悪くなって「うわ～！」て感じで出てきました。	I didn't feel well, so I was like "Ahhhh!" and left (of the building).
11.	#	感覚(かんかく)	touch (sensation)

373. 想 そう　　conception, idea, thought　　想

1.	感想(かんそう)	
2.	感想を言いかけたその時に電話が入った。	The call came when I was about to share my thoughts.
3.	自分なりの感想を言わせてもらうと、正直言ってあまり楽しくなかった。	When you allowed me to share my own thoughts, to tell you the truth, it was not much fun.
4.	予想(よそう)(する)	predict
5.	予想外(よそうがい)	unexpected
6.	この映画、タイトルのイメージで予想したのと違ってたよ。	This movie was different from what I expected from the image that I got from the title.
7.	今年の天気は予想しづらいらしい。	I heard that this year's weather is difficult to predict.
8.	理想的(りそうてき)(な)	ideal
9.	犬にだって理想的な家族はあるんじゃない？	There are ideal families even for dogs.
10. #	空想(くうそう)	imagination, fantasy

374. 笑 わら(う)　ショウ　　laugh, smile　　笑

1.	笑(わら)う	laugh
2.	他の人に笑われるのはだれだっていやなものです。	You know, being laughed at by other people is unpleasant for anyone.

3.	日本の映画館では声に出して笑う人があまりいないけど、アメリカの映画館では違う。	There are not many people who laugh out loud in Japanese movie theaters, but it is different in American movie theaters.
4.	+ 笑い声	laughter
5.	公園から子どもの笑い声が聞こえてくる。	I hear children's laughter from the park.
6.	(笑)	LOL
7.	ビーチに来てやったぞ！冬でめちゃくちゃ寒いけど(笑)	I came to the beach! But it's winter and extremely cold (LOL).
8.	# 失笑(する)	scornful laughter

375. 泣 な(く) キュウ — weep, cry, grieve

1.	泣く	cry
2.	大声で泣いた。	I cried loudly.
3.	全米が泣いた心温まる感動のストーリー	a story so heart-warming and touching that everyone in the U.S. cried
4.	泣ける話	tear-jerker
5.	聞けば聞くほど泣ける話ですね。	The more I hear the story, the more it makes me cry.
6.	女の子を泣かせちゃだめだよ。	You shouldn't make girls cry.
7.	+ 泣き声	tearful voice, crying sound
8.	あの家、毎晩泣き声が聞こえて心配だ。	I'm worried about that house because I hear someone crying every night.
9.	(泣)	Sad (similar to :-(in English)
10.	あの問題また間違えた (泣)	I got that question wrong again :-(
11.	# 号泣(する)	wailing

376. 化 カ — process of making something happen, transforming

| 1. | 文化 | culture |

2.	今日は日本とアメリカの文化の違いについてお話しさせていただきます。	Today I'm going to talk about the difference between Japanese and American culture.
3.	温暖化(おんだんか)	global warming
4.	温暖化というと?	What about global warming?
5. +	映画化(えいがか)(する)	cinematize
6.	この本、ついに映画化されることになりました。	This book will finally be made into a movie.

Now go to the Activity Book for 練習.

Then do 評価 activities, including 読んでみよう, 書き取り, and 書いてみよう.

21-9R 典型的(てんけいてき)な夜型(よるがた)です。

第22幕
Act 22

これさえできれば大丈夫(だいじょうぶ)。

If we can do just this much it will be fine.

雨(あめ)降(ふ)って地(じ)固(かた)まる。
April showers bring May flowers.
(lit. 'The ground firms up after rain.')

◆ 話す・聞く

Scene 22-1 プリントしたばっかりだったのに。
Even though I just finished printing it now.

Ikebe-san, the part timer, spills coffee all over a document that Sasha has just printed.

The script

サーシャ	池辺
ああ！	わ、すいません！
たった今、プリントしたばかりだったのに……。	申し訳ありません。どうしよう。
とにかく、やりなおしますから、できたら直ちにコピーしてもらえます？	はい。超特急でコピーさせてもらいます。
あと、そのコーヒー、できるまで我慢してもらえます？	あ、はい、すいません。
「すいません」「すいません」って、「すみません」じゃないの？	すいません、じゃなくてすみません。

Sasha	Ikebe
Aaah!	Whoa, I'm sorry!
Even though I just now finished printing it . . .	I am so sorry. What to do.
I'll reprint it, anyway, so when it's finished can I have you make copies right away?	Yes. Let me make the copies super fast.
Also, until those copies are finished can I have you hold off on that coffee?	Oh, yes, sorry.
"Sorry," "Sorry," shouldn't it be "I am sorry?"	Sorry, I mean I am sorry.

単語と表現

名詞

| 超特急(ちょうとっきゅう) | super fast |

動詞

こぼす (-U; こぼした)	spill something
汚す(よごす) (-U; 汚した)	get X dirty, pollute X
汚れる(よごれる) (-RU; 汚れた)	become dirty

表現

たった今(いま)	just now
Past sentence + ばかり・ばっかり	just X-ed
直(ただ)ちに	immediately, right away

Behind the scenes

BTS 1 Past sentence + ばかり・ばっかり

In this Act, you will see that ばかり (ばっかり for emphasis) has a number of uses. Following a past sentence, it indicates that the event described by the sentence just happened.

| 今月入(はい)ったばかりのメンバーです。よろしくお願いします。 | I am a member who just joined this month. |
| ついさっきやり直(なお)したばかりなのに、また変更(へんこう)するんですか? | Even though I just now fixed it, you're going to change it again? |

BTS 2 Expressing frustration in a professional setting

Expressing emotions is one of the most culture-bound aspects of life in Japan. In this Scene, Sasha expresses her frustration with Ikebe-san's job performance. Keep in mind that she is talking to a part-timer and not her supervisor. When she makes demands with 「もらえます？」 (not the more polite いただけますか), she is not really asking a question.

If there is a person who frustrates you and you express yourself directly, be aware that emotional outbursts are embarrassing to Japanese people. Don't be surprised if, after the fact, apologies are repeated over and over, especially to higher-ups. Also keep in mind that actually losing one's temper is a last resort in Japan. In fact, when someone gets angry, rather than confronting the other person directly, they are apt to vent their frustration to other in-group members. In some cases, they may expect, or ask, the third party to convey their feelings. It would not be unusual for a colleague to come to you to report that another co-worker complained about your behavior. Try not to judge this behavior as you would if it happened in your own culture. Ask a trusted 先輩 or teacher what you should do.

Now go to the Activity Book for 練習 and 腕試し.

Scene 22-2 コンビニ弁当ばかり……。
Nothing but convenience store bento...

Brian has just finished dinner with his host family.

The script

ブライアン	お母さん
ごちそうさま！何と言ってもお母さんの手料理が一番！僕、ホームステイにしてよかった。	え？留学生はみんなホームステイじゃないの？
むしろ、ホームステイの方が少ないです。約4割程度でしょうね。あとは寮、アパートなどで……。	へえ。みんな何食べてるのかしら？
コンビニ弁当。	ええ？毎日？
ばかりっていう訳ではないけど、多いみたいです。	そうなの。

Brian	Host mother
It was delicious! No matter how you look at it Mom's homemade food is the best! I'm glad I opted for the homestay.	Huh? Aren't all the exchange students doing a homestay?
On the contrary, homestays are fewer. About 40 percent or so, I'd imagine. The rest (live) in dorms, apartments, and the like.	Huh. I wonder what they are all eating?
Bento from convenient stores.	What? Everyday?
Not only bento, but it seems they have them a lot.	Really.

単語と表現

名詞

手料理(てりょうり)	home cooking
家庭料理(かていりょうり)	home cooking
程度(ていど)	about (following a number), degree
コンビニ弁当(べんとう)	bento from a convenience store
インスタント	instant

助詞

など	and the like, et cetera
かしら	I wonder

表現

何(なん)と言っても	no matter what people say, in the end
むしろ	rather, on the contrary
約(やく) + Quantity	about, approximately
(Noun +) ばかり・ばっかり	just, only X

Behind the scenes

BTS 3 Exclusivity: Noun + ばかり・ばっかり

ばかり alone or the combination of Noun plus ばかり means 'only X' or 'nothing but X.'

インスタントのものばっかり食(た)べるのは不健康(ふけんこう)じゃないですか。	Isn't it unhealthy to eat nothing but instant stuff?
仕事(しごと)ばかりして、子供(こども)と遊(あそ)ぶ時間がない。	All I do is work; I have no time to play with the children.

You will also find particles before or after the [Noun + ばかり] combination.

ただ調子が悪くて、うちにばかりいたくなった。	I just felt bad and wanted nothing more than to be at home.
私ばかりにやらせないで、少しは自分で責任持ってやってもらえませんか？	Don't make just me do it; why not assume the responsibility yourself and do it?

ばかり・ばっかり may appear at the beginning of an utterance, the way Brian uses it in this Scene, when the presumed noun (コンビニ弁当) has already been mentioned.

A: え？ラーメン？また？ B: ばっかりだよね、この頃。じゃあ、カレーにする？	A: What? Ramen? Again? B: Nothing but that recently, isn't it? Well, shall we have curry then?

BTS 4 むしろ

むしろ is used between Nouns or Sentences to indicate that one alternative is more acceptable or accurate than another. The less preferable alternative is often preceded by より.

先生というより、むしろコーチのような方です。	She's more like a coach than a teacher.
よく失敗します。むしろ失敗しないことの方が珍しいです。	I make mistakes often. Rather, it's rare that I don't make mistakes.

BTS 5 など

You saw なんか used to mean 'something like.' など is its more formal equivalent. Both follow Nouns as well as 〜て forms.

工学が専攻ということは、数学なども得意なんですか？	You major in engineering, so does that mean you are also good at math and the like?
授業は終わりましたけど、来週は試験ですから、遊んでなどはいられませんよ。	Classes are over, but next week is exams, so I can't play (and relax), you know.

BTS 6 かしら

かしら follows a Sentence to mean 'maybe' or 'I wonder.' It is similar to かなあ but much softer sounding. Note that だ disappears before かしら.

曇ってきたわね。午後は雨かしら。   It's turning cloudy, isn't it? Maybe it's going to rain in the afternoon.

こちら、いただいていいかしら。   I wonder if it's alright for me to accept this.

Now go to the Activity Book for 練習 and 腕試し.

Scene 22-3 コピーさえできれば……。
If we can just get the copies done . . .

Sasha has finished reprinting the document that Ikebe-san ruined earlier. All that remains is to make copies.

The script

池辺	サーシャ
じゃあ、コピーしてきます。	お願いします。コピーさえできればあとはまとめて届けるだけですから。
コピー機のコード、拝借します。	どうぞ。

Ikebe	Sasha
Okay, I'll go make copies.	Please. If we can just get the copies done, all we have left to do is put it together and deliver it, so . . .
I'll borrow the copy machine code.	Go ahead.

単語と表現

名詞

拝借(する)↓	borrow (humble)
拝見(する)↓	look (humble)
頂戴(する)↓	receive (humble)
コピー機	copy machine
コード	code

動詞

揃える (-RU; 揃えた)	arrange, complete
揃う (-U; 揃った)	be a full set, become complete

助詞

さえ	if only

表現

Noun + さえ + 〜れば	if and only if X

Behind the scenes

BTS 7 Special humble nouns: 拝借

You have seen a number of humble polite Verbs earlier: いただく in Act 3, 伺う and 参る in Act 5, 申す, おる, and 存じる in Act 6, and 差し上げる in Act 12. Three additional examples that use [Noun する・いたす] come up with this Scene: 拝借する, 拝見する, and 頂戴する. 頂戴します is the standard formal expression when accepting someone's business card. In this Scene, Ikebe-san is being extra polite (コピー機のコード、拝借します。) because she botched an earlier job.

よろしければ、こちら、ちょっと拝見します。すぐお返しいたしますから。	If it is all right, I'll take a look at this. I'll give it back to you right away.
恐れ入りますが、お名刺を頂戴できますでしょうか。	Sorry to impose, but may I please have your business card?
大切な資料をずっと拝借しっぱなしで申し訳ありませんでした。お蔭様で論文が仕上がりました。	I'm sorry to have borrowed your valuable materials for such a long time without returning them. Thanks to you, my research paper is complete.

BTS 8 Noun + さえ + 〜ば

In this Act, you will see that the Particle さえ occurs in a number of patterns. The first of these is following a Noun, emphasizing the need for that Noun ('if only . . . , as long as . . .') for what follows (typically in the provisional 〜ば form).

典型的(てんけいてき)な例(れい)さえあれば、それでいいですから。	If only we have a typical example, that would be enough.
体(からだ)さえ丈夫(じょうぶ)なら、なんでもできますよ。	If only your body is strong, you can do anything.
お客様(きゃくさま)さえこれでよろしければ、私(わたし)の方(ほう)はいつでもこれで進(すす)めさせていただけます。	As long as our clients are satisfied, for my part I can promote this any time.
もっと練習(れんしゅう)さえしていれば、失敗(しっぱい)しなかったと思います。	I think if only we had practiced more, we wouldn't have failed.

Now go to the Activity Book for 練習 and 腕試し.

Scene 22-4 社長がいいって言いさえすれば……。 If only the president would just say okay...

Sasha and Kanda-san are becoming impatient about a time-sensitive project for which they are eagerly awaiting final approval by the president.

The script

サーシャ	神田
なかなかゴーサインが出ませんね。	うん。
一体いつになったら始められるんでしょうか。	さすがに焦りますね。ただ時間が過ぎていくばかりのようで、
社長がいいって言ってくれさえすれば進められるんですね。	そう聞いてます。すでに社長のところまで上がっているから、あとは社長次第だって。

Sasha	Kanda
The "go" signal doesn't seem to be forthcoming, does it.	Yeah.
How far out does it have to get for us to be able to start?	It's frustrating even for us. It feels as if time is just moving ahead with nothing else happening.
If the president would just give us the okay, we could move ahead, right?	That's what I hear. [The proposal] has already reached the president, so the rest is up to the president.

単語と表現

名詞

ゴーサイン	"go" signal
非常 (に)	extraordinary; emergency

139

委員	committee member
委員会	committee meeting
委員長	committee chair
役員会	officers' meeting
理事	governing board
理事会	governing board meeting
理事長	governing board chair
オーケー(する)	okay
許可(する)	permission
理解(する)	understanding
承諾(する)	consent, agree
検討(する)	consider, investigate, examine
選挙(する)	election
投票(する)	vote
効率的(な)	efficiently
能力	ability
完璧(な)	perfect

表現

一体	what in the world, what the heck
時間が過ぎる	time passes
Non-past Sentence + ばかり	all it does is X
Verb stem + さえ + 〜れば・たら	if and only if X
すでに	already
X次第	depending on X

Behind the scenes

BTS 9 Non-past Sentence + ばかり

When ばかり follows a non-past Sentence, it indicates that 'nothing but X happens' or 'all (someone/something) does is X.'

「ダメだ」というばかりで、ちっともやり方を教えてくれないから、どうすればいいかわからないんです。	All she says is, "It's wrong," and doesn't tell us how to do it at all, so we don't know what to do.
初めの３ヶ月は慣れないから苦しいばかりでしたけど、楽しい思い出が一つもないかというと、そうでもないんですよね。	I wasn't used to it for the first three months so it was nothing but misery, but it's not as if I don't have a single happy memory.
部屋とか家具が立派なばかりで、あまりすみやすい家とは言えませんでした。	The rooms and furniture were nothing but splendid; I couldn't say it would be a house that's easy to live in.

BTS 10 Verb stem ＋さえ

Much as Nouns can be emphasized in combination with さえ, a Verb can be emphasized in the sequence [Verb stem ＋ さえ] to mean 'if only X happens.' This combination is probably most frequently followed by すれば.

ここにいさえすれば、みんなが面倒見てくれますから。	If only you were here, everyone would take care of you.
毎日１０分でいいですから散歩などの軽い運動をなさりさえすれば、いいかと思います。	Ten minutes every day is fine, so as long as you do some light exercise like a walk or something – I think that would be okay.

Now go to the Activity Book for 練習 and 腕試し.

Scene 22-5 そう言えば……。 Come to think of it...

As Sasha and Kanda-san finish their briefing, Kanda-san realizes that his calculator is missing.

The script

神田	サーシャ
それはそうと、僕の計算機、見ませんでした？	いえ？
確かつい３０分ぐらい前までここで使ってたはずなんだけど……。	そう言えば、さっき使ってられましたね。で、部長と話しながら書類持って……
あ、会議室だ！どうも、どうも。	

Kanda	Sasha
By the way, have you seen the calculator?	No?
I thought for sure I was using it here until just 30 minutes ago, but . . .	Come to think of it, you were using it a while ago, weren't you. And while you were talking to the division chief you were holding some documents . . .
Ah, the conference room! Thanks.	

単語と表現

名詞

計算機	calculator
計算(する)	calculate
職員室	staff room
事務室	office

社長室 (しゃちょうしつ)	president's office
秘書室 (ひしょしつ)	secretary's office
秘書 (ひしょ)	secretary

動詞

探す (-U; 探した)	look for X
見つける (-RU; 見つけた)	find X
見つかる (-U; 見つかった)	X is found

表現

それはそうと	by the way
ところで	by the way, incidentally
つい３０分	just 30 minutes
そう言えば、	speaking of that, come to think of it

Behind the scenes

BTS 11 Connectives

In this Scene, note the useful expressions それはそうと and そう言えば that connect a related thought to the context at hand. You have seen other expressions that accomplish the same thing, including ちなみに and ところで.

ごちそうさまでした。それはそうと、来週の会の場所はもう決まってます？	I'm finished (thanks for the meal). By the way, has the location of next week's gathering been decided?
インスタントの食べ物も、この頃のは味が良くなりましたね。そう言えばグルメの神田さんも、インスタントカレー、食べるそうですよ。	Even if they are instant food, the ones these days have much improved flavor, don't they? Speaking of which, I heard that even Kanda-san, the gourmet, eats instant curry.

Now go to the Activity Book for 練習 and 腕試し.

Scene 22-6 池辺さんの話 (失敗談)
Ikebe-san's story (explaining failure)

Ikebe-san reports to Kanda-san about what happened earlier in the day.

The script

池辺	神田
失敗してばっかりですいません。	え？どうかしたの？
さっきサーシャさんがプリントされたばっかりの文書にコーヒーこぼしちゃって……。	ありゃ。
それもバアーっと	そうなんだ。
さすがのサーシャさんもかなり頭にきたみたいで、怖かったです。	へえ。
言葉遣いまで直されました。	サーシャさんに？今ちょっとプロジェクトのことで気が立ってるからね
私が気をつけてさえいればと思うと、申し訳なくて……。	まあ、そんなに気を落とさなくたって、そのうち慣れますよ。

Ikebe	Kanda
I'm sorry that I do nothing but fail.	What? Did something happen?
A while ago, I spilled coffee all over documents that Sasha had just printed.	Oh dear.
It went all over the place.	Wow, really.
Even Sasha must have gotten really ticked off – it was scary.	Really.
I even got corrected on my language.	By Sasha? She's all worked up over this project, so . . .

| I keep thinking if only I had been careful, and I feel bad . . . | There, there. No need to be so discouraged; you'll get used to things soon enough. |

単語と表現

名詞

順調(な)	doing well, favorable, okay
興奮(する)	excitement
感情	emotion
感情的(な)	emotional
言葉遣い	language use
プロジェクト	project

動詞

悲しむ (-U; 悲しんだ)	be sad
慰める (-RU; 慰めた)	console, comfort (someone)
踏む (-U; 踏んだ)	step on, tread on

形容詞

| 情けない | pathetic, miserable |

表現

ありゃ	oh dear, oh my
バアーっと	[expression of dismay], all over and rapidly
頭にくる	get angry
言葉遣いまで	even the choice of words
気が立つ	get worked up, get excited

〜てさえいれば	as long as you keep doing X, as long as it keeps doing X
気を落とす	get discouraged, become disheartened
気を落とさなくたって	even if you don't get discouraged

気を入れる	set your mind to
やる気を出す	become enthusiastic

Behind the scenes

BTS 12 Verb 〜て + ばかり・ばっかり

A 〜て form plus ばかり・ばっかり may be followed by some form of いる or by some form of です to mean 'doing only X' or 'doing nothing but X.' When the combination is [Noun する] you are more likely to hear [Noun してばかり] than [Noun ばかりして].

いつまでも泣いてばかりいないで、元気出して！	Don't be crying all the time, cheer up!
ハワイに行ったのに、働いてばかりだった。	In spite of going to Hawaii, all I did was work.

BTS 13 〜て + さえ

Yet another combination with さえ is following a 〜て form, 'if only X.' This combination emphasizes the absolute necessity of doing X. When the combination is [Noun する] you are more likely to hear [Noun さえしていれば] than [Noun してさえいれば].

もう少し健康に気をつけてさえいればよかったと、思います。今になってそんなこと考えても遅いんですけど……。	If only I had taken better care of my health. It's too late now to think about that sort of thing, but . . .
子供の勉強を手伝ってさえくださるのでしたら、いついらしてくださっても結構です。	If you are here <u>only</u> to help our children study, it's fine to come any time.

ええ？論文の締め切り、明日って本当ですか？それ知ってさえいれば、週末もうちょっと頑張ったんですけど……。	What? Is it true that the deadline for the paper is tomorrow? If only I'd known that, I would have done more over the weekend, but . . .

BTS 14 ～たって

The suffix ～たって combines with all Core Sentences to mean something like 'even if.' Note that

a   the Noun form [Noun だったって] is frequently shortened to [Noun だって];
b   the Adjective is built on the ～く form;
c   the Verb is built on the Past form.

Noun だっ(たっ)て	本当だっ(たっ)て	even if it's true
Adjective ～くたって	安くたって	even if it's cheap
Verb ～たって・～だって	行ったって 読んだって	even if we go even if we read it

～たって is primarily a spoken pattern, similar to ～ても but more assertive.

部長に頼んだって無駄だね。	There's no point even asking the division chief, is there.
高くたって、必要なんだろう？買おうよ。	Even if it's expensive, we need it, right? Let's buy it.
このテストはね、特に前の日に勉強しなくたってできます。	This test, y'know, you can manage even if you don't study the day before.
社長だって「やれ」っておっしゃってるじゃないですか。やりましょうよ。	Even the president is pushing us to do this. Let's do it.

You may hear 何だって added to a question, indicating disbelief or mystification.

何だってあんな時間にあんなところに行ったんだろう。	How in the world did you end up going to that sort of place at a time like that?

When どんなに precedes 〜たって, the meaning becomes 'no matter how (much) . . .'

マラソン？冗談でしょう。どんなに行きたくたって、今の状態じゃあ無理だよ。 — Marathon? You're joking. However much you want to run, in your current condition, it's impossible.

Now go to the Activity Book for 練習 and 腕試し.

Then do 評価 activities.

◆ 読み書き

シーン 22-7R 発送(はっそう)のお知(し)らせ Shipping notice

Sasha ordered something from an online store and received the following email.

テキスト Text

件名：ご注文の「FUKUZAWA おしるこ味プロテイン」その他1点の発送

発送のお知らせ

注文番号: 123-475934 19038402

サーシャ・モリス様

ジャパンショップをご利用いただき、ありがとうございます。ご注文のお手続きが完了しましたので、お知らせいたします。何かご不明な点や質問などがございましたら、ご連絡ください。お問い合わせはメールにてお願いいたします。「発送済み」のご注文はキャンセルができませんのでご注意ください。

お届け予定：

金曜日、07/05

お届け先：

サーシャ・モリス様

330-1234

埼玉県

福沢市大山５－５－５アパートナウ２０１号室

発送の詳細

- 【オンライン限定】FUKUZAWA おしるこ味プロテイン【200g】 ¥1980
- 【単行本】実はウソばかり？むしろしない方がいいダイエット ¥972

Subject: Your order "FUKUZAWA sweet red-bean flavored protein (powder)" and one more item has shipped

Shipping Notice

Order Number: 123-475934 19038402

Sasha Morris,

Thank you for using Japan Shop. We are letting you know that your order has been processed. If anything is unclear or if you have questions, please contact us. Please send all inquiries via email. Please note that orders that have been "shipped" cannot be cancelled.

Scheduled Delivery:

Friday, 07/05

Ship to:

Sasha Morris

330-1234

Saitama Prefecture

Fukuzawa City, Oyama 5-5-5, Apartment NOW #201

Shipping Details

- [Limited Online] FUKUZAWA sweet red-bean flavor protein (powder) [200g] ¥1980
- [Book] In fact, is it all lies? Diets you should avoid ¥972

Between the lines

BTL 1 にて・まで in business writing

In written style, rather than で or によって, you may see にて.

お問い合わせはメールにて、お願いいたします。	Please send your inquiries via email.
メールにて失礼いたします。	I'm sorry to bother you via email (instead of talking to you).

Similarly, まで is used to mean 'for the time being' when you don't have time to write more.

以上、取り急ぎのご報告まで。	The above was just a quick report.
取り急ぎご挨拶まで。	This is just a quick greeting. (Let me send you further details later.)

BTL 2 Japanese addresses

Generally, Japanese address information is organized from general (postal code, city name) to specific (house number). The postal codes used in Japanese generally contain seven digits (i.e., 123-4567). Below are some kanji characters associated with Japanese addresses. Many of these characters will not be formally introduced here, but they might be helpful when you travel or move to Japan or send something to Japan.

市 (し)	city	丁目 (ちょうめ)	neighborhood subdivision
町 (まち・ちょう)	town	番 (ばん)	number (in a series)
区 (く)	ward (subdivision of a large city)	県 (けん)	prefecture
郡 (ぐん)	district	～号室 (ごうしつ)	classifier for room numbers

文字と例 Kanji with examples

377. 点　テン　　point, dot, punctuation, item　　点

1.	１００点 (てん)	100 points (perfect score)
2.	その他１点の発送	one more item has shipped
3.	歴史のテストでは０点ばかり……。	He frequently gets zero points on his history tests …
4.	以下の点を直してください。	Please fix the following points.
5.	授業ではこの点に集中して教えるようにしてください。	Please focus on this point as you teach in class.
6.	初めて１００点を取った感想は？	How do you feel about getting a perfect score for the first time?
7.	名前を書き忘れたから０点にされたらしいよ。	I heard that he forgot to write his name and got no points.

378.	用	ヨウ		purpose, business, use	用
	1.	+	用がある	have something to do	
	2.		お姉様に用があるのですが……。	There's a matter I need to attend to with your older sister, but . . .	
	3.		実用的(な)	practical	
	4.	+	X用	for the purpose of X	
	5.		男用のスリッパ	slippers for men	
	6.	+	使用(する)	use	
	7.		あの部屋は今使用中です。	That room is being used right now.	
	8.	+	利用(する)	making the most of	
	9.		ATMをご利用いただきありがとうございました。	Thank you for using the ATM.	
	10.	+	用事	something to do, errand	
	11.		さっき用事を終えたばかりで疲れています。	I just finished my errands, so I'm tired.	
	12.		用事があったのですが、子どもが熱を出して家で寝ているもので……。	I had some errands to run, but my child got a fever and is sleeping at home, so . . .	
	13.	+	用意(する)	preparation	
	14.		朝食にはパンやヨーグルトなどをご用意させていただいています。	We have prepared things like bread and yogurt for breakfast.	
379.	続	つづ(く) つづ(ける) ゾク		continue	続
	1.		続く	X continues	
	2.		ダイエット始めてみたけど、三日も続かなかった。	I started a diet, but it didn't even last three days.	

3.	続ける	continue X
4.	これ以上は続けられないですよ。	We can't continue anymore.
5.	続き	continuation, succession
6.	続きはまた今度ということで……。	We will continue once again next time, so . . .
7.	手続き(する)	procedure
8.	去年手続きを済ませたばかりです。	I just finished the procedure last year.
9.	さっき手続きを済ませた ところ・ばかり です。	I just finished the procedure a short while ago.
10.	連続(する)	continuous, consecutive
11.	悪い事、いやな事が連続して起こるのはなぜだと思いますか。	Why do you think things that are bad and unpleasant happen in succession?
12.	# 継続は力なり	Continuation is power.

380. 完 カン finish 完

1.	完	finish
2.	¥ 完璧(な)	perfect
3.	¥ 完成(する)	complete, bring to perfection
4.	完全(な)	perfect, complete
5.	乗り物が完全に止まるまでもうしばらくお待ちください。	Please wait a while until the ride comes to a complete stop.

381. 了 リョウ finish, completion, the end 了

| 1. | + 完了(する) | completion |
| 2. | 試験は先ほど完了したばかりです。 | The exam just finished a short while ago. |

3.	+	終了(する)		termination, end
4.		映画はもう終了しております。		The movie is already over.
5.		その研究は開始から終了までどのぐらいかかると思いますか。		How long do you think that research will take from beginning to end?
6.		工事は予定通りに終了したようです。		The construction was completed as planned.
7.	¥	了解(する)		understanding, agreement

382. 届 とど(く) とど(ける) — report, deliver, reach

1.	届く		X is delivered
2.	最悪な場合、届くのは来週になってしまうかと思います。		In the worst case scenario, I think the day that it will get delivered to you is next week.
3.	先日送ったばかりですが、もう届いたんですか。		I just sent it the other day, but has it already been delivered?
4.	届ける		deliver X
5.	これ、明日までに届けておいてもらえませんか。		Could I have you deliver this for me by tomorrow?
6.	+	(お)届け先	shipping address
7.		届け先が間違っていたらしく、まだ届いてないんです。	I heard that the shipping address was mistaken and it hasn't been delivered yet.
8.	#	届け出	notification

383. 詳 くわ(しい) ショウ — detail

1.	詳しい	well-informed, detailed
2.	詳しければ詳しいほどいいです。	The more well-informed you are, the better.
3.	あの意見に反対するのにはもう少し詳しく知らないと難しいんじゃないかな。	I think it would be difficult to oppose that opinion unless we know a little more.

4.	+	Xに詳(くわ)しい		be familiar with X
5.		八木部長って実は歴史に詳しいって知ってました？		Did you know that Yagi-buchō actually knows a lot about history?
6.	+	詳細(しょうさい)		detail
7.		詳細が分かってから後日連絡いたします。		I'll contact you later after I find out the details.

384. 質　シツ　quality

1.	+	質(しつ)がいい・よい	of good quality
2.		今日の魚は質がいいよ〜。	The fish today is good quality.
3.		質問(しつもん)	question
4.		日本のこれからの経済について何か質問のある人はいますか。	Is there anyone who has questions about the future economy of Japan?
5.		この質問に答えられる人いますか？	Is there anyone who can answer this question?
6.		その質問ですが、ちょっと調べてみないと答えるのは難しいかと思います。	I think it would be difficult to answer that question unless I do some searching.
7.		その質問にはこの論文の内容を読むといいと思います。	It would be good to read the contents of this thesis for that question.
8.		受験のことで質問してもいいですか。	May I ask a question about the college exam?

385. 限　かぎ(る)　ゲン　limit, restrict

1.	限(かぎ)る	set a limit to X
2.	予定通りに行くとは限らない。	Things don't necessarily go as planned.
3.	今度の試合、あのチームが負けるとは限らないよ。	That team won't necessarily lose in the next match.

4.	+	限定	limitation
5.		このデザインは春限定でございます。	This design is limited to the spring only.
6.		この絵を限定で５名様にプレゼントいたします。	We will give this picture as a present for just five people.
7.	#	限度	a limit

Now go to the Activity Book for 練習.

シーン 22-8R 履歴書 Resume

The following is the first page of a resume that Amy wrote for her internship in Japan.

テキスト Text

履歴書

令和〇X年 12月 23日現在

ふりがな	えいみー・じょんそん	生年月日		性別
氏名	エイミー・ジョンソン	平成XX年 8月 30日生 (現 24歳)		男・㊛

ふりがな	おれごんしゅう くりんとんし かれっじろーど 5771 ひがてぃーびれっじ 245
現住所	〒97207 オレゴン州 クリントン市 カレッジロード 5771 ヒガティービレッジ 245
自宅：	614-555-6446
携帯番号：	同上

E-mail: amyjohnson555@cu.edu

年	月	学歴
平成XX年	6	アメリカ合衆国オハイオ州オハイオアカデミー高等学校 卒業
平成XX年	9	アメリカ合衆国オレゴン州クリントン大学 人文学部 言語学科 入学
令和X年	4	アメリカ合衆国オレゴン州クリントン大学 人文学部 言語学科 卒業予定

年	月	職歴
平成XX年	9	アメリカ合衆国オハイオアカデミー高等学校 特別支援教育プログラムアシスタント 入職
平成XX年	6	アメリカ合衆国オハイオアカデミー高等学校 特別支援教育プログラムアシスタント 離職
平成XX年	1	サンスケマーケット アルバイト勤務 (レジ打ち・品出し・販売スタッフ)
		現在に至る

22-8R これさえできれば大丈夫。

単語と表現

#	人文学(じんぶんがく)	study of the humanities
#	特別支援教育(とくべつしえんきょういく)	special support education
#	レジ打(う)ち	cash register
#	品出(しなだ)し(する)	stock, goods
#	販売(はんばい)(する)	sale

Resume	as of year Reiwa X, month 12, date 23		
Furigana: eimii jonson	Year, month, and date of birth		Gender
Name: Amy Johnson	Year XXXX August 30th (current age 24)		M・F
Furigana: oregon-shuu kurinton-shi karejji-roodo 5771 hagatii-birejji 245			
Current address 〒97207 5771 College Road, 245 Hagerty Village, Clinton City, Oregon			
Home:　　Cell: 614-555-6446	E-mail: amyjohnson555@cu.edu		

Year	Month	Educational background
Heisei XX	6	Graduated from Ohio Academy High School, Ohio, U.S.A.
Heisei XX	9	Entered Clinton University in Oregon, U.S.A. College of Humanities, Linguistics
Reiwa X	4	Anticipated graduation from Clinton University in Oregon, U.S.A. College of Humanities, Linguistics

Year	Month	Work Experience
Heisei XX	9	Started working as an assistant in special education at Ohio Academy High School, Ohio, U.S.A.
Heisei XX	6	Left working as an assistant in special education at Ohio Academy High School, Ohio, U.S.A.
Heisei XX	1	Sansuke Market part-time (cash register, stocking, sales staff)
		Applies up to the present

BTL 3 履歴書 (りれきしょ)

Japanese resumes are traditionally written by hand, but typed ones are becoming more common. Whether you type it or write it by hand, be sure to draft it first and then prepare a clean version with no errors. In professional settings, documents with erasures, cross-outs, and whiteouts are not received well.

Note that 学歴 (がくれき) and 職歴 (しょくれき) are written in chronological order.

The expression 同上 (どうじょう) is used to avoid redundancy when you are using the same number for your home phone and cell phone, and the same address for your mailing address and home address. However, you should avoid using 同上 for full names and titles in the 学歴 and 職歴 sections even though it may seem unnecessary to write the same names and titles repeatedly.

When you fill out your own resume, you will need to become familiar with kanji characters that are not introduced in in this textbook such as the following expressions with the # symbol:

	Expressions used in labels			Useful expressions for filling out your resume	
+	生年月日 (せいねんがっぴ)	date and month of birth	+	同上 (どうじょう)	same as above
+	X 生 (うまれ)	born on/in X	#	令和 (れいわ)	Reiwa
#	X 歳 (さい)	age X	#	平成 (へいせい)	Heisei
#	性別 (せいべつ)	gender	#	アメリカ合衆国 (がっしゅうこく)	U.S.A.
#	氏名 (しめい)	name	+	X 学部 (がくぶ)	college/faculty of X
#	現在 (げんざい)	present	#	X 学科 (がっか)	department X
	自宅 (じたく)	home		入学 (にゅうがく)・卒業 (そつぎょう)	start/graduate from school

¥	携帯番号 (けいたいばんごう)	mobile number	
#	入社・退社 (にゅうしゃ・たいしゃ)		enter/leave a company
#	入職・離職 (にゅうしょく・りしょく)		start/leave employment
#	就職・退職 (しゅうしょく・たいしょく)		employment/retirement
#	X 勤務 (きんむ)		work as/at X
#	現在に至る (げんざいにいたる)		applies up to the present

文字と例 Kanji with examples

386. 住 す(む) ジュウ   live, dwell

1. 名古屋に住む — live in Nagoya
2. 日本に行ったらどこに住むつもりなんですか。— Where are you planning to live when you go to Japan?
3. このエリアに住めさえすればどこでもいいです。— Anywhere is fine as long as I can live in this area.
4. 便利なところに住んでるもので、運動もせずに食べてばかりだから太るばかり(笑)。— I live in a convenient place, and I just eat without exercising, so I'm only gaining weight (LOL).
5. # 衣食住 (いしょくじゅう) — clothing, food, and housing
6. + 住所 (じゅうしょ) — address
7. 名前が書いてなくても住所さえあれば届くらしいですよ。— Even if the name is not written, I heard that things get delivered if they have an address.
8. 住めば都 (すめばみやこ) — There is no place like home.
9. 駅から遠くて不便だっていうから心配してたけど、住めば都だね。— Someone said that it's far from the station and inconvenient and I was worried, but it turns out to be great.

387. 職 ショク   work, position, job

1. + 職員 (しょくいん) — staff
2. 職員室 — staff room, teacher's lounge
3. + 職歴 (しょくれき) — work experience
4. 新しい社長さん、職歴がすごいですね。— the new company president's work experience is amazing.
5. + 職業 (しょくぎょう) — job, occupation

6.		どの職業にしますか？	Which occupation would you choose?
7.	#	住職 (じゅうしょく)	the chief priest of a Buddhist temple
8.	+	転職(する) (てんしょく)	job change
9.		転職は５０代になってからでも遅くないはず(泣)。	I expect that it's not late to switch my job even after I am in my fifties (sad).
10.	#	入職(する) (にゅうしょく)	start work
11.	#	退職(する) (たいしょく)	leave work

388. 卒 ソツ graduate 卒

1.		卒業(する) (そつぎょう)	graduation
2.		卒業さえできれば……。	If only I can just graduate . . .
3.		最後のプロジェクトも終わり、あとは卒業するばかりだ。	The last project is completed, so the only thing left to do is to graduate.
4.	#	中卒 (ちゅうそつ)	middle school graduate
5.	#	高卒 (こうそつ)	high school graduate
6.	+	大卒 (だいそつ)	college graduate
7.		大卒でも仕事がない人って多いらしいですよ。	I heard that there are a lot of people, even college graduates, without work.
8.	+	卒業生 (そつぎょうせい)	students who graduated
9.		卒業生が会いに来てくれるというのは先生としてうれしいことだ。	It's a happy thing for teachers when their former students come to visit.

389. 等 など トウ etc., rank, level 等

1.		X 等 (など・とう)	X, etc.
2.		返していない本等がありましたら、図書館に行ってきてください。	If you have books and other things that you haven't returned, please go to the library.
3.		趣味は合気道やフラワーアレンジメント等です。	My hobbies are aikido, flower arranging, etc.
4.		大雪による電車の運休等ございますので、お確かめください。	There are things like cancellations of trains due to heavy snow, so please check.
5.	+	高等学校 (こうとうがっこう)	high school

6.	#	平等(な) びょうどう			equal
7.	#	X等 とう			X class, rank

390. 別　わか(れる)　ベツ　separate　別

1.		別 べつ	different, separate
2.		男女別ランキング「40代の社会人が転職したい会社」 てんしょく	ranking by gender, "(a list of) companies to which working adults in their forties want to change their jobs"
3.		別に	not particularly
4.		意味は別にありません。	There is no meaning in particular.
5.		別れる わか	part from, separate from
6.		彼女と別れた日の思い出	memories of the day I broke up with her
7.	+	分別(する) ぶんべつ	separate
8.		ゴミの分別	garbage separation
9.	#	分別がある ふんべつ	having good sense, discrete
10.	#	性別 せいべつ	gender

391. 現　あらわ(れる)　ゲン　reality, present　現

1.	+	現場 げんば	the scene (of a crime/an accident)
2.		工事現場	construction site
3.	+	現代 げんだい	the present day
4.		現代の若者は「ミレニアル世代」と呼ばれているそうだ。	I hear that young people nowadays are called millennials.
5.	+	現金 げんきん	cash
6.		現金ないんだけど、送金アプリ持ってる？	I don't have cash, but do you have an app to transfer money?
7.	+	現住所 げんじゅうしょ	current address
8.	+	現職 げんしょく	current job
9.		転職を考えているんだけど、現職よりいい仕事ってなかなかないんだよね。	I'm thinking about changing my job, but it's difficult to find a job that is better than my current job.
10.	¥	現地 げんち	place, destination

162

11.	#	現実 (げんじつ)		reality
12.	#	現れる (あらわれる)		appear

392. 存 ソン　exist　存

1.		存じる (ぞんじる)	know, find out, think (humble)
2.		お名前は存じております。	I am familiar with the name.
3.		お仕事をお辞めになったことは存じませんでした。	I didn't know you quit work.
4.		ご存知 (ごぞんじ)	know (honorific)
5.		白井さんもご存知ですか。	Shirai-san, do you know, too?
6.	¥	保存 (ほぞん)(する)	preserve, save
7.	#	現存 (げんそん)(する)	in existence

393. 借 か(りる)　シャク　borrow　借

1.		借りる (かりる)	borrow X from (someone)
2.		研究のためなら図書館の本借りたければ借りたいだけどうぞ。	When it's for your research, if you want to borrow the books in the library, you may borrow as many as you want.
3.		借りた本の感想は？	What are your thoughts on the book you borrowed?
4.		勝負に勝ったら借りたお金全部返してやるよ。	If you win the match, I will return all of the money that I borrowed from you.
5.		もうこれ以上借りるわけにはいかないよ。	I can't and I won't borrow anymore.
6.	+	借金 (しゃっきん)(する)	debt, loan
7.		借金さえしなければ最悪なことにならなかったのに……。	Things wouldn't have turned out to be so bad if I hadn't borrowed money.

394. 拝 ハイ　bowing one's head (in respect), worship　拝

1.	拝見 (はいけん)(する)	see, read, watch (humble)
2.	教授が書かれた論文、拝見させていただきました。	I read the thesis that the professor wrote.
3.	拝借 (はいしゃく)(する)	borrow (humble)

4.		申し訳ありませんが、トイレを拝借してもよろしいでしょうか。	I'm terribly sorry, would it be all right to use your restroom?
5.	#	それでは「お手を拝借」「いよぉーっ」（一本締め）	All right then, can I have you put your hands together [hand-clapping performed to celebrate the completion of something: 3-3-3-1 rhythm, done once]
6.	#	拝啓	[opening phrase of business correspondence]
7.	#	礼拝(する)	a religious service

395. 特 トク.   special   特

1.	特急	limited express
2.	たとえ特急に乗れたとしても、必ずしも間に合うとは限らないですよ。	Even if we are able to ride on the limited express, we won't necessarily make it in time.
3.	特に	especially, particularly
4.	特に心配なのは足と首ですね。	What I'm especially worried about is my legs and neck.
5.	ボタンを押してみたけど、特に何もなかった。	I pushed the button to see, but nothing in particular happened.
6.	みんな大卒なので、特に説明する必要もないとは思いますが……。	Everyone has graduated from college, so I think there is no particular need to explain, but . . .
7. +	特別(な)	special
8.	この公園には家族との特別な思い出があるんです。	I have a special memory of my family in this park.

Now go to the Activity Book for 練習.

シーン 22-9R 自己(じこ) PR Promoting your strengths

This is the second page of Amy's resume for her internship in Japan.

テキスト Text

学業で力を入れたこと
大学では言語学を勉強し、第2言語として日本語を学びました。高校の時に日本からの留学生と友達になったことがきっかけで日本文化に興味を持ち、日本に行ってみたいと思い、留学も経験しました。最初はコミュニケーションを取ることさえ難しかったのですが、ホームステイ先のラーメン屋さんでお手伝いをさせてもらい、コミュニケーションには相手を思いやる行動と心が大切だということに気付きました。貴社でも、お客様やチームの信頼を得られるように思いやりの心を忘れずに行動したいと考えています。
学業以外で力を入れたこと
JLC(ジャパニーズ ランゲッジ クラブ)の会長として、日本語の会話クラスや、運動会、春祭りなどの文化活動を2年間まとめました。最初の年は失敗もありましたが、2年目はサークルのメンバーに相談し、活動内容を決めるようにしたことによって、始めの年と比べて2倍から3倍の人が活動に集まるようになりました。JLCの経験を活かし、貴社でもわからないことは話し合い、チームワークを大切にすることによって活躍したいと考えています。
趣味・特技・資格 等
日本語実力試験 3級 令和X年6月24日 日本語スピーチコンテスト 2位 令和X年3月21日 マラソン 令和X年4月16日 ボストンマラソン完走
補足(志望動機・自己PR 等)
貴社では、日本人だけでなく、外国人や留学生のインターンシップ プログラムを通して、グローバル化する社会に合ったサービスを提供されています。私も大学やJLCの経験を活かして貴社のグローバルなプロジェクトのチームメンバーとして仕事したいと思い志望しました。
本人希望
貴社の規定に従います。

22-9R これさえできれば大丈夫(だいじょうぶ)。

Expressions

+	学(まな)ぶ	learn	#	実力(じつりょく)	ability
#	興味(きょうみ)	interests	#	～級(きゅう)	level
#	貴社(きしゃ)	your company	#	～位(い)	placement
#	信頼(しんらい)(する)	trust	#	完走(かんそう)(する)	complete run
#	運動会(うんどうかい)	Sports Day	#	提供(ていきょう)(する)	provide
#	X祭(まつ)り	X festival	#	志望(しぼう)(する)	aspire, apply
#	活躍(かつやく)(する)	active	#	貴社(きしゃ)の規定(きてい)に従(したが)います。	I will abide by your company's rules.

Things you focused on in your study
I studied linguistics in college and studied Japanese as a second language. I started to have an interest in Japanese culture when I became friends with an exchange student from Japan in high school, so I thought I would like to go to Japan and do a study abroad. At first even just communicating was difficult, but I was given a chance to help at the ramen shop of the homestay family, which helped me notice the importance of considerate action and heart in communication. I want to gain the team's trust by being considerate in my actions and taking an active role in the company.

Things you focused on besides study
As the president of JLC (Japanese Language Club), I organized activities such as Japanese conversation class, Sports Day, Spring Festival, etc. for two years. I made a lot of mistakes the first year, but I consulted with the members of the club the second year and made decisions about the activities with everyone, and the number of people gathered for activities was more than three times what it was the first year. By using my experience with JLC, I plan to consult about things that are unfamiliar to me and take an active part while valuing teamwork.

Hobbies・Skills・Qualifications etc.
Japanese Ability Test: Level 3 (June 24th, Reiwa X)
Japanese Speech Contest: 2nd place (March 21st, Reiwa X)
Marathon: April 16th, Reiwa X, completed Boston Marathon

Additional materials (Reasons for application・Description of your strengths etc.)
Through its internship program for Japanese as well as international visitors and students, your company provides service suited to a globalized society. I, too, would like to use my experiences from college to work as a team member in your global projects (and that is why I am applying).

Personal request
I will abide by the rules of your company.

Between the lines

BTL 4 Talking about your strengths in Japanese

In certain contexts, such as on your resume and in job interviews, you want to appropriately promote yourself. When describing your strengths, provide concise yet specific examples to illustrate them, and tell how they can be of benefit to the company. The following prompts appear in typical Japanese resume templates:

- 学業で力を入れたこと　　things you focused on in your studies
- 学業以外で力を入れたこと　things you focused on besides your studies

In the 学業で力を入れたこと section, Amy briefly talks about how she started learning Japanese. She then describes a challenge she faced and how she overcame it, and she wraps up with a description of her plans to apply what she has learned to the job she is applying for.

This section is where you tell your story. Make it personal, specific, and concise. Prior to writing your narrative, look for a good model to follow. Pay close attention to how ideas are connected with transition words.

- 趣味・特技・資格等　　hobbies・skills・qualifications etc.

When you list your skills and qualifications, indicate when you obtained them. As much as possible, accompany your hobbies with a notable accomplishment such as completing a marathon. This is an effective way to promote yourself.

- 補足(志望動機・自己PR)　　additional materials (reasons for application・self-promotion etc.)

The PR in 自己PR stands for 'public relations.' Another way to effectively promote yourself in a resume is to show that you are familiar with the company to which you are applying. For instance, to show that she is familiar with the company's operations, Amy describes 大垣商会 as a company that provides service suited to a globalized society.

- 本人希望　　　　　　　　personal request

In this section you should write your personal preferences such as what kind of job you want or where you would like to work (when there are multiple locations).

営業または企画関係の仕事を希望します。 'I request work related to sales or planning.'
東京支部を希望します。 'I hope to work at the Tokyo branch.'
You may also put down a date and time you can start working.
令和X年より就業可能。 'I can start working from year X of Reiwa.'

If you do not have any requests, write 貴社の規定に従います。 'I will abide by your company's rules.'

In preparation for writing your own resume in Japanese, look for ways to describe your own strengths by looking at other models. You may do so by using keywords in the search such as 履歴書, 自己PR, etc.

BTL 5 Using the appropriate terms of address: 当社 vs. 弊社 and 御社 vs. 貴社

Amy uses 貴社 in her resume to address the company she is applying to. In spoken settings, such as during a job interview, you should use 御社. On the other hand, you should use a term such as 弊社 to refer to your own company when talking to representatives from other (out-group) companies. You can use 当社 to refer to your company in both spoken and written communication within the company or when referring to companies in the same industry. Terms like 当校 and 弊校 are used by representatives of academic institutions such as college presidents, school principals, and teachers. The following provides a summary of terms used in professional settings for companies and schools. Note that other types of institutions use different terminology. Kanji characters such as 御 and 貴 are not formally introduced here, but they are useful in professional settings.

	In-group		Out-group	
			Spoken	Written
Company	(Polite) 当社・わが社 (Humble) 弊社・小社・私ども		御社	貴社
School	(Polite) 当校・本校・わが校 (Humble) 弊校 (used by private schools)		御校・ 御(大)学	貴校・ 貴(大)学

文字と例 Kanji with examples

396. 相 あい ソウ (See kanji #397.)　mutual(ly), phase, minister　相

　1.　相手　　　　　　　　　　　other party, companion, opponent (in sports)

　2.　相手の事ばかり心配してないで、自分のこともちゃんと気にした方がいいよ。　You shouldn't worry just about the other party, but also about yourself.

3.	相変(あいか)わらず		as usual
4.	相変わらず忙しそうですね。		You seem busy as usual.
5.	¥ 相槌(あいづち)		interjections to indicate one is listening
6.	首相(しゅしょう)		prime minister, chancellor
7.	首相さえ出席するほどの集まりなんだって。		I heard that the (scale of the) gathering is so great to that even the prime minister is attending.

397. 談　ダン　　story, talk　　談

1.	(ご)相談(そうだん)(する)	consultation
2.	ちゃんと相談できていればこんな間違いはしなかったはずなのに……。	Had we had a chance to consult, I suppose we wouldn't have made this kind of mistake.
3.	卒業のことで、教授とご相談したいのですが……。	I'd like to consult with you (professor) about graduation.
4.	必ずしも相談する時間が持てるとは限らないですが、明日はどうですか？	I don't necessarily have time to consult, but how about tomorrow?
5.	¥ (ご)冗談(じょうだん)	joke
6.	# 談話(だんわ)	discourse

398. 活　い(かす)　カツ　　vigor, live　　活

1.	+ 活動(かつどう)(する)	activity
2.	今度の音楽活動っていつの予定？	When is the schedule for the next music activity?
3.	+ 生活(せいかつ)(する)	(everyday) life
4.	今の経済では、生活するために必要なお金が足りなくなるだろう。	The money necessary for living will not be enough with this economy.
5.	# 終活(しゅうかつ)(する)	making preparations for one's death
6.	+ 活(い)かす	make use of X
7.	工事の経験を活かしてがんばりたいです。	I want to do my best by making the most out of my construction experience.

399. 第　ダイ　　ordinal number　　第

1.	X次第(しだい)	depending on X

これさえできれば大丈夫(だいじょうぶ)。

2.		あとは手続き次第ですね。		The rest depends on the procedure.
3.	+	第2言語		second language
4.		中国語を第2言語として勉強中です。		I'm in the middle of studying Chinese as my second language.
5.	#	第X課		lesson X
6.	#	落第(する)		fail (an examination)

400. 敗 やぶ(れる) ハイ　　lose　　敗

1.		失敗(する)		failure, blunder
2.		大失敗(する)		big failure
3.		最初は失敗してばかりでも平気ですよ。		It's okay to fail a lot in the beginning.
4.		例の研究、失敗に終わって死にそう。		I am about to die because the research ended up failing.
5.	#	敗れる		lose to
6.	+	X 勝 Y 敗		X wins and Y losses
7.		これで5勝6敗になりました。		This makes it five wins and six losses.
8.	¥	失敗は成功のもと		failure is the foundation of success
9.	+	勝敗		winning and losing, result
10.		勝敗はまだ決まってない。		The results of the match haven't been decided yet.
11.	#	連敗(する)		consecutive loss
12.		失敗談		a story about failure
13.		先生の失敗談を聞くのを楽しみにしている。		I'm looking forward to hearing the teacher's story about learning from experience.
14.		受験の失敗談はもう聞きたくない。		I don't want to listen to stories about failing college exams.

401. 得 え(る) トク　　advantage, profit, benefit　　得

1.	+	(お)得(な)		profitable
2.		家族みんながお得なプラン		a plan that benefits everyone in the family

170

3.	+ 得(を)する	benefit
4.	こんなことをしてだれが得するんだろう？	Who would benefit from doing this kind of thing?
5.	得意(な)	strong point, specialty
6.	得意なスポーツは何ですか。	What sports are you good at?
7.	# 得る	gain X
8.	あり得る	is in the realm of possibility
9.	そんなのあり得ないでしょ。反対です。	I can't accept that. I oppose.
10.	得手(な)	strong point, one's forte
11.	不得手(な)	inept, awkward
12.	だれでも得手不得手があるでしょうから……。	No matter who it is, they've got their strengths and weaknesses so . . .

BTL 6 Verb stem 〜得る・得る

You saw あり得る and あり得る 'be possible' in an earlier Act. Both of these are originally literary forms, related to the Potential. Both are more commonly used in the written language, but there are unusual constraints on the forms that you will see and hear. あり得る probably occurs more frequently than あり得る, but you will never see あり得る in the 〜ます form (while you do hear あり得ます). Nor will you see あり得る in the negative; rather you will see あり得ない.

The 〜得る suffix may be used as a written-style potential expression with other verbs: 考え得る, 行い得る, for example. As you continue your study of Japanese, be on the lookout for more expressions involving 〜得る, 〜得る, and 〜得ない.

病気の症状が見えなくても、実は病気になっているということもあり得るので、注意しましょう。	Even when there are no visible symptoms, it is possible that you are in fact sick, so let's be cautious.
考え方の違う人だけど、うまくまとめ得る力のあるリーダーですよ。	Although she has a different way of thinking, she is a leader who has the power to be able to bring matters to fruition.

	あり得ないと思っていたことを目の前で見せられて、本当に驚いた。			I was astonished when right before my eyes I was shown something that I thought was not possible.

402. 比　　くら(べる)　ヒ　compare　比

1. 比べる — compare
2. どうして人って比べたがるんでしょうね。 — Why do people tend to want to compare, I wonder.
3. どちらの絵の質がいいかなんて、比べられるわけないですよ。 — It's not possible to compare which paint has better quality.
4. 話してばかりいないでちゃんと比べてみてください。 — Don't just talk, compare and see.
5. # 比較(する) — comparison

403. 倍　　バイ　double, multiple, -fold　倍

1. 倍 — double, -fold
2. これの倍にしてください。 — Please make it double the size of this.
3. 〜倍 — multiple, -fold
4. 何倍も上手 — many times better at
5. ブライアンの日本語の方が僕の英語の何倍も上手だよ。 — Brian's Japanese is far better than my English.
6. ３０点の２倍は６０点だから……。 — The doubled amount of 30 points is 60 points, so . . .
7. さっき１０倍にしたばかりだけど、まだ足りないんですか。 — I just multiplied it by ten, but is it still not enough?

Now go to the Activity Book for 練習 and 腕試し.

Then do 評価 activities, including 読んでみよう, 書き取り, and 書いてみよう.

第 23 幕
Act 23

理想(りそう)を言えばキリがないけど……。

When it comes to ideals, there is no end, but . . .

切磋琢磨(せっさたくま)

Learn from experience.

◆ 話す・聞く

Scene 23-1 １０時以降は洗濯するな。
It is forbidden to do laundry after 10:00.

Kawamura-senpai tells Brian about his residence.

The script

ブライアン	川村
川村さんのアパート、住み心地はどうですか。	いいよ。ただ、結構規則がやかましくて……。
例えば？	１０時以降は洗濯するなとか、ゴミは当日まで出すなとか。

Brian	Kawamura
How does your apartment feel?	Good! Only the rules are pretty strict . . .
For example?	Things like it's forbidden to do laundry after 10:00, and you can't put your garbage out until the day of (pick-up).

単語と表現

名詞

(お)住まい	dwelling, housing
心地	feeling, sensation
住み心地	feeling of living (in a place)

居心地（いごこち）	comfort
着心地（きごこち）	ease of wearing something
履き心地（はきごこち）	ease of wearing something on the feet
座り心地（すわりごこち）	easy to sit in/on
使い勝手（つかいかって）	usability, ease of use
環境（かんきょう）	environment, circumstance
自然（しぜん）	nature
池（いけ）	pond
湖（みずうみ）	lake
川（かわ）	river
山（やま）	mountain
海（うみ）	sea, ocean
森（もり）	forest
林（はやし）	woods
規則（きそく）	rules, regulations
洗濯（せんたく）(する)	(do) laundry
洗濯物（せんたくもの）	laundry
洗剤（せんざい）	detergent
燃える（もえる）ゴミ	burnable garbage
当日（とうじつ）	the day of
リサイクル(する)	recycle
ベランダ	veranda
植木（うえき）	plants, shrubs

動詞

干す (-U; 干した)	air out, dry
別ける (-RU; 別けた)	divide, split
燃える (-RU; 燃えた)	burn
臭う (-U; 臭った)	smell
咲く (-U; 咲いた)	bloom
枯れる (-RU; 枯れた)	wither, wilt

形容詞

騒がしい	noisy
汚い	dirty
緩い	loose, lax
臭い	smelly

表現

ただ	only, just, but
心地が いい・悪い	good/bad feeling

Behind the scenes

BTS 1 Negative imperative: Verb + な

You saw negative requests in Act 8 with the 〜ないで form: 心配しないで(ください) 'please don't worry.' A much blunter, somewhat aggressive imperative is made up of the Verb plus な.

ここにゴミをすてるな。	Don't leave trash here.
走るな！	Don't run!

When the imperative is embedded in a longer Sentence, it is the longer sentence that determines the overall tone of the imperative. Note also in this Scene that when Kawamura-san lists the rules for his new residence it is an impersonal report – part of the description of his new place.

すっかり治るまで使うなって言われたんです。	I was told not to use it until it's completely cured.
資料は何も持っていくなということです。	The order is not to take any of the materials.
心配するなって。大丈夫だよ。	I'm telling you, don't worry. It's going to be all right.

BTS 2 Rules and regulations

When you hear announcements or see signs for prohibited or required behavior in Japan, they are not always spelled out with imperatives (such as するな). Some expressions you are likely to see or hear include 禁止 'forbidden,' ご遠慮ください 'please refrain from,' ……〜ないようにしてください 'please don't behave such that . . .' and お控えください 'please refrain from.' Likewise, rules for required behavior such as putting out garbage (location and hours), getting in line, giving up your seat on the train to the disabled, and even writing an academic term paper are very often phrased in very indirect, polite terms, making it seem as if you have an option. This is not how Japanese people see it. Rules can be ironclad in Japan, and you should keep in mind that going against them can have serious repercussions that might taint your experience of your neighborhood, your school, and your host family.

図書館の中での飲んだり食べたりはお控えください。	Please refrain from eating and drinking in the library.
黄色い線の内側にお立ちくださるようお願いいたします。	We request that you stand inside the yellow line.
ドアを開けたままでのご使用はご遠慮ください	Please refrain from using it while keeping the door open.
エスカレーターでは歩かず、手すりにおつかまりください。	While on the escalator, please don't walk and hold on to the railing.

Now go to the Activity Book for 練習 and 腕試し.

Scene 23-2 行け！ Go!

Brian and Ichiro are at a baseball game, cheering for the opposite teams.

The script

一郎	ブライアン
しっかり応援しようぜ。	うん。あ、ヒット！打った！
ウソ！拾え！	行け！走れ！回れ！
投げろ！そこ違う！あああ……。	セーフ！やった！成功！
やられた。	ドンマイ、ドンマイ！

Ichiro	Brian
Let's do our part and cheer them on.	Yeah. Ah, a hit! He smacked it!
No! Pick it up!	Go! Run! Turn the corner!
Throw it! Not there! Ahhhh . . .	Safe! We did it! Success!
Beaten.	Never mind, never mind!

単語と表現

名詞

応援(する)	support, cheer on, assistance
ヒット	hit
ホームラン	home run
くよくよ(する)	fret, worry

動詞

拾う (-U; 拾った)	pick up, gather
投げる (-RU; 投げた)	throw
当てる (-RU; 当てた)	hit
動かす (-U; 動かした)	move X
下ろす・降ろす (-U; 下ろした・降ろした)	take down, drop off (a passenger)
隠す (-U; 隠した)	hide X
叩く (-U; 叩いた)	strike, hit
逃げる (-RU; 逃げた)	escape
隠れる (-RU; 隠れた)	hide, disappear
向かう (-U; 向かった)	head towards
転ぶ (-U; 転んだ)	fall down
立ち上がる (-U; 立ち上がった)	get up, stand up
立ち直る (-U; 立ち直った)	recover (one's footing)
引っ張る (-U; 引っ張った)	drag, pull
やっつける (-RU; やっつけた)	beat (an opponent)
行け	go (imperative)
拾え	pick X up (imperative)
走れ	run (imperative)
回れ	go around (imperative)
止めろ	stop (imperative)
投げろ	throw (imperative)
受けろ	catch (imperative)

助詞

ぜ	[particle for emphasis or force, blunt]

表現

ドンマイ	never mind, don't worry

Behind the scenes

BTS 3 Affirmative imperative

To form the affirmative imperative for -RU Verbs, change the -*ru* to -*ro* (食べろ, 鍵かけろ); for -U Verbs change the final -*u* to -*e* (飲め, 止まれ). In fact, you have seen the imperative form of a ～ます style Verb in いらっしゃいませ 'welcome,' which literally means something like 'come (in).' The imperative form of する is しろ and 来る is 来い. You should recognize the imperative form of some of the special polite Verbs: ください, なさい, いらっしゃい, and おっしゃい (the final -*ru* changes to -*i*). Because they are honorific Verbs they are not blunt, as an ordinary imperative might be. Just like negative imperatives, when the affirmative imperative is embedded in a longer sentence, it is the longer sentence that determines the overall tone of the sentence. Similar to the negative imperative, affirmative imperatives are often framed as impersonal reports, which softens the harshness.

他の先生にも音を聞いて覚えろってよく言われます。	I've also often been told by other teachers to listen to the sound and then memorize.
今すぐここで書けって言われても、それは不可能ですよ。	Even if I were told to write it here right now, it would be impossible.
食べてみなさいって。きっと気にいるから。	I'm telling you, try it 'cause I'm sure you'll like it.
プロジェク頑張って今週中にやっつけちゃえ！	Hang in there and beat the project deadline this week!
「悪いのはそっちなんだから謝れ」って言われて困ってます。	I'm stuck because I was told, "It's your fault, apologize!"
太郎ちゃん、はっきりおっしゃい。行くつもりあるの？ないの？	Taro, speak clearly. Do you intend to go? Or not?

Another notable expression is the honorific imperative form of 見る, which is based on ご覧. In this case, the imperative is simply ご覧 or ご覧ください. This is especially frequent in the ～てみる 'try doing' pattern that you saw earlier.

| 始(はじ)めから説明(せつめい)してご覧。 | Try explaining from the beginning. |
| いつやってくれるか聞(き)いてご覧ください。 | Please ask her when she's going to do it for us. |

BTS 4 Sentence particle ぜ

You saw ぞ in Act 21 and here you see ぜ. Both of these are particles that add emotional emphasis in casual conversations. You may hear that these are considered to be "masculine" particles, but you will also find that more and more (especially younger) women use them just as men do.

| やってみずに「やりたくない」なんて言うなよ。面白(おもしろ)いぜ。 | Don't tell me to do it without trying it (yourself). It's fun! |
| 待(ま)っても来ないんじゃない？始(はじ)めようぜ。 | Isn't it the case that they aren't coming, even if we wait? Let's get started. |

Now go to the Activity Book for 練習 and 腕試し.

Scene 23-3 おんなじことばっかりさせられて……。
Being made to do the same thing . . .

Brian started a part-time job, permitted on his student visa.

The script

一郎	ブライアン
どう？バイトの方は。条件良さそうだって言ってたよね。	ところが、始めてみたら、毎日おんなじことばっかりさせられて、ちょっとうんざり。
まだ始めたばかりじゃない。	まあね。「文句言うな」って自分で自分に言い聞かせてる。
そのうち慣れるよ。	

Ichiro	Brian
How is it – your part-time job? You said that it looked like it would be a good setup.	As a matter of fact, now that I've started, I'm made to do the same thing every day, so it's a little boring.
Didn't you just start?	Well, you know. "Don't complain," I always say to myself.
You'll get used to it soon.	

単語と表現

名詞

条件	condition, terms, set-up
待遇	treatment, working conditions

給料 (きゅうりょう)	salary
有給休暇 (ゆうきゅうきゅうか)	paid vacation
時給 (じきゅう)	hourly wage
提示(する) (ていじ)	presentation, suggestion
おんなじ	same (an emphatic form of 同じ)
うんざり(する)	fed up, tedious
挫折(する) (ざせつ)	setback
解決(する) (かいけつ)	resolution, solution, settlement
当たり前 (あたりまえ)	common, obvious

動詞

雇う (-U; 雇った) (やと)	hire, employ
繰り返す (-U; 繰り返した) (く かえ)	repeat, do over
言い聞かせる (-RU; 言い聞かせた) (き)	tell (someone) to do X
宥める (-RU; 宥めた) (なだ)	soothe, calm

表現

ところが、	as a matter of fact, even so

Behind the scenes

BTS 5 Causative passive

You have seen both causative (使わせる 'make/allow to use') and passive (使われる 'be used') forms of the Verb. These two combine in a causative passive (使わせられる 'be made to use') which is an involuntary passive, meaning 'someone is made to do something' (the 'allowed to do something' interpretation is not likely in the case of causative passives).

For U-verbs you may also hear a shorter form of the causative-passive in which ASARERU is attached to the Verb stem (使わされる). Note that this shorter form is not used with U-verbs that end in す nor with -RU verbs.

Causative	Passive causative	Alternative passive causative
食べさせる	食べさせられる	
やめさせる	やめさせられる	
話させる	話させられる	
出させる	出させられる	
来させる	来させられる	
させる	させられる	
払わさせる	払わさせられる	払わされる
払わさせる	払わさせられる	払わされる
帰らせる	帰らせられる	帰らされる
行かせる	行かせられる	行かされる

今日の講演は素晴らしかったです。色々考えさせられました。

Today's lecture was fabulous. It made me think about various things.

できればやりたくなかったんですが、4月から委員長をさせられることになりました。

I didn't want to do it, if at all possible, but it's been decided that I'm going to be made to serve as the committee chair from April.

Now go to the Activity Book for 練習 and 腕試し.

Scene 23-4 LDK にこだわるの？
You are set on an LDK?

Eri is considering relocating when Sasha leaves Japan.

The script

恵理	サーシャ
3月で契約も切れるから、もうちょっと駅に近いところ探して移ろうかな。	ハハ、バス使わずに行ける距離でしょ？
そう、そう。	大きさは？
理想を言えばキリがないけど……	LDKにこだわるの？
いや、ワンルームでもいいけど、日当たりだけは譲れない。	恵理らしい。

Eri	Sasha
Since my contract ends in March, I'd like to move someplace closer to a station.	Right, you mean a distance that you could get to without using the bus, right?
Right, right.	Size?
Ideally speaking there's no end to (what I want).	You're set on an LDK, are you?
No, a studio apartment would be fine, but I can't compromise on sunlight.	That's so like you.

単語と表現

名詞

契約	→	contract

期限（きげん）	term, time frame
都会（とかい）	city
田舎（いなか）	rural area
実家（じっか）	home (where one grew up)
ふるさと	hometown
理想（りそう）	ideal
キリ	end
LDK	living room, dining room, kitchen
2LDK	two rooms plus living room, dining room, kitchen
1DK	one room plus dining room, kitchen
ワンルーム	studio apartment
日当たり（ひあたり）	sunlight, sunny place
X向き（むき）	facing X, suitable for X

動詞

移る（うつる）(-U; 移った)	move (house), transfer (department)
切れる（きれる）(-RU; 切れた)	expire, wear off, break
目指す（めざす）(-U; 目指した)	look for, search
(Xに)こだわる (-U; こだわった)	be particular about X, have one's mind set on X
譲る（ゆずる）(-U; 譲った)	turn over, concede
(Xに)向く（むく）(-U; 向いた)	turn toward X, suitable for X

表現

理想（りそう）を言えば	ideally speaking
キリがない	endless, boundless
キリがいい	good place to end or make a cut

一人きり	on one's own, by oneself
キリをつける	put an end to (the matter)
Past Sentence ＋ きり	doing X and ending there
上を目指せば	provided one aims high
上を見れば	if one were to look up

Behind the scenes

BTS 6 キリ

キリ refers to an outer limit or ending. You will see it combined with other elements such as the phrases you see in 表現 above. Note also that [past sentence ＋ キリ] indicates that something was done and then left – usually in an undesirable state.

ちょうど会議が終わったところでしょう。キリのいいところでお茶、飲みませんか？	You just finished your meeting, right? A perfect timing for a break. Would you like some tea?
こんなに広いアパートに一人きりで住むのはちょっと寂しいから。	It's lonely to live all by myself in a big apartment like this, so . . .
え？何度頼んでも何も言ってこない？じゃあ、私が電話で直接話して、キリをつけますよ。待っててください。	What? They haven't contacted you even after repeated requests? Then I'll call to talk to them directly and put an end to this nonsense. Just wait.
一度電話してきたきり、何の連絡もありません。一体どうしているのか……。	We got one phone call and then no communication at all. I wonder what in the world could have happened . . .

Now go to the Activity Book for 練習 and 腕試し.

Scene 23-5 こんなに払わせられるくらいなら
If I'm to be made to pay this much

Brian heard that Kawamura-senpai has moved.

The script

ブライアン	川村
引っ越されたそうですね。	うん。ちょうどキリがよかったし、前のところ、家賃が上がるって言われてね。
そうなんですか。	こんなに払わせられるくらいなら、もっといいところ探そうと思って。
で、いいところが見つかったんですね	うん、前と同じくらいの家賃で、前より交通の便のいいところで。
規則は？	それも、前ほど厳しくないよ。

Brian	Kawamura
I hear you moved.	Yeah. The timing was right, and I was told that the rent in my old place would go up.
I see.	I thought if I'm going to be made to pay this much, I'm going to look for a better place.
And I guess you found a good place.	Yeah, the rent is about the same as the last place, and the commute is easier.
How about the regulations?	Those also aren't as strict as the last place.

単語と表現

名詞

引っ越し(する)	move (residence)
家賃	rent (charge)
交通	traffic
交通の便	transportation facilities
安全(な)	safety
交渉(する)	negotiation
妥協(する)	compromise

動詞

引っ越す (-U; 引っ越した)	move (houses), change residence

数詞

軒	classifier for counting buildings

表現

払わせられるくらいなら	if one is to be made to pay

Behind the scenes

BTS 7 Sentence + くらい

You saw くらい used to approximate quantity earlier. くらい can also combine with Sentences to indicate extent or degree.

大変だったんです。途中で諦める人が何人も出るくらい。	It was awful. To the degree that a number of people gave up in the middle.

| 高校生なら誰でも知っているくらい有名なアーチストですよ。 | She is such a famous artist that every high school student knows her. |
| タクシーで３０分かかるくらいなら、歩いた方が早いですよ。 | If it takes as much as 30 minutes by taxi, it'd be faster to walk. |

Now go to the Activity Book for 練習 and 腕試し.

23-5 理想を言えばキリがないけど……。

Scene 23-6 ブライアンの話(新情報)
Brian's story (new information)

Brian reports to Ichiro what happened earlier in the day.

The script

ブライアン	一郎
先輩の川村さんね？	うん。
最近引っ越したんだって。	へえ。なんで？
前のところも住み心地はよかったけど。	うん。
この４月以降に家賃が上がることになったそうで……。	ああ、そうか。で？
で、家賃の点も問題なくて交通の便が良くって、規則に関しても前ほど厳しくないところが見つかったんだって。	ふうん。でも大変だよね、家探しに始まって、引っ越し、住所変更、その他の手続き。場所は？
あ、それは聞いてない。	

Brian	Ichiro
(You know) my *senpai* Kawamura-san?	Yeah.
He says he moved recently.	Oh. Why?
The place he lived in before had a good feeling, but ...	Yeah.
It seems the rent was going to go up after April.	Oh, I see, So?

So he says that he found a place where the thing about the rent was not an issue and the commute was easier, plus as far as the regulations went, they weren't as strict as before.	Got it. But it's tough, isn't it. Starting with finding housing, then moving, changing address, and besides that the paperwork. Where is it?
Oh, I haven't asked him that.	

単語と表現

名詞

新情報	news, new information
(ご)新居	new home, new place
新住所	new address
新人	new person
家探し	house-hunting, looking for housing
光熱費	utility costs, heat and electricity
以降	hereafter, after X
以前	before X
(ご)苦労(する)	hardship
住所	address
住所変更(する)	change of address
その他	besides that

動詞

建てる・立てる (-RU; 建てた・立てた)	build X, erect X
(X に)関する (-U; 関した)	regarding X

表現

Xに始まって、Y、Z、	starting with X, then Y, Z

Behind the scenes

BTS 8 Xに関して

The combination [Xに関する] is unusual in that 関 never occurs as an independent Noun, and the combination itself never occurs in the negative. Probably most common is the ～て form: Xに関して 'with regard to X.'

先月出した論文に関して、先生からまだ何もコメントが来ません。	With regard to the paper that I submitted last month, I still haven't received any comment from the professor.
地球温暖化に関する論文をいくつも読みました。	I read any number of research papers about global warming.

BTS 9 Xに始まって、Y、Z

Xに始まって starts a list of things about which a comment is made, where X is the subject and is the most important item.

机の片付けに始まって、窓拭き、冷蔵庫の掃除、ゴミ出しなど、引越しの前にはすることが山のようにありますから。	Starting from tidying up the desk to window washing, refrigerator cleaning, trash disposal, etc., there is a mountain of things to do before moving.
ナイフ、フォークに始まって、お皿、コップなど、今プラスチックに頼っているものはいっぱいあります。	From knives and forks to plates and cups, there are a great many things that rely on plastic.

Now go to the Activity Book for 練習 and 腕試し.

Then do 評価 activities.

◆ 読み書き

シーン 23-7R　ゴミを捨てるな。
Don't throw away trash here

This is a poster in front of the trash station next to Sasha's apartment.

テキスト Text

ゴミの出し方

ゴミは必ず分別して当日の午前8時までに決められた場所に出すようにしてください。前日の夜のゴミ出しはお控えください。入居者以外のゴミ捨ては禁止です。

燃えるごみ	毎週火・金曜日
燃えないごみ ペットボトル	毎週木曜日
プラスチックごみ	毎週水曜日
あきかん・びん 古着類、古紙類 その他リサイクルごみ	第1・第3水曜日
落ち葉・草木ごみ	第1・第3・第5月曜日
有害ごみ・小型家電	第4月曜日
大型家電	電話受付またはクリーンセンターへ

カラスに注意！

やったぜ！

前日の夜にゴミを出すな！
ゴミは必ずネットの中に！

How to put out trash

Please be sure to sort trash and put it out at the designated location at 8 a.m. on the assigned day.

Please refrain from throwing out trash the night before. Non-residents may not throw away trash here.

Burnable garbage	Every Tuesday and Friday	
Noncombustible garbage・plastic bottles	Every Thursday	
Plastic trash	Every Wednesday	Beware of crows
Empty cans and bottles old clothes, old paper other recycles	First and third Wednesday	Yeah
Fallen leaves and plants (yard debris)	First, third, and fifth Monday	Don't put out trash the night before! Be sure to put the trash inside the net!
Hazardous waste・small appliances	Fourth Monday	
Large appliances	Call or (bring it) to Clean Center	

BTL 1 Sorting trash: ゴミの分別

There are community rules to follow when you live in Japan and handling trash is one of them. Trash is carefully sorted in Japan. Here are the common types of trash.

燃えるごみ (可燃物)	burnable garbage	燃えないごみ (不燃物)	nonburnable/noncombustible garbage
プラスチックごみ	plastic trash	ペットボトル	plastic bottles
あきかん・びん	empty cans and bottles	リサイクルごみ	recyclables
古着類	old-clothing	古紙類	old paper
新聞	newspapers	雑誌	magazines

落ち葉・草木ごみ	fallen leaves and plants (yard waste)	有害ごみ	hazardous waste
小型家電	small appliances	大型家電	large appliances

Each community has its own rules and some places require residents to buy designated trash bags for trash that cannot be recycled. When you live in Japan, be sure to follow the rules carefully. The garbage collectors will not take the trash if you put it out on the wrong day or if your trash is not appropriately sorted. A neighbor is usually designated to leave notes for the owners of garbage that is not properly put out.

文字と例 Kanji with examples

404. 居　い(る)　キョ　exist, reside　居

1. 居る — stay, exist, live (often written in hiragana)
2. 家に居ながらできる仕事 — work you can do at home
3. + 入居(する) — moving in
4. 入居中 — currently occupied
5. 入居の手続きさえまだ終わってないんです。 — I haven't even finished the moving-in process yet.
6. + 入居者 — tenant
7. ご入居者様ご相談ページ — a (web) page for residents' consultation

405. 有　あ(る)　ユウ　possess, own　有

1. 有名(な) — famous
2. 有名人 — celebrity, public figure
3. これ、日本語の勉強が１００倍楽しくなるって有名だよ。 — This is known for making Japanese study a hundred times more fun.
4. この料理、特に有名でもないのにうま！ — This dish isn't popular in particular but is way delicious!
5. 知ってる？ここって、あの映画で有名な場所なんだぜ！ — Do you know? This place is known for that movie!
6. + 有利(な) — advantageous, profitable

7.		正社員になると転職活動でも有利な点がある。		There are merits for full-time employees even when they are looking for a new job.
8.	¥	共有(する)		co-ownership, sharing
9.	#	有る		have X, there is X, (often written in hiragana)

406. 捨　す(てる)　シャ　dispose, throw away

1.		捨てる	throw away X
2.	+	ポイ捨て	littering
3.		捨てろ捨てろと言われても、こりゃさすがに捨てられないぜ。	I can't throw these things away even if I'm told repeatedly to throw them away.
4.		捨てないでゴミと一緒にあなたの心	don't throw your heart out with the trash
5.		要らない物、捨てろって何度言ったら分かるの？	How many times do I have to tell you to get rid of things that are unnecessary?
6.		ゴミは捨てずにお持ち帰りください。	Please take your trash home without throwing it away.
7.	#	四捨五入(する)	round off
8.	#	断捨離(する)	living with the bare minimum by getting rid of the clutter in your life

407. 禁　きん(ずる)　prohibit, ban

1.	+	禁止(する)	prohibition
2.		タバコのポイ捨て禁止	Cigarette butt littering is prohibited.
3.		飲酒運転は禁止されています。	Driving while intoxicated is prohibited.
4.		日本と違ってハワイではビーチの飲酒が禁止されているので、要注意！	Be aware that drinking is prohibited on the beach in Hawaii, unlike Japan.
5.	+	立(ち)入(り)禁止	no entry, no trespassing
6.		入居者以外立入禁止	no entry except for residents
7.	#	禁ずる	prohibit X

408.	控	ひか(える)		avoid, wait, put down	控
	1.	控える		avoid, wait for, put down X	
	2.	これから２週間お酒を控えるようにしてください。		Please refrain from drinking alcohol for the next two weeks.	
	3.	相手の車のナンバーをメモに控えておいてください。		Please put down the other person's car plate number on a memo.	
	4.	コンサート中は席をお立ちになることはお控えください。		Please refrain from standing up during the concert.	
	5.	試合を明日に控えているんだから、今日は早く寝た方がいいですよ。		You had better go to sleep early today because the match is waiting for you tomorrow.	
	6.	車内でのご飲食はお控えください。		Please do not eat and drink inside the car.	
	7.	+	控えめ(な)		modest, reserved	
	8.		あまさ控えめの大人のスイーツ		mildly sweet candy for adults	
	9.		控えめに言っても最悪でしたね。		Even if we put it mildly, it was the worst.	

409.	然	ゼン　ネン		so, thus	然
	1.	全然		not at all, entirely	
	2.	あの有名人、名前ばかりで何やらせても全然下手なんだって。		That person is a celebrity in name only and is entirely unskilled in things he is asked to do.	
	3.	この問題が全然分からなくて、まだ宿題が終わっていません。		I don't understand this problem at all, so I'm not finished with the homework yet.	
	4.	当然		of course, naturally	
	5.	知らないなんてあり得ない。日本人なら知ってて当然のマナー		Not knowing is not acceptable. Manners that you should know naturally if you are Japanese	
	6.	自然		nature	
	7.	ゴミを捨てるな！自然を大切に！		Don't litter! Take care of the environment!	
	8.	#	天然		natural(ly), airhead (someone who lacks common sense)	

410.	燃	も(える) ネン		burn	燃
1.		燃える		X burns	
2.		燃えるゴミっていつだったっけ？		When is (the day to put out) burnable garbage, do you remember?	
3.		燃えないゴミは毎週水曜日です。		Noncombustible garbage is every Wednesday.	
4.		これは燃えないゴミだから、こっちに入れちゃだめだよ。		This is non-burnable trash, so you shouldn't put it here.	
5.	#	不燃物		noncombustible things	
6.	#	可燃ごみ		burnable garbage	
7.	#	燃料		fuel	

411.	葉	は ば		leaf	葉
1.		言葉		word, language	
2.		質問する時には言葉に気を付けてください。		When you ask questions, be careful of your words.	
3.	#	言葉遣い		choice of words, wording	
4.	+	葉(っぱ)		leaf	
5.		葉っぱごみは第1月曜日のはずです。		Leaf debris is supposed to be on the first Monday.	
6.	+	落ち葉		fallen leaves	
7.		落ち葉よ、燃えろ〜。		Burn, you fallen leaves!	
8.		落ち葉を入れるとよく燃えますよ。		It will burn better if you put in fallen leaves.	

412.	類	ルイ		sort, class, group	類
1.	+	X類		X-sort of things	
2.		書類		documents, papers	
3.		この書類を届けてもらいたいんだけど。		I want you to deliver these documents, but . . .	
4.		書類全部拝見させていただきました。		I looked through all of the documents.	

5.		大事な書類を忘れるなんて、そりゃないぜ。	Forgetting the important documents, that's not okay.
6.	+	紙類(かみるい)	paper things
7.		紙類はこっちにしまっておかなくちゃ。	We should put away paper things here.
8.	¥	種類(しゅるい)	type
9.		類(るい)は友(とも)を呼(よ)ぶ	like attracts like (birds of a feather flock together)
10.		類は友を呼ぶって言うけど、ここに集まっている人みんな控(ひか)えめだね。	People say that like attracts like – people who gathered here are all reserved.
11.	+	人類(じんるい)	humankind
12.		人類の歴史と文化についての本	a book about the history and culture of humankind

Now go to the Activity Book for 練習.

シーン 23-8R 残業(ざんぎょう)させられることナシ！
You won't be forced to work overtime!

Brian is looking for a part-time job in the area of Fukuzawa Station.

 テキスト Text

アルバイト募集中

◆残業させられることナシ！◆

人間関係がいい職場。フリーター、学生さん、留学生、大歓迎☆
働きやすいシフト相談可。語学スキルも活かせるオシゴト！

ショップナウ福沢駅東口駅前店
ショップナウスタッフ

詳細を見る ＞

職種	コンビニ、レジ、staff
給与	時給 1288 円～（22 時～8 時）　時給 1030 円～ ※食事付き♪
交通	「福沢駅」より徒歩 1 分
勤務時間	２２：００～８：００内で働ける時間 ★日数・時間はご相談下さい。「平日のみ」「土日のみ」等のシフトも OK。

大学生 フリーター	留学生	残業無し	英語 中国語	研修有り （一度きり）	シフト 相談可	駅チカ

Now Hiring Part-timers

◆ No overtime ! ◆
A workplace with a great team. Freeters (job hoppers), students, exchange students welcome ☆
Can consult for shifts around your schedule.
Work where you can use your linguistic skills.

	Shop NOW in front of Fukuzawa Station East Entrance Shop NOW staff	See details >
Job type	Convenience store, cash register work, staff	
Wages	Hourly pay 1288 yen ~ (22 o'clock ~ 8 o'clock) Hourly pay 1030 yen ~ ※ a meal included ♪	
Transportation	1 minute on foot from Fukuzawa Station	
Working Hours	Hours within 22:00 ~ 8:00 that you can work ★ Please consult about the days and hours. Shifts such as "weekdays only," "weekends only," etc. are okay.	

College student freeter	Exchange student	No overtime work	Use of English・Chinese	Job training (only once)	Shift negotiable	Close to station

Between the lines

BTL 2 Job hunting

You will find posters and websites that announce recruitment for workers in Japan (募集中 'now recruiting'). They will include a set of descriptions about the work, often targeting specific types of workers (X 大歓迎 'X welcome'). When you search for a job online, you can narrow your search by various factors such as 職種 'job type,' 給与 'wages,' and 勤務時間 'working hours.' Under 交通 'transportation' you will find information about the closest station and how long it takes to walk there (徒歩 'go on foot'). A summary of features and characteristics is often provided. For example, 残業なし 'no overtime work' and 駅チカ 'close to a station.'

BTL 3 More on より

You have learned that より is used in comparisons such as パソコンより高い。 'It's more expensive than a computer.' In writing, [Noun より] can also be used instead of

[Noun から]: 「福沢駅」より徒歩１分 and １０時より始まります where より marks the Noun as the starting location or time. Note that より in this usage is different from から in that it does not occur with まで as in 福沢駅から東京駅まで 'from Fukuzawa Station to Tokyo Station.' You may also hear より in place of から in formal speeches and by tour guides.

名古屋駅よりバス１本	One bus ride from Nagoya station
ライブイベント – 明日の午前９時より	A live event – starting at 9 a.m. tomorrow

BTL 4 のみ

Noun + のみ can be used instead of だけ in writing (平日のみ 'only weekdays').

東京で１日のみのアルバイト	a part-time job in Tokyo for only one day
物理の勉強は自分が学生である間のみする予定です。	Studying physics is something I plan to do only while I am a student.
夜のプールは、夏の間のみオープン。	The pool is open in the evening only in summer.
以上、ご報告のみにて失礼いたします。	Please excuse the fact that this is the extent of my report.

のみ can also follow a Sentence.

えっ？ラーメンとギョーザを食べたのみで２０００円？高くない？	What? I just had ramen and gyoza and it's 2,000 yen? Isn't it expensive?
要らないものはどんどん捨てるのみ！	Let's just throw away the things we don't need.

文字と例 Kanji with examples

413.	無	な(い) ム		nothing	無
1.		無い		there is none; I have none	
2.		無理(な)		impossible, unrealistic	
3.		無理なお願いだとは存じておりますが。		I know that it's an unreasonable request.	

4.		卒業なんて無理、無理！		Graduation – impossible!	
5.		無理(する)		try/work too hard	
6.		送金アプリがあるんだから、別に無理してみんなから現金集めることないよ。		We have an app to transfer money, so you shouldn't work especially hard to collect cash from everyone.	
7.	#	無駄(な)		wasteful	
8.	+	無料		free of charge	
9.		すごくない？無料で授業が受けられるんだってさ。		Isn't it great? I hear that you can take lessons for free.	
10.	+	年中無休		open all year round	
11.		最近人が足りなくて年中無休のお店の数が少なくなってきた。		Having fewer people in recent years, the number of stores that are open all year round is decreasing.	

414.	給	キュウ		give, confer, wage	給
1.		給料		wage	
2.		給料が下げられて泣けてきた。		I'm going to cry after having my pay cut.	
3.		あの人、給料もらうだけもらっていなくなっちゃったよ。		That person was gone immediately after he got his pay.	
4.		有給		paid (leave)	
5.		有給取って、旅行でもしようかな。		I wonder if I should travel or something by taking a paid leave.	
6.		時給		hourly pay	
7.		時給が上がったご感想は？		What are your thoughts on pay raises?	
8.		時給１０円でもいいから上げてくれ！		Only ten yen will do, please raise my hourly pay.	

415.	可	カ		passable, acceptable, fair	可
1.	+	可		passable, acceptable (condition)	
2.		コミック￥１９２ 中古本 – 可		Comic books – 192 yen used books – acceptable condition (some wear)	
3.		相談可		consultation accepted	
4.	+	不可		not acceptable	

5.		おトイレはまだ使用不可になっております。		The toilet is still inoperable.
6.	¥	可愛い		cute, likable
7.	¥	可愛い子には旅をさせよ。		If you love your child, send them on a journey (spare the rod and spoil the child).
8.	¥	許可(する)		permit
9.	#	可燃(物)		combustibles

416. 能 ノウ — competence, ability 能

1.	(お)能		noh (traditional theater)
2.	可能(な)		possible
3.	可能な限りがんばります。		I'll do my best as long as possible.
4.	可能であれば今すぐ辞めたい。		I'd like to quit immediately if possible.
5.	不可能(な)		impossible
6.	不可能かどうか確かめてみないと分からないよ。		We won't know if it's impossible unless we check it.
7.	不可能でない限り研究は続けるべきです。		As long as it's not impossible, we should continue our research.

417. 交 コウ — meet, intersect 交

1.		交番	police box
2.		サイフ落としたんだけど、交番に届いてるといいな。	I dropped my wallet. I hope it's been turned in to the police box.
3.		交通	transportation
4.		今度の活動に行くのには交通費が２０００円以上かかる。	In order to go to the next activity, the transportation cost will be more than 2,000 yen.
5.		交通費は半分返してもらえるらしいよ。	I hear that half of the transportation cost will be returned.
6.	¥	交際費	entertainment expense
7.	#	交換	exchange
8.	¥	交差点	intersection

206

418.	働	はたら(く)　ドウ		operate, work	働
1.		働く		work	
2.		今はバイトとして働いているが、早く正社員になれればいいと思っている。		I'm working as a part-timer now, but I'm thinking that it would be good if I could become a full-time employee soon.	
3.		実は理絵ちゃんにも働いてもらってたんだ。		I actually had Rie-chan work for us, too.	
4.		明日は働く予定はなかったからいいようなものの、そういうことはもっと早く知らせてくれよ。		Good thing I am not scheduled to work tomorrow, but do tell me those kinds of things sooner.	
5.		一日中工事現場で働いていたから疲れたぜ。		I'm tired of working all day at the construction site.	
6.		仕方なく働いているけど、実は危ないって反対されているんだ。		I'm working on it reluctantly, but it's dangerous and I'm running into opposition, so...	
7.	#	稼働		work, operation	
419.	関	かか(わる)　せき　カン		connect, relate	関
1.	+	関		[family name]	
2.		Xに関する		related to X	
3.		お金に関することならおまかせください。		Leave the things related to money up to me.	
4.		歴史に関しては全然詳しくない。		I'm not familiar at all with the things related to history.	
5.		関わる		related to X	
6.		自然に関わる仕事		work related to nature	
7.		あの人には関わらない方がいいよ。		It's better if you don't associate with that person.	
8.	¥	玄関		entryway	
420.	係	かかり　ケイ		duty, section	係
1.	+	係		(person) in charge	
2.		係の者と代わりますので少々お待ちください。		Please hold for moment as I transfer you to the person in charge.	

3.	+	X 係(がかり)	person in charge of X
4.		受付係(うけつけがかり)	receptionist
5.	+	係長(かかりちょう)	subsection head, assistant manager
6.		１０年も働(はたら)いているのにまだ係長なんです。	Even though I've worked for all of ten years, I'm still an assistant manager.
7.		関係(かんけい)(する)	relate, relationship
8.		関係無い話だからあっち行けよ。	It's none of your concern, so go away.
9.		関係者(かんけいしゃ)	the people involved
10.		関係者の話によるとって新聞にあるけど、信じていいの？	The newspaper says it is according to the persons concerned, but is it okay to believe that?
11.		X 関係(かんけい)	related to X
12.		人間関係(にんげん)	human relations
13.		日中経済関係(にっちゅう)の問題	problems associated with economics between Japan and China

421. 修 シュウ — repair, master 修

1.		研修(けんしゅう)(する)	training
2.	+	研修生(けんしゅうせい)	intern
3.		研修生じゃ相手にならないぜ。	Interns are no match.
4.		社内研修と比べるとまだ全然楽ですよ。	This is entirely easy compared to the company training.
5.	+	修理(しゅうり)(する)	repair
6.		自分は修理に出していて車が無いから他の人の車で送ってもらわないと。	I need to have someone give me a ride with their car because I'm having my car repaired so I don't have one.
7.	+	修行(しゅぎょう)(する)	training
8.		勝負に負けたからこれからまた修行するのみ！	I lost the match, so I'm just going to train again.

Now go to the Activity Book for 練習.

シーン 23-9R　スカイタワーズナウ
Sky Towers NOW

Here is one of the search results for Eri's new apartment.

テキスト Text

検索したエリア	東京都 ・ 足立区（1）
お探しの条件	☑南向き　☑日当たりがいい　☑海が見える　☑駅から近い ☑住み心地のいいエリア　☑クレジットカード払い可

1件中　1件〜1件を表示

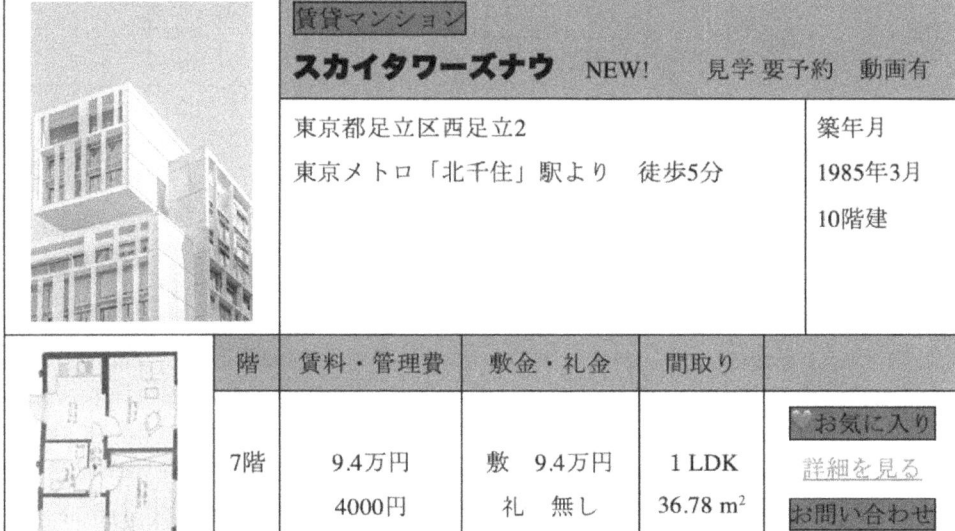

	階	賃料・管理費	敷金・礼金	間取り	
	7階	9.4万円 4000円	敷　9.4万円 礼　無し	1 LDK 36.78 m²	お気に入り 詳細を見る お問い合わせ （無料）

賃貸マンション
スカイタワーズナウ　NEW!　見学 要予約　動画有

東京都足立区西足立2
東京メトロ「北千住」駅より　徒歩5分

築年月
1985年3月
10階建

23-9R 理想を言えばキリがないけど……。

Areas searched	Tokyo • Adachi Ward (1)
Search conditions	☑ facing south ☑ good exposure to sun ☑ view of the ocean ☑ close from the station ☑ areas comfortable to live in ☑ credit card payment okay

Results Displaying 1 result ～ 1 result

	Rental Unit **Sky Towers NOW** NEW! Reservation needed for visits Video available			
	Tokyo Adachi Ward West Adachi 2 5 minute walk from Tokyo Metro "Kita-Senju" Station			Year and month built Year 1985 March ten-story building
	floor	rent・ management fee	deposit・service charge	layout	
	7th	94,000 yen 4000 yen	Deposit 94,000 yen service change not applicable	1 LDK 36.78 m²	♥favorite See details inquiries (free)

文字と例 Kanji with examples

422.	払	はら(う)		pay	払
	1.	払う		pay	
	2.	交通費払ってもらえたら考えるよ。		I'll think about it if someone pays for my transportation cost.	
	3.	食事代、払わせられるくらいなら行かなきゃいいじゃん。		If you are being forced to pay for the meals, it's better that you don't go.	
	4.	いつもお世話になってばかりいるので、今日は僕に払わせてください。		I've been taken care of all the time, so please let me pay today.	
	5.	お金を払えば払うほど質がいいサービスが受けられるって言うけどねえ。		People say that the more you pay the better service you get, but . . .	
	6.	たとえ電話代払わなかったとしても今月もうヤバいよ。		We are doomed for this month even if we don't pay the phone bill.	

7.		生活費払えなくて、電気も止められてしまいました。		I couldn't pay the living cost, and the electricity was also shut off.
423.	探	さが(す)	search, look for	探
1.		探す		search for X (by sight)
2.		家探し		house hunt
3.		一人用の部屋を探しているんですけど。		I'm looking for a room for one person.
4.		控えめの赤のコートを探し中です。		I'm in the middle of searching for a light red coat.
5.		お部屋探しならこちらのサイトをクリック。		If you are looking for a room, click this site.
424.	件	ケン	subject, matter, case	件
1.	+	件		matter, case
2.		例の件に関する書類、拝借しました。		I borrowed the documents related to that matter (in question).
3.	+	件名		subject
4.		件名：スピーチコンテストの勝敗		Subject: Speech contest results
5.	¥	条件		condition
6.	+	物件		estate, investment
7.		見つけた物件が入居中だから見学できない。		The property I found is currently occupied, so we can't visit.
8.	+	事件		matter, case, incident
9.		同じ日に何度も違う事件が起きるのなんてあり得ない。		It's impossible that different incidents occur many times on the same day.
425.	向	む(こう) む(かう) む(く)	direction	向
1.		向こう		opposite side, other side
2.		あの雲の向こうに僕たちを待っている何かがあるんだ。		There is something awaiting us beyond those clouds.
3.		方向		direction
4.		Xに向かう		head X, face X
5.		あとは南の方向に向かうのみ。		Now we just have to head south.

6.		向く	face (something, some direction)
7.		Xに向く	good at X
8.		趣味でやってるけど、自分は音楽にはあまり向いてないと思う。	I'm doing it as a hobby, but I think I'm not good at music.
9.		X向き	facing X
10.		南向きだから日当たりがいい。	It's facing south so it has good sun exposure.
11.	#	向ける	point (in the direction), turn toward
12.	+	X向け	intended for
13.		大人向けの映画	movies intended for adults
14.		入居者向けのページ	A (web) page designated for residents

426. 海 うみ　カイ　　ocean, sea　　海

1.		海	ocean
2.		海の向こうに明日がある。	There is a "tomorrow" on the other side of the ocean.
3.		危ないから海の方には行くな。反対の方へ向かえ。	It's dangerous, don't go towards the ocean. Head in the opposite direction.
4.	+	日本海	Sea of Japan
5.		地中海	Mediterranean Sea
6.		日本海は地中海と比べると小さめだ。	The Sea of Japan is relatively smaller than the Mediterranean Sea.
7.	#	上海	Shanghai

427. 地 チ　ジ　　ground　　地

1.		現地	the place, destination
2.		じゃあ朝8時に現地に集合ね。	Let's meet at the site at eight in the morning.
3.		地下	basement, underground
4.	+	地下室	basement room
5.		上と比べて地下室は寒い。	The basement is colder than the upstairs.

6.	+	地元（じもと）	local
7.		地元の人による自転車ツアー	a cycling tour hosted by the locals
8.		心地（ここち）	feeling
9.		住（す）み心地（ごこち）	comfortability of living
10.		居心地（いごこち）	be comfortable (to live in)
11.		心地が悪いと思ったらだれかに押されてたんだ。	No wonder I was feeling uncomfortable, I was being pushed by someone.
12.		地元はやっぱり居心地がいい。	After all, my hometown is comfortable to live in.
13.	#	土地（とち）	land
14.	¥	地域（ちいき）	area
15.	¥	雨（あめ）降（ふ）って地固（じかた）まる	rain settles the soil (adversity strengthens the foundation)

428. 貸　か(す)　タイ (See kanji #429.)　lend, loan　貸

1.	貸（か）す	lend X
2.	雨降ってるけど、私のかさ貸してあげようか。	It's raining, shall I lend you my umbrella?
3.	友人にお金を貸したけど返ってきそうにない。	I lent some money to my friend but it doesn't seem that it will come back.
4.	借りた物は返すのが当たり前でしょう？	It's common sense to return things that you borrow.
5.	夜寝ようとすると「貸した金返せ〜。」って声が聞こえるんだ。	When I try to go to sleep at night, I hear a voice saying, "return the money I loaned you."

430. 階　カイ　floor　階

1.	Ｘ階（かい）	Xth floor
2.	+	最上階（さいじょうかい）	top floor
3.	４階の４０２号室のお客様	a guest in room 402 on the fourth floor
4.	地下の階は黒で、上の階は青にしようと考えています。	I'm thinking of making the downstairs black and upstairs blue.

5. # 階段(かいだん)   stairway
6. # 段階(だんかい)   phase, step

Now go to the Activity Book for 練習.

Then do 評価 activities, including 読んでみよう, 書き取り, and 書いてみよう.

第 24 幕
Act 24

<ruby>挨拶<rt>あいさつ</rt></ruby>[1]

Formal speeches

<ruby>初心忘るべからず<rt>しょしんわすれ</rt></ruby>

Do not forget the spirit of your original intention.

---

1 The word 挨拶 is usually translated into English as 'greeting(s),' but this does not do justice to the pervasiveness and importance of this phenomenon in Japanese. 挨拶 covers not just 'good morning' and 'hello' but also remarks made at the beginning of meetings and ceremonies, along with set expressions of apology, sympathy, and congratulations. This Act will give you some idea of the breadth of 挨拶.

◆ 話す・聞く

Note: The Scene Scripts in this Act aim to provide the discourse structure for each type of speech in context. Use them as a guide to compose your own speeches for similar occasions. For each scene, identify your scene clearly, draft your own speech using the general structure and appropriate expressions, have it checked by a competent user of Japanese and/or your instructor, then practice your speech. You may need to have notes to help you remember the points, but your speech should be smooth and fluid, and you should maintain appropriate body language and eye contact.

Scene 24-1 ブライアンの挨拶（感謝）
Brian's remarks (gratitude)

Brian's program is ending and there is a farewell party for all the students and their host families.

The script

ブライアン

えー、ブライアン・ワンです。1年ぶりにオレゴンの家族に会えるのは楽しみですけど、日本の家族と離れるのは正直悲しいです。楽しい思い出をいっぱい、ありがとうございます。お母さん、タマちゃんを看病して、長生きさせてあげてください。一郎くん、いつかアメリカで野球を見に行こう。それから、先輩の川村さん、就活で忙しい間も面倒見てくれてありがとうございます。最後になりましたが、日本語の先生方、これからも必ず日本語の勉強を続けます！ありがとうございました。

Brian

Umm, my name is Brian Wang. I am looking forward to seeing my family in Oregon who I haven't seen for a year, but to be honest it is sad to leave my Japanese family. Thank you for all the wonderful memories. Mom, please take care of Tama-chan and give her a long life. Ichiro, let's go watch baseball sometime in the U.S. Kawamura-senpai, thank you for looking after me even when you were job hunting. And last but not least: all my Japanese teachers, I will definitely continue my Japanese study from here on! Thank you.

単語と表現

名詞

挨拶(する)	greeting, speech (expressing congratulations, appreciation, sympathy, etc.)
感謝(する)	appreciation, gratitude
思い出	memories, reminiscence
看病(する)	nursing (a patient)
長生き(する)	long life, longevity
就活(する)	job hunting
婚活(する)	searching for a (marriage) partner
終活(する)	making preparations to die
活動(する)	activity

形容詞

懐かしい	nostalgic, remembered fondly

表現

DURATION ぶり	after (a period of time)
面倒(を)見る	take care of someone
面倒(を)かける	trouble someone
最後になりましたが、	lastly

Behind the scenes

BTS 1 Structure of a simple gratitude speech

In this this Scene Brian gives a farewell speech. Typical of such speeches, it includes multiple overt expressions of appreciation, concluding with one in the past form (emphasizing the finality of this occasion). A typical farewell speech includes: a statement acknowledging one's departure, reflection on the shared experience in the current place, a description of one's feelings about the next stage, and a conclusion (thanks). In his speech Brian states that he is returning to Oregon after a year. He begins the second part with his gratitude for many fun memories and goes on to enumerate experiences that some of the listeners share. His future plan is linked to the preceding list of memories with 最後になりましたが (in the sense of 'last but not least'). He concludes his speech with a simple ありがとうございました。

Here are a few more examples of conclusions to farewell remarks.

最後になりましたが、お集まりの皆様のご健康を祈りたいと思います。	Last but not least, I wish for the health of all of those gathered here.
最後になりましたが、今回のプロジェクトのためには、社長からも多くのアドバイスをいただいたことをお伝えしておきます。	Last but not least, I wish to report that for the project this time, we also received a good deal of advice from the president.

Now go to the Activity Book for 練習 and 腕試し.

Scene 24-2 乾杯の音頭 Leading a toast

At the farewell party for Brian's program, Professor Sakamoto has been assigned to lead the toast.

The script

坂本

皆様、本日はお忙しい中、福沢大学留学プログラムの修了式にお集まりくださいまして、ありがとうございます。留学生たちは、一年の間、授業に、クラブ活動にと忙しい日々を過ごしてまいりました。その間、大学関係者はもとより、ホストファミリーの皆様、地域の皆様にも大変温かいご支援を賜りました。プログラムを代表いたしまして、心から御礼申し上げます。留学生の皆さん、それぞれの大学に戻っても、この一年間の経験を大切にしてください。これからの皆さんのさらなる成長を願って、乾杯をいたしたいと思います。皆様、グラスのご用意はよろしいでしょうか。では、皆様の飛躍と、プログラムの成功を祝って、乾杯！

Sakamoto

Everyone, thank you for taking time out of your busy schedules to gather here today for the close of Fukuzawa University's exchange program. The exchange students have passed one year with busy days (full of) classes and club activities. During that time, they were blessed with the warm support of those associated with the university, but also their host families and everyone in the area. As a representative of the program, thank you from the bottom of our hearts. Exchange students, even though you return to your various colleges, please treasure the experiences of this one year. Hoping for your continued development, I would like to propose a toast. Is everyone's glass ready? To everyone's progress and the success of the program, cheers!

単語と表現

名詞

音頭（おんど）	leading a group
皆様・みなさま	everyone

本日(ほんじつ)	today (formal)
修了式(しゅうりょうしき)	closing ceremony
クラブ活動(かつどう)	club activities
日々(ひび)	days
人々(ひとびと)	people, persons
国々(くにぐに)	countries
個々(ここ)	one by one, individually
間(かん)	during the time, meanwhile
X関係者(かんけいしゃ)	associates of X
地域(ちいき)	region, area
市(し)	city
町(まち)	town
村(むら)	village
県庁(けんちょう)	prefectural office
(ご)支援(しえん)(する)	support
代表(だいひょう)(する)	representative
(お)礼(れい)	gratitude, thanks
御礼(おんれい)	gratitude, thanks
それぞれ	each, respectively
(ご)経験(けいけん)(する)	experience
(ご)体験(たいけん)(する)	personal experience
さら・更(さら)(なる)	further, even more
(ご)成長(せいちょう)(する)	growth, development
(ご)用意(ようい)(する)	preparation
飛躍(ひやく)(する)	great progress, great strides, leap
(ご)発展(はってん)(する)	development

(ご)活躍(する)	activity, thrive
(ご)期待(する)	expectation

動詞

過ごす (-U; 過ごした)	pass time
賜る↓ (-U; 賜った)	be given, be granted (humble)
祝う (-U; 祝った)	celebrate, congratulate
祝す (-U; 祝した)	celebrate, congratulate
讃える (-RU; 讃えた)	extol, praise
応える (-RU; 応えた)	answer, meet (expectations or demands), respond

数詞

〜杯(はい・ばい)	classifier for counting cup-fuls, glass-fuls

表現

音頭を取る	take the lead
Sentence + 中	in the midst of X
X に Y に	from X to Y
X はもとより、Y	of course X, but also Y
X を代表して	as a representative of X
さらなる・更なる	furthermore, even more
X を祝って	celebrate X, congratulate X

Behind the scenes

BTS 2 Leading a toast (discourse structure)

This toast follows a typical four-part structure: introduction, body, lead-up to the toast, and the toast itself (乾杯！). An introduction may include a statement of intention such as では、チームを代表して乾杯の音頭を取らせていただきます 'Well then, representing the team, I will lead the toast.' This might also include a self-deprecating remark such as ご指名に預かりましたので、僭越ながら乾杯の音頭を取らせていただきます 'Since I have the honor of being asked, though I'm not the most qualified, I will lead the toast.' The body of the toast usually reviews events that have culminated in the gathering. In this Scene, Sakamoto-sensei extends her gratitude for the help of the community members. The lead-up to the toast urges all attendees to fill their glasses. Sometimes, it will include a request to chime in when the toast is voiced. Finally, the toast itself is delivered with enthusiasm.

Here are some examples of the final portion of toast speeches.

お二人のご結婚を祝って、乾杯！	Congratulations to you both on your marriage, cheers!
インターンシップの成功を期待して、乾杯！	Wishing for the success of the internship, cheers!
チームのこの一年の素晴らしい成績を讃え、新たな発展に乾杯！	Congratulations on the team's brilliant results this year. To the prosperous development of the team – cheers!

BTS 3 X に Y に

X に Y に is used to emphasize the range or scope of something. It is similar to と but the suggestion is 'X and on top of that Y.' A classic example is a vendor walking around the seats in a stadium, calling 「おセン (=おせんべい) にキャラメル、ジュースにサイダー」 'Crackers to caramels, juice to cider!'

海に、空にと活躍している。	She is doing well, from start to finish (lit. 'from sea to sky').
市の代表に、政治家にとすごい人が集まってますから、挨拶は気をつけてください。	From city representatives to politicians, some amazing people have gathered, so be mindful as you give your remarks.
アルバイトに、ボランティア活動にと毎日忙しいけど、満足しています。	I'm busy with everything from part-time work to volunteer activities, but I am satisfied.

BTS 4 X はもとより、Y、Z

When listing things in a set, sometimes one thing is primary or is an obvious starting point. That Noun is followed by もとより and the rest of the list follows.

部長はもとより、チームの全員がこの意見には賛成しています。 — Of course, the division chief, but all the team members are in favor of this opinion.

ミステリーはもとより、コメディ、サイエンスフィクションと、色々な種類の本を書いている作家です。 — Of course, mystery, but including comedy, science fiction, and others, he is an author who is writing a number of different types of books.

Now go to the Activity Book for 練習 and 腕試し.

Scene 24-3 サーシャの挨拶(新たな出発)
Sasha's farewell (moving on)

Sasha is leaving Ogaki Trading and the division is having a farewell party for her.

The script

サーシャ

3年間という短い間でしたけれど、大変お世話になりました。改めてお礼申し上げます。今月末で帰国し、シカゴにある貿易会社に就職することになりました。八木部長始め、神田さん、みなさんに助けていただきながら、ここまでやってくることができました。至らないことも多々あったと思いますが、皆さんに励ましていただいたお陰で楽しく仕事ができました。毎日充実していました。ここで学んだことは一生忘れません。新しい職場ではまた初心にかえって頑張ります。シカゴの方においでになる機会がありましたら、是非ご連絡ください。本当にありがとうございました。

Sasha

It was a short three years, but I am incredibly grateful. Let me thank you again. I will return home at the end of this month and have gotten a job at a trading company in Chicago. I was able to come this far while being helped by everyone, starting with Division Chief Yagi and then Kanda-san. I think I had many weaknesses, but thanks to everyone's encouragement I was able to enjoy doing my work. I can never forget what I learned here. In my new job I will go back to being a beginner, and do my best. If you have a chance to come to Chicago, please get in touch. Thank you very much.

単語と表現

名詞

新た(な)	new, fresh
(ご)出発(する)	departure

225

(ご)到着(する)	arrival
今月末	end of this month
今週末	end of this week
今年度末	end of this school year, end of this fiscal year
年度	fiscal year
(ご)帰国(する)	return to the home country
貿易	trade
国際	international
多々	very much, very many, more and more
無事(に)	without incident, safety
一生	life
充実(する)	completion, fullness
職場	workplace
初心	original intention, basics

動詞

改める (-RU; 改めた)	change X, do something anew
改まる (U; 改まった)	something changes; act formally
励ます (U; 励ました)	encourage
学ぶ (U; 学んだ)	learn
生かす・活かす (U; 生かした・活かした)	make use of, make the best of

表現

改めて	again
X末	the end of X

X (を) 始め Y	beginning from X to Y
至らない	imperfect, inadequate
Sentence + ことができる	can do X
初心にかえって	returning to the basics, returning to the original intention

Behind the scenes

BTS 5 Formal speech when moving on (discourse structure)

This Scene represents Sasha's final remarks as she leaves one post and moves on to the next. It has six parts, starting with a word of thanks. This is followed by an explanation of the departure – that her time at the company is coming to an end and that Sasha has a new job lined up. Next Sasha reflects on her experience as an intern and an employee, giving credit to her colleagues for making it meaningful. In the fourth part Sasha expresses her own feelings about her future, connecting it to what she learned. In the fifth part, Sasha invites those in attendance to come and visit her in her new location. She concludes with another expression of thanks – the concluding thanks being in the past form, giving her remarks finality.

Here are a few more examples of giving credit to others while mentioning one's accomplishments.

わからないことが多くて大変でしたが、親切に教えていただいたお陰で、完璧に仕上げることができました。	There were a lot of things I didn't understand, and it was rough, but thanks to your kind instruction, I was able to completely finish.
非常に難しいプロジェクトでしたが、皆さんの頑張りのお陰で、思っていなかったくらいの素晴らしい結果を出すことができました。	It was a very difficult project, but thanks to everybody's persistent effort, we have been able to produce a fantastic result that we hadn't even imagined.

BTS 6 X (を) 始め Y、Z

You saw Xに始まって earlier where X is the subject and starts a list of things about which a comment is made. When the list of items are things that are altered as a result of an action, they are listed with Xを始め. Again X is the most important item in the list, but in this case X may be a subject or an object.

小林先生はじめ、クラブのメンバーの皆さんには大変お世話になりました。

近くのコンビニを始め、駅の側には充実したスーパーもあるので、非常に便利です。

Starting from Professor Kobayashi, to all of the members of the club, I am indebted for their kindness.

Starting from the convenience stores nearby, there is also a well-stocked supermarket, so it's very convenient.

Now go to the Activity Book for 練習 and 腕試し.

Scene 24-4 孝の挨拶(振り返り) Takashi's reflection

Takashi is completing his study at Clinton University. His friends at the Japanese Language Club are holding a farewell party for him.

The script

孝

えーと初めて来たばかりの頃は、分からないことだらけで、失敗の連続でした。でもみんなと親しくなれ、慣れてくるとともに、このキャンパスでの生活を心からエンジョイできるようになりました。みんな、ありがとう!留学、または仕事で日本に来ることがあったら、絶対に連絡してください。ありがとうございました。

Takashi

Umm, when I had first arrived, (life here) was full of things I didn't understand, and (I made) a string of mistakes. But as I was able to become friends with all of you, and at the same time get used to things, I truly became able to enjoy life on this campus. Thanks, everyone! If you come to Japan to study or to work, be sure to contact me. Thank you for everything.

単語と表現

名詞

振り返り	reflection, reminiscence
連続(する)	series, continuation
生活(する)	life, daily life
エンジョイ(する)	enjoy

動詞

| 振り返る (-U; 振り返った) | look back, reflect, reminisce |

形容詞

| 親しい | close, familiar, intimate |

表現

X だらけ	full of X, riddled with X
X の連続	series of X
Non-past Sentence + とともに	along with X
X または Y	X or Y

Behind the scenes

BTS 7 Impromptu farewell speech structure

The speech in this Scene has four parts. Takashi first recalls how life was at the beginning of his stay in the U.S. He then contrasts that with how he enjoyed his experience, implicitly suggesting his sense of gratitude to those who helped him become accustomed to the ways of life in the new place. Since he is moving back to his home country, the third part consists of his open invitation for his friends to visit him there. As with Brian and Sasha's speeches, the last part is his concluding expression of thanks.

BTS 8 Non-past Sentence + とともに

A Noun in combination with とともに means '(along) with.'

| 神田さん、池辺さんとともにどこかに出かけたんだ。 | Kanda-san went off somewhere with Ikebe-san. |
| 父は年とともに弱くなってきた。 | My father got weaker with age. |

In combination with a non-past Sentence, とともに indicates that one event follows closely along with another.

仕事が増えてくるとともに、家族と一緒に過ごす時間が減ってきた。	As my work becomes fuller, the time that I can spend with my family has begun to decline.
嫌な経験をしたので、新しいアパートを探すとともに、今のところでは隣の人と話さないようにした。	I had a bad experience, so I looked for a new apartment and, moreover, I took care not to talk to neighbors.

BTS 9 X、または Y

または is used between Nouns as well as Sentences. Between Nouns it is almost always equivalent to 'or.' It is a much stronger contrast than か、and is often used in addition to か to reinforce the contrast.

ここからは、山田さん、または水野さんに代わっていただきます。	From here on, I'm going to ask Yamada-san or Mizuno-san to take over.
ご家族、または親しい人のお名前を書いてください。	Please write the name of a family member or someone you are close to.
水か、またはお湯は飲んでもいいですけど、コーヒー、紅茶、ジュースなんかは明日まで控えてください。	It's all right to drink either water or hot water but please hold off until tomorrow on things like coffee, tea, and juice.

または can also be used between Sentences to introduce an alternative when the context makes it clear. Note that sentences connected by または are almost always sentence modifiers.

自分の車がない、またはあっても運転したくないという人にはとても便利なサービスです。	For people who don't have their own car or who don't want to drive even if they own a car, this is a very convenient service.
面白いと思う、または賛成する方は青いボタンを押してください。	Those who think it's interesting or who agree with it, please press the blue button.

Now go to the Activity Book for 練習 and 腕試し.

Scene 24-5 エイミーの挨拶（自己紹介）
Amy's remarks (self-introduction)

Amy has just arrived in Japan, where she will be an intern. She has been asked to introduce herself.

The script

エイミー

アメリカのクリントン大学を卒業して日本にやって参りましたエイミー・ジョンソンでございます。ニューヨークで育ちましたが、大学は西海岸でした。インターンとしてこちらで2年間お世話になることになりました。アメリカでも、友人や先生と日本語を使うチャンスはありましたが、日本に来て、仕事をしながらさらに上達できるよう、頑張るつもりです。仕事の方も、早くいろいろ覚えて、この研究所の戦力になれるよう、励んで行く決意です。ご指導、ご鞭撻のほど、どうぞよろしくお願いいたします。

Amy

I am Amy Johnson. I have come to Japan after graduating from Clinton University in the U.S. I grew up in New York but went to college on the West Coast. I will be grateful for your assistance for two years as an intern. I had a chance to use Japanese in the U.S. with my friends and my teachers, and I have come to Japan (ready) to do my best to improve even more while I am working. I am determined to learn quickly at work, and will try my best to become an asset to this research institute. I very much appreciate your guidance and support.

単語と表現

名詞

西海岸	West Coast
東海岸	East Coast

中西部 (ちゅうせいぶ)	the Midwest
南部 (なんぶ)	the South
ロッキー山脈 (さんみゃく)	Rocky Mountains
東北 (とうほく)	northeast
南西部 (なんせいぶ)	the Southwest
表日本 (おもてにほん)	the Pacific Ocean side of Japan
裏日本 (うらにほん)	the Japan Sea side of Japan
友人 (ゆうじん)	friend
チャンス	chance
上達(する) (じょうたつ)	improve
進歩(する) (しんぽ)	progress
実力 (じつりょく)	ability, strength
戦力 (せんりょく)	asset
(お)力 (ちから)	power
決意(する) (けつい)	determination
(ご)指導(する) (しどう)	guidance, leadership
(ご)鞭撻 (べんたつ)	encouragement

動詞

やって来る (やって来た)	come along
磨く (-U; 磨いた) (みが)	polish
(X に)励む (-U; 励んだ) (はげ)	strive to X

表現

ご指導、ご鞭撻のほど (しどう、べんたつ)	your guidance and encouragement

Behind the scenes

BTS 10 Workplace self-introduction (discourse structure)

A self-introduction typically has four parts: name and identifying information, background, aspirational statements, and a conclusion. The name is often given with a lengthy set of sentence modifiers. The background can include some information about where the person came from or what the person used to do. The aspirational statement outlines what the person hopes to do in the new place. Self-introductions typically end with よろしくお願いします, a more polite variation, よろしくお願いいたします, or a more explicit request for help and guidance, as expressed by Amy in this Scene.

Here are other examples of self-identification that may be used at the beginning of self-introductions.

ただいまご紹介いただきました、大垣商会のサーシャモリスでございます。	I'm Sasha Morris from Ogaki Trading, who has just been kindly introduced.
先月からこちらのゼミでお世話になることになった、3年生の松浦と言います。	I'm Matsuura, a junior who has been a member of this seminar since last month.

Now go to the Activity Book for 練習 and 腕試し.

Then do 評価 activities.

◆ 読み書き

シーン 24-6R　失敗談(しっぱいだん) Learning experiences

Here is a message that Brian wrote for a collection of essays (文集(ぶんしゅう)) that departing international students wrote.

テキスト Text

失敗談

　　　　　　　　　　　　　　　　　　ブライアン・ワン

　僕の心に残っていることは、坂本先生が授業で話してくれた失敗談です。留学生の名前を間違えて呼んでしまったことや、電車を間違えて家に帰れなくなってしまって初めて気付いたこと等、今でも思い出すと笑ってしまう話ばかりです。でも、僕たちが失敗した時に先生が言ってくれた「失敗は成功のもと」、「七転び八起きでがんばれ～！」という言葉が一番うれしかったです。また、先生は時間をとって読み書きの勉強の仕方を教えてくださったり、僕の大切にしていたトトロの話を聞いてくださったり、相談にのってくださったりした。正直母親のような存在でした。両親が離婚している僕にとって、忙しいのにも関わらず、僕たちのことを第一に考えてくれた先生に感謝しています。このご恩は一生忘れません。

Failure Stories

Brian Wang

What will remain in my heart are the stories of learning experiences that Sakamoto-sensei shared in class. Many of her stories are ones that make me smile as I remember them, such as noticing the fact that she was saying the exchange student's name wrong at the graduation ceremony, and not being able to get home because she took the wrong train. However, what made me happiest was the warm words she always shared with us when we failed, which are, "Failure is the essence of success, do your best with the spirit of falling seven times but rising up eight." Sakamoto-sensei did other things such as taking time to teach us how to study reading and writing, listening to my story about the trading cards that I cherished, and giving me advice. To tell the truth, Sakamoto-sensei was like a mother-figure to me (whose parents are divorced). I'm grateful that she gave priority to us. I will never forget this indebtedness.

BTL 1 恩と義理

The concepts of 恩 'indebtedness' and 義理 'obligation, duty' play an important role in Japanese society. 恩 is what you feel when someone does something for you or helps you in some way. You become indebted to them for their kindness. People naturally feel a sense of 恩 to their parents, their teachers, their *senpai* – anyone who has done something that benefits them, even a small favor. 恩 is not to be taken lightly, and indeed the benefactor is thereafter called 恩人 or, in the case of a teacher, 恩師.

義理 on the other hand is a sense of duty or obligation to someone with whom you have a formal relationship (employee, co-worker, 後輩). If a supportive supervisor asks you for a favor, it is your duty to comply as repayment for their support. To take another example, on Valentine's Day (February 14th) employees often give 義理チョコ 'obligation chocolate' to their co-workers and supervisors to show their appreciation. There is nothing romantic about this gift; it is simply a matter of acknowledging the relationship. One month later (March 14th), the gesture is reciprocated on "White Day" when recipients give white chocolate or some other small gift in return.

文字と例 Kanji with examples

431. 式 シキ ceremony, technique, formula 式

1. 修了式 — completion ceremony
2. お金を探していたらバスから降りられず、修了式に間に合わなくなってしまった。 — I couldn't get off the bus as I was looking for the fare, and so I didn't make it to the completion ceremony.

3.	+	卒業式 (そつぎょうしき)		graduation ceremony
4.	+	入学式 (にゅうがくしき)		school entrance ceremony
5.		春は卒業式に入学式にと、忙しいシーズンだ。		Spring is a busy season with graduation and entrance ceremonies.
6.	+	入社式 (にゅうしゃしき)		company welcoming ceremony
7.		入社式と言っても名前ばかりで、特別なことは何も無い。		The welcoming ceremony is just the name of the event, and there is nothing special happening.
8.	+	式場 (しきじょう)		ceremonial hall
9.		式場はもとより日付等の詳細は何も決まっていない。		We haven't decided on the details such as the date, or even the place for the ceremony.
10.	#	方式 (ほうしき)		system, method, form, technique
11.	#	数式 (すうしき)		mathematical formula
12.	#	和式・洋式 (わしき・ようしき)		Japanese style and Western style

432. 成　な(る)　セイ　accomplish　成

1.	+	成田空港 (なりたくうこう)	Narita Airport
2.		平成 (へいせい)	Heisei era (1989–2019)
3.		平成最後の日は成田空港で過ごした。	I spent the last day of Heisei at Narita Airport.
4.		完成(する) (かんせい)	complete
5.		正直予定通りに完成させられるとは思ってなかったよ。	To tell you the truth, I didn't think we could have it completed as scheduled.
6.		成長(する) (せいちょう)	grow
7.		育てれば育てるほど成長するからおもしろい。	It's interesting because the more I nurture it the more it grows.
8.		成人の日 (せいじん の ひ)	Coming of Age Day (second Monday of January)
9.	¥	成績 (せいせき)	results, grades
10.	¥	賛成(する) (さんせい)	agreement

433.	功	コウ		merit	功
1.		成功(する)		succeed	
2.		失敗は成功のもと		Failure is the foundation of success.	
3.		この件、正直失敗するかと思ってたけど、無事に成功してよかったですね。		To be honest, I thought we were going to fail in this case, but I'm glad that we succeeded safely.	
4.		成功するわけないじゃん。		There is no way that it will succeed.	
5.		大成功		big success	
6.		おかげさまで実験大成功です！		Thanks to you, the experiment is a big success!	

434.	謝	あや(まる) シャ		apologize	謝
1.		家族に謝る		apologize to the family	
2.		自分は関係ないのに、どうして謝らなくちゃいけないの？		I'm not involved, so how come I have to apologize?	
3.		勝手に働いてしまったことは謝らせてください。		Please allow me to apologize for working without your permission.	
4.		死んでも謝るもんか。		I won't ever apologize even if I die.	
5.		感謝(する)		appreciate	
6.		いい賃貸アパートを探してくれて本当に感謝しています。		I'm truly grateful that you found a good rental apartment.	
7. ¥		勤労感謝の日		Labor/Thanksgiving Day	
8. ¥		謝罪(する)		apologize (formal)	

435.	離	はな(す) はな(れる) リ (See kanji #436.)		depart	離
1.		離れる		be away, separate from	
2.		可能であればできるだけ離れてください。		To the extent possible, please stay as far away as you can.	
3.		早く海から離れたところに行け！		Go quickly to a location far from the ocean!	
4.		離す		divide something	
5.		あの２人を早く離さないと！		We have to separate those two.	

	6.		だれが一番長く手を離さずにいられるか勝負です。		Let's have a match to see who can hold it the longest without letting go.
436.	婚	コン		marriage	婚
	1.		婚活(する)		marriage hunting
	2.		今婚活アプリで手続きを終えたところです。		I just finished the registration for the marriage app now.
	3. +		離婚(する)		divorce
	4.		離婚することになってしまいました。		It's been decided they'll get divorced.
	5. +		婚約(する)		wedding engagement
	6.		婚約する時に彼女にどんな質問したの？		What kind of question did you ask when you got engaged?
	7.		婚約さえすれば変わると思ったけど、むしろ悪くなるばかり。		I thought things would change if we got engaged, but instead it's getting worse.
437	親	おや　した(しい)　シン		parent, close, kind	親
	1.		親		parent
	2.		親に生活費を払って一緒に住むのも悪くはない。		It's not bad to live with my parents by paying the cost of living there.
	3.		親が７０過ぎたら１階に住んでもらう予定です。		We plan to have my parents live on the first floor when they are past 70.
	4.		親から借りているお金、早く返したい。		I want to return the money I borrowed from my parents.
	5.		母親		mother
	6.		父親		father
	7.		父親も母親も働いていたから、家にいることは少なかった。		Both my father and mother were working, so they were rarely home.
	8. ¥		親孝行(な)		filial piety (dedication to parents)
	9. ¥		親不孝(な)		lack of filial piety
	10.		親しい		close, intimate

11.		あの2人、一度キリのデートで親しい関係になったみたい。	It seems that those two became really close after just one date.
12.		親切(な)	kind, gentle
13.		あの歴史の教授ってけっこう親切にメール返してくれるよ。	That history professor replies to emails quite kindly.
14.	¥	両親	parents
15.	¥	親戚	relative, family (in-group)
16.	¥	親睦会	informal gathering, meet-and-greet

438. 在　あ(る)　サイ　presence　在

1.	+	現在	current, present
2.		この電話は現在使われておりません。	This phone is not being used currently.
3.	+	存在(する)	existence, presence
4.		離れられない存在	inseparable existence
5.		そんな名前の場所、地図にも存在しないよ。	A location with that name doesn't even exist on the map.
6.	+	不在届け	undeliverable notice
7.		向こうのポストに不在届が入ってたよ。	There was a delivery notification in the mailbox over there.
8.	#	在る	occur, exist
9.	¥	在来線	conventional train

439. 恩　オン　aindebtedness, favor, kindness　恩

1.	+	(ご)恩	indebtedness, favor, kindness
2.		このご恩は一生忘れません。	I will never forget your kindness.
3.	+	恩返し(する)	repaying kindness
4.		このお礼はただの恩返しです。	This expression of gratitude is just to return a favor.
5.		『つるの恩返し』という話を読んでもらった。	Someone read to me a story called "The Grateful Crane."

Now go to the Activity Book for 練習.

◆ シーン 24-7R

お祝いの言葉 Congratulatory words

Here is a message that Sakamoto-sensei contributed to a collection of essays for departing international students.

テキスト Text

先生からのお祝いの言葉

留学生の皆様

教師として皆様に出会えた機会に感謝しています。これからも勉強に就職、結婚など色々な経験が皆様を待っています。人生問題だらけと感じることもあるかと思いますが、日本での経験が皆様の役に立ちますように。

学校の試験と違って人生の問題に対する答えは一つだけではありませんし、結果が全てではありません。日本での経験を活かし、皆様がそれぞれにあった「正解」を見つけられるよう願っています。

また日本に来る機会があればぜひ顔を出してください。

坂本

Congratulatory words from teacher

Dear international students,

I'm grateful for the opportunity to have met all of you as a teacher.

From now on, too, there will be various experiences such as studying, employment, and marriage awaiting you. I think there will also be times when you feel that life is full of problems, but I hope that your experiences in Japan will be useful.

Unlike school exams, there is not just one answer to the problems of life, and results may not always be everything you wish for. I hope that you can take advantage of your experience in Japan and you will find the answers that suit each of you.

Please drop by if you have an opportunity to come to Japan again.

Sakamoto

文字と例 Kanji with examples

440.	祝	いわ(う) シュク	celebrate, bless	祝
1.		祝う・祝す	celebrate X	
2.		日本では二十歳(はたち)になると成人の日をお祝いする。	In Japan people celebrate Coming of Age Day when they turn 20.	
3.		研究の成功を祝う会	a party to celebrate the success of research	
4.	#	祝福(しゅくふく)(する)	blessing	
5.		(お)祝(いわ)い	celebration	
6.		今晩はおいしいお酒とビールでお祝いだぜ！	Tonight let's celebrate with good sake and beer!	
7.		お祝いがあった部屋に行ったら、ゴミだらけでびっくりしました。	I went to the room that had the party, but it was full of trash and I was astonished.	

441.	皆	みな	everyone	皆
1.		皆様(みなさま)	everyone	
2.		学生を始め、ご家族、ご友人の皆様、本日はお集りくださってありがとうございます。	To students, family, and friends, thank you for gathering today.	
3.		皆様とお祝(いわ)いすることができることに感謝しています。	I'm grateful that I could celebrate with everyone.	
4.		学生の皆様への感謝の気持ちをお伝えするとともに、皆様のさらなる成長を願っております。	I'd like to express my feeling of gratitude to the students and wish for their continued growth.	

442.	師	シ	teacher	師
1.		教師(きょうし)	teacher	
2.		教師または教授として学生の質問に答えるには	ways for a teacher or professor to answer students' questions.	
3.		今度の政治の授業の教師って知ってる？	Do you know the instructor who is teaching politics next time?	
4.		失敗だらけでしたが皆さんの教師になれた機会に感謝しています。	It was full of failures (on my part), but I'm grateful for the opportunity to be able to be your teacher.	

5.	+	恩師(おんし)		former/beloved teacher
6.		恩師に手紙を書くべきだと言われた。		I was told that I should write a letter to my former teacher.
7.	¥	看護師(かんごし)		nurse
8.	#	師走(しわす)		twelfth month of the lunar calendar

443. 機　キ　machine, opportunity　機

1.	コピー機(き)	copying machine
2.	このコピー機でプリントしようとしたらインクだらけ！	I tried to print it with this copier, but there was ink all over!
3.	コピー機が直らないんだけど、修理頼んでくれる？	The printer hasn't been fixed – can you request a repair?
4.	機会(きかい)	opportunity
5.	皆様(みなさま)とお祝(いわ)いできる機会に心より感謝しております。	I'm grateful from my heart that I have the opportunity to celebrate it with all of you.
6.	来週またはその次の機会に参りたいと思っております。	I'm thinking of going next week or the next chance after that.
7.	¥	計算機(けいさんき)	calculator
8.	¥	飛行機(ひこうき)	airplane
9.	¥	自動販売機(じどうはんばいき)(自販機(じはんき))	vending machine
10.	#	機械(きかい)	machine

444. 就　つ(く)　シュウ　occupy, fill　就

1.		就活(しゅうかつ)(する)	job hunting
2.		就活での失敗談	mistakes in job hunting
3.		就職(しゅうしょく)(する)	employment
4.		この会社に就職することに家族から反対されている。	I've been opposed by my family about being employed in this company.
5.		実用的なスキルが無いと就職は難しい。	Getting employed is difficult if you don't have practical skills.
6.		就職は経済関係の仕事がいい。	As for employment, I'd like a job related to economics.
7.	#	就(つ)く	attain (a position)

445.	役	ヤク	role, part, duty	役
	1.	役員	officer	
	2.	役員会	officers' meeting	
	3.	あの役員と相談してみたら？	Why don't you consult with that officer?	
	4.	役員なのに役員会に出席せずに何考えてるの？	You are an officer but you aren't attending the officers' meetings, what are you thinking?	
	5.	役者	actor, actress, star	
	6.	あの映画、内容はおもしろそうなんだけど、役者さんがちょっとね……。	The content of that movie seems interesting, but I'm not sure about the actors...	
	7.	役に立つ	useful	
	8.	役に立たなそうだったから、授業には一度しか出席しなかった。	It didn't seem useful so I only attended class once.	
	9.	この書類はもう役に立たないから捨てちゃいましょう。	These paper documents are no longer useful, so let's throw them away.	
	10.	役に立てる	make good use of	
	11.	これ、新しい職場で役に立ててください。	Please make good use of this at your new job.	
	12. #	役目	mission, duty	
446.	結	ケツ	join, tie	結
	1.	結婚(する)	marriage	
	2. +	結婚式	marriage ceremony	
	3.	結婚するならこれぐらいの給料が必要となるらしい。	If I were to get married, I hear that I need this amount of salary.	
	4.	自分の結婚を他の人と比べてしまうことってありませんか？	Don't you sometimes compare your own marriage with other people's?	
	5.	結婚式には親を始め、家族や友人が来てくれる。	For the marriage ceremony, people like my parents, family, and friends are coming.	
	6.	去年離婚したばかりのくせにもう結婚相手見つけたの？あり得ない！	You just got divorced last year, but you already found a marriage partner? That can't be right.	
	7. #	完結(する)	complete	
	8. ¥	結構(な)	nice, wonderful, quite, sufficient	

447.	果	くだ　カ		end, limit, fruit	果
1.		果物		fruit	
2.		果物、野菜、魚、肉、あとは何を買うんだったっけ？		Fruits, vegetables, fish, and meat, what else am I buying?	
3.		古くなった果物は燃えるゴミに出せばいいんだよね？		We just have to put the spoiled fruit out in the burnable garbage, right?	
4.		結果		result	
5.		たとえ今日結果が出せなくても明日があるさ。		Even if we can't get the results today, we have tomorrow.	
6.		受験の結果っていつ分かるの？		When do you find out about the results of the college exam?	
7.		親からゲームを禁止されて育てられた結果、ゲームしかしない大人になってしまった。		As the result of my parents restricting me from playing video games growing up, I became an adult who does nothing but play video games.	
8.	¥	効果		effect	
9.	¥	効果的(な)		effective	

448.	表	あらわ(す)　ヒョウ		display, express, present	表
1.		表現(する)		expression	
2.		ちょっとあいまいな表現ですね。		The expression is a little ambiguous.	
3.		発表(する)		present, announce	
4.		日付はいつ発表しますか？		When are you going to announce the date?	
5.		みんなの前で発表するとドキドキします。		Presenting in front of everyone makes me nervous.	
6.	#	表す		show, express	

449.	解	と(く)　カイ		solve	解
1.		正解(する)		correct	
2.		正解が書かれている用紙、ちょっと拝借。		Let me borrow that paper with the correct answers written on it.	

3.		不正解(する)	incorrect
4.		お決まりになったお答えは、残念ながら不正解です。	The answer you decided on is unfortunately incorrect.
5.		理解(する)	comprehend
6.		授業に出るだけ出てみたけど、寝不足で全然理解することができなかった。	I tried to attend class, but being deprived from sleep I could not understand it at all.
7.		温暖化の事、実はまだよく理解できてないんです。	I haven't actually understood global warming very well.
8.		了解(する)	understanding, consent, agreement
9.		論文の件、了解しました。	About that thesis, I got it.
10.	#	解く	solve X
11.	¥	誤解(する)	misunderstand

450. 顔 かお　ガン   face   顔

1.		顔	face
2.		人は顔がきれいでも心がきれいとは限らないよ。	The fact that someone's face is pretty doesn't necessarily mean that their heart is pure.
3.		顔に何か黒い点がついてるよ。	There is a black spot or something on your face.
4.		お客様、顔が細く見えるようになったご意見ご感想をお聞かせください。	Dear customer, please let us hear your opinions and thoughts on having your face look thinner.
5.		では、お顔を拝見させていただきます。	Well, let me see your face.
6.	¥	顔を潰す	make somebody lose face
7.	#	顔面	facial surface
8.	+	泣き顔	crying face
9.	+	笑顔	smiling face
10.		最後に笑顔で一枚、ハイチーズ！	For the last picture, smile and say cheese!

Now go to the Activity Book for 練習.

Then do 評価 activities, including 読んでみよう, 書き取り, and 書いてみよう.

Appendix A: Japanese-English glossary in *gojuuon* order

List of abbreviations

N = Noun
V = Verb
Adj = Adjective
Sp. Exp. = Special Expression
Inst. Exp. = Instructional Expression

	あ、	あ、	Sp. Exp.	Oh	1	10
	ああ	ああ	Sp. Exp.	ahh, oh	2	7
	あいかわらず	相変わらず	Sp. Exp.	as usual, as ever	19	3
	あいきどう	合気道	N	aikido (martial art)	6	1
	あいさつ	(ご)挨拶(する)	N	greeting, speech (expressing congratulations, appreciation, sympathy, etc.)	24	1
	あいだ	間	N	interval, space between; XとYの間 between X and Y; Scene 8-6 during, between; 夏休みの間 during summer vacation; Scene 14-3 混ぜて(い)る間(に) while mixing it in	7	6
+	あいだ	会田	N	[family name]	10	9R
+	あいづち	相槌	N	interjections to indicate one is listening (BTS 14); Scene 11-6 ～を打つ provide back-channel comments and nods	8	5
	あいて	相手	N	other party, companion, opponent (in sports)	15	1
+	アイティー	IT	N	IT	9	3

247

+	あいまい	曖昧(な)	N	ambiguity (BTS 12)	4	2
+	あう	会う (-U; 会った)	V	see, meet	3	4
+	あう	合う (-U; 合った)	V	merge, match, fit; 言い合う say to one another; 話し合う discuss; 見せ合う show one another	16	5
	アウト	アウト	N	out (from baseball)	19	5
+	あおい	青い	Adj	blue; Scene 6-4 青 blue, green (N)	3	5
+	アオイしゅっぱん	アオイ出版	N	Aoi Publishing	3	1
	あおき	青木	N	[family name]	13	7R
	あかい	赤い	Adj	red; 赤いの the red one; Scene 6-3 赤 red (N)	3	5
+	あかちゃん	赤ちゃん	N	baby	7	2
	あがる	上がる (-U; 上がった)	V	rise, go up, enter a house	8	3
+	あかるい	明るい	Adj	light, bright	7	1
+	あき	秋	N	autumn, fall	8	6
+	あきらめる	諦める (-RU; 諦めた)	V	be reconciled, give up	10	6
+	あきる	(Xに) 飽きる (-RU; 飽きた)	V	get tired of X	20	5
	あく	空く・あく (-U; 空いた・あいた)	V	become free, empty	6	5
+	あく	開く (-U; 開いた)	V	X opens	14	1
	アクション	アクション	N	action	19	2
+	アクセサリー	アクセサリー	N	accessory	11	4
	あくび	あくび・欠伸	N	yawn	13	1
+	あけましておめでとうございます	明けましておめでとうございます	Sp. Exp.	Happy New Year	10	8R
	あける	開ける (-RU; 開けた)	V	open X; 開けてみる try opening and see	8	1

+	あける	空ける (-RU; 空けた)	V	empty, make room for, remove X	14	1
	あげる	あげる・上げる・挙げる (-RU; あげた・上げた・挙げた)	V	give (to out-group); Scene 16-6 raise X	12	6
+	あげる	揚げる (-RU; 揚げた)	V	deep fry	14	3
+	あさ	朝	N	morning; Scene 2-3 朝ごはん breakfast; Scene 12-4 朝型 morning person; 朝に強い morning type (lit. 'strong in the morning')	3	4
	あさって	あさって・明後日	N	day after tomorrow	3	4
+	あし	足/脚	N	feet/leg	11	5
+	あじ	味	N	flavor, taste	14	4
+	あした	あした・明日	N	tomorrow	2	2
	あす	あす	N	tomorrow (slightly more formal than あした)	5	1
+	あずかる	預かる (-U; 預かった)	V	keep X in custody; look after X	15	5
+	あずける	預ける (-RU; 預けた)	V	place X in someone's custody, deposit X	15	5
	あすのひゃくよりきょうのごじゅう	明日の百より今日の五十	Kotowaza	A bird in the hand is worth two in the bush.; also in Scene 20-2	6	0
+	あせる	焦る (-U; 焦った)	V	hurry	19	6
+	あそこ	あそこ	N	over there, there (away from both of us), that place (that we both know about)	2	7
	あそぶ	遊ぶ (-RU; 遊んだ)	V	play; 遊び play, fun	9	3
	あたたかい	暖かい・温かい	Adj	warm (climate); 暖かくて気持ちがいい warm and good feeling; Scene 18-8R 温かい warm (personality); Scene 18-7R 暖か(な)・温か(な)	7	1
+	あたたまる	温まる・暖まる (-U; 温まった・暖まった)	V	X heats up, warms; Also in Scene 18-7R	14	4

	あたためる	温める・暖める (-RU; 温めた・暖めた)	V	heat up, warm X	14	3
	あたま	頭	N	head; Scene 12-3 頭が/のいい intelligent, smart; Scene 22-6 頭にくる get angry	11	5
+	あたらしい	新しい	Adj	news	4	1
+	あたりまえ	当たり前	N	common, obvious	23	3
	あたる	当たる (-U; 当たった)	V	hit on target; 当たり！ right (on target)!; you got it!	8	1
+	あちら	あちら	N	there (away from both of us), that thing (away from both of us), in that direction (away from both of us), that alternative (of two away from both of us), that place (that we both know about), that person over there (polite)	2	4
+	あつい	暑い・熱い	Adj	hot (weather, climate) / hot (non-weather, non-climate); Scene 14-4 熱い・暑いうち(に) while it's hot	7	1
+	あっち	あっち	N	there (away from both of us), in that direction (away from both of us), that alternative (of two away from both of us), that place (that we both know about)	2	7
	あつまる	集まる (-U; 集まった)	V	get together, assemble	7	5
+	あつめる	集める (-RU; 集めた)	V	gather together, collect X	14	1
	あてはまる	当てはまる (-U; 当てはまった)	V	apply (a rule); Scene 21-3 Xに当てはまる apply to X	21	3
+	あてる	当てる (-RU; 当てた)	V	hit	23	2
	あと	あと	Sp. Exp.	lastly, remaining, and then	4	2
	あと	あと・後	N	time after; Scene 2-2 あとで later; Scene 5-6 Nのあとで after N; Scene 14-4 食べた後で after eating	5	6
+	アドバイス	アドバイス	N	advice	5	6

+	アドレス	アドレス	N	(email) address	6	4
+	あなた	あなた	N	you	1	7
+	あに	兄↓	N	older brother (humble)	7	2
+	あね	姉↓	N	older sister (humble)	7	2
+	あの	あの+N	Sp. Exp.	that N over there	3	5
	あのう	あのう	Sp. Exp.	umm (hesitation noise)	2	2
+	アパート	アパート	N	apartment	2	5
+	あびる	浴びる (-RU; 浴びた)	V	take (a shower) (lit. 'bathe in' or 'be covered in')	9	5
+	あぶない	危ない	Adj	dangerous	7	6
	あぶら	油;	N	oil; 油を引く coat the surface with oil	14	3
+	アプリ	アプリ	N	app, application	3	3
+	アフリカ	アフリカ	N	Africa	8	4
+	アポ	アポ	N	appointment	6	5
	あまい	甘い	Adj	sweet	10	3
+	あまやかす	甘やかす (-U; 甘やかした)	V	pamper, spoil	18	2
+	あまり	あまり・あんまり	Sp. Exp.	+ NEGATIVE not very much; Scene 11-5 + AFFIRMATIVE so, to such an extent	4	2
	あめ	雨	N	rain	3	6
	あめふってじかたまる	雨降って地固まる	Kotowaza	April showers bring May flowers. (lit. 'The ground firms up after rain.')	22	0
	アメリカ	アメリカ	N	America; Scene 3-1 アメリカ人 American (person)	6	1
+	あやしい	怪しい	Adj	painful, stressful	21	5
+	あやまり	誤り	N	mistake, error	21	4
	あやまる	謝る (-U; 謝った)	V	apologize	9	1
+	あらう	洗う (-U; 洗った)	V	wash	9	1
	あらた	新た(な)	N	new, fresh	24	3
+	あらたまる	改まる (-U; 改まった)	V	something changes; act formally	24	3

	あらためる	改める (-RU; 改めた)	V	change X, do something anew; 改めて again	24	3
+	ありがたい	ありがたい	Adj	grateful, thankful	7	1
+	ありがとう。	ありがとう。	Sp. Exp.	Thank you. (non-past or past, informal); Scene 0-0 ありがとうございました。 Thank you. (past, formal); Scene 1-2 ありがとうございます。 (non-past formal)	1	2
	ありゃ	ありゃ	Sp. Exp.	oh dear, oh my	22	6
	ある	ある (-U; あった; ない)	V	exist (inanimate); Scene 10-4 あるかもしれません。 There may be.; Scene 15-5 あり得る・ありえる (-RU; あり得た) is in the realm of possibility; ありえない impossible, that can't be; Scene 21-1 あり there is/are	2	8
	あるく	歩く (-U; 歩いた)	V	walk; 歩いて on foot; Scene 7-5 歩き walk; 歩く人 people who (will) walk; Scene 17-1 歩きながら while eating	5	4
	アルコール	アルコール	N	alcohol, alcoholic beverage	10	3
+	アルバイト	アルバイト(する)	N	part-time work, part-timer	9	3
+	あれ	あれ	N	that (thing over there)	2	1
	あれ？	あれ？	Sp. Exp.	What? Huh?	7	6
	アレルギー	(X)アレルギー(＋ある)	N	(have an) allergy (to X)	13	4
+	あわせる	合わせる (-RU; 合わせた)	V	match, face, connect with (someone)	16	5
+	あん	案	N	design, plan, idea	16	8R
+	あんしん	(ご)安心(する)	N	relief, peace of mind	20	6
+	あんぜん	安全(な)	N	safety	23	5
	あんない	(ご)案内(する)	N	show around; 案内してあげる I'll do you the favor of showing you around	12	6
+	い	胃	N	stomach	20	4
+	いい	いい	Adj	good; Scene 2-3 よかったら if it's all right; Scene 3-6 よくわかりませんけど…… I'm not sure, but . . .	2	1
+	いいえ	いいえ	Sp. Exp.	no	2	1

+	いいん	委員	N	committee member; 委員会 committee meeting; 委員長 committee chair	22	4
	いう	いう・言う (-U; いった・言った)	V	is called, say; 0-0 (Inst. Exp.) 言ってください。 Please say it.; Scene 2-0 PERSON に言ってください。 Please say it to PERSON.; Scene 10-4 言った時 when I have said; Scene 13-2 言う・おっしゃる 通り just as you say; Scene 13-3 言った通りに as you said; Scene 16-1 言っておくべき should have said something; Scene 16-5 言い合う say to one another; Scene 18-6 言っていいことと悪いことがある there are things that are okay to say and things that are not okay to say; Scene 21-6 言ってやった said back to, (did the favor of) telling; Scene 23-3 言い聞かせる tell (someone) to do X	3	1
+	いえ; ～さがし	いえ・家	N	house, home; Scene 23-6 家探し house-hunting, looking for housing	2	5
+	いえ	いえ	Sp. Exp.	no; いえいえ no, no	2	1
	いか	X 以下	N	below X	10	6
	いがい	X 以外	N	outside of X; besides X	12	5
	いがい	意外(な)	N	unexpected; 意外と unexpectedly	15	4
	いかが	いかが	Sp. Exp.	how (polite)	6	5
+	いかす	活かす・生かす (-U; 活かした・生かした)	V	make use of X; also in Scene 24-3	22	9R
+	イギリス	イギリス	N	England, U.K.	6	1
+	いきる	生きる (-RU; 生きた)	V	live, exist, come to life	14	5
+	いく	行く (-U; 行った)	V	go; Scene 9-2 cover (as in a task); Scene 1-8 行ってきます。 See you later. (lit. 'I'll go and come back.'); 行って(い)らっしゃい。 See you later. (lit. 'Go and come back.'); Scene 6-3 行きますよ。 Here we go!; Scene 7-2 行くんだ。 The fact is, I'm going; Scene 10-1 行こう let's go (informal); Scene 12-6 行くことになりました。 It has been decided I will go.; Scene 15-1 行ける (-RU; 行けた) can go; Scene 15-2 PLACE 行き bound for PLACE	2	2

	いくつ	(お)いくつ	Classifier	how many things/items	5	3
	いくら	いくら	N	how much	3	5
+	いけ	池	N	earth, soil	23	1
	いけない	いけない	Adj	won't do	13	2
	いけん	意見	N	opinion	17	5
+	いご	以後	N	hereafter	17	7R
	いこう	以降	N	hereafter; X 以降 after X	23	6
+	いごこち	居心地	N	comfort	23	1
+	いじめる	いじめる (-RU; いじめた)	V	bully, tease; いじめ bullying, teasing	18	6
+	いしゃ	医者	N	(medical) doctor	6	2
+	いじょう	以上	N	above; X 以上 above X	10	6
	いじょう	異常	N	abnormal	18	1
	いしんでんしん	以心伝心	Kotowaza	Meeting of the minds.	18	0
+	いす	椅子	N	chair	12	1
	いずれ	いずれ	N	another time, at some future date	18	4
+	いぜん	以前	N	before; X 以前 before X; also in Scene 23-6	17	7R
	いそがしい	(お)忙しい	Adj	busy; Scene 10-7R お忙しい中 when you are busy	2	4
	いそがばまわれ	急がば回れ	Kotowaza	More haste, less speed. (lit. 'If you are in a hurry, go the long way.'); also in Scene 20-2	3	0
+	いそぐ	急ぐ (-U; 急いだ)	V	hurry	5	1
	いたい	痛い	Adj	painful	11	5
+	いたす	いたす (-U; いたした)	V	do (humble)	6	5
	いただく	いただく↓ (-U; いただいた)	V	eat; receive (humble); Scene 1-6 いただきます。 I humbly receive. (eating ritual); Scene 5-3 いただける (-RU; いただけた) can/may have someone do X; Scene 5-6 そうしていただけますか? Can I have you do that?; Scene 17-4 X させていただく・もらう・ください let me X	2	3

+	いたむ	痛む (-U; 痛んだ)	V	become painful	11	5
	いたらない	至らない	Sp. Exp.	imperfect, inadequate	24	3
	いち	一・1	Numbers	one; Scene 6-3 いち、に、さん！ One, two, three!	3	2
	いちおう	一応	N	for the time being, tentatively, more or less	5	3
	いちごいちえ	一期一会	Kotowaza	Once in a lifetime or 'carpe diem' (seize the day).	1	0
+	いちばん	一番	Sp. Exp.	most, best; Scene 9-4 CATEGORY の中で一番行ってみたいの within/ among CATEGORY the one I want to go to most	4	5
	いちろう	一郎	N	[given name]; 一郎君 Ichiro (addressing or referring to)	1	7
	いつ	いつ	N	when?; Scene 6-5 いつか sometime	4	3
	いっしょ	一緒	N	together	3	4
	いっしょう;〜けんめい	一生	N	life; Scene 10-6 一生懸命 all out, for all one is worth	24	3
+	いっせい	一世	N	first generation	17	1
	いっせきにちょう	一石二鳥	Kotowaza	Two birds with one stone.	17	0
	いったい	一体	Sp. Exp.	what in the world, what the heck	22	4
+	いっぱい	いっぱい	N	a lot, much, full	12	1
+	いっぱん	一般	N	general, average; 一般的(な) generally	21	3
+	いっぽう	一方	N	on the other hand	13	7R
	いつも	いつも	N	always, usual(ly); いつものN the usual N (e.g., 場所 place, 時間 time, ところ place; Scene 6-4 いつもお世話になっております↓. we are always in your debt.	4	4
	いとう	伊藤	N	[family name]	3	9R
+	いとこ	いとこ	N	cousin (in-group); おいとこさん cousin (polite)	11	4
+	いない	X以内	N	within X	17	7R

+	いなか	田舎	N	rural area	23	4
+	いぬ	犬	N	dog	12	3
+	いのうえ	井上	N	[family name]; also in 39R BTL	13	8R
+	いのる	祈る (-U; 祈った)	V	pray, wish	18	5
+	イベント	イベント	N	event	4	4
	いま	今	N	now	2	2
+	イマイチ	イマイチ(な)	N	not quite, lacking	16	6
	いみ	意味	N	meaning; Scene 11-4 どういう意味 what do you mean? what does that mean?	11	4
	イメージ	イメージ	N	image	11	4
+	いもうと	妹↓	N	younger sister (humble); 妹さん younger sister	7	2
	いや	いや	Sp. Exp.	no (informal); uhh (hesitation noise)	2	4
	いや	嫌(な)	N	disagreeable, unpleasant; Scene 18-6 嫌がらせ harassment	8	2
+	イヤリング	イヤリング	N	earring	11	2
+	いらい; 〜しょ	依頼(する)	N	request; Scene 20-1 依頼書 application, written request	16	4
	いらっしゃる	いらっしゃる↑, いらっしゃって↑・いらして↑(-ARU; いらっしゃった・いらした)	V	go, come (honorific); Scene 6-4 be; Scene 8-4 いらしたこと have gone; the experience of having gone; Scene 10-3 いらっしゃいませ。 Welcome.	5	5
+	いりぐち	入り口・入口	N	entrance	6	3
+	いる	いる (-RU; いた)	V	be, exist (animate)	2	2
+	いる	いる (-U; いった)	V	need	4	6
	いれる	入れる・いれる (-RU; 入れた・いれた)	V	put X in; brew or infuse (tea)	8	4
	いれる	淹れる・いれる (-RU; 淹れた・いれた)	V	brew or infuse (tea)	8	4

+	いろ	色	N	color	6	3
	いろいろ	いろいろ(な)	Sp. Exp.	various	8	1
	いわう	祝う (-U; 祝った)	V	celebrate X, congratulate X; Scene 8-4 (お)祝い congratulations, celebration; Scene 17-2 X を祝う会 congratulatory celebration for X	24	2
	いわゆる	いわゆる	Sp. Exp.	so-called	17	1
+	いん	院	N	(medical) institution, clinic	17	9R
+	いんしゅ; 〜うんてん	飲酒(する)	N	drinking; Scene 20-7R 飲酒運転 driving while intoxicated	14	9R
+	インスタント	インスタント	N	instant	22	2
+	インターン	インターン	N	intern	10	4
+	インタビュー	インタビュー(する)	N	interview (television, media, also job)	11	2
+	インドネシアご	インドネシア語	N	Indonesian (language)	8	8R
+	インフルエンザ	インフルエンザ	N	influenza	13	4
	う〜ん	う〜ん	Sp. Exp.	well (hesitation)	2	7
+	ウーロンちゃ	ウーロン茶	N	oolong tea	2	3
	ううん	ううん	Sp. Exp.	no (informal)	7	1
+	うえ	上	N	top, over Scene 23-4 上を見れば if one were to look up; 上を目指せば provided one aims high	6	2
+	うえき	植木	N	garden	23	1
+	うえだ	上田	N	[family name]	10	8R
+	うえやま	上山	N	[family name]	9	9R
+	うえる	植える (-RU; 植えた)	V	plant, grow	20	5
	うかがう	伺う↓ (-U; 伺った)	V	visit (humble); Scene 10-3 inquire, hear; 伺って↓おります↓. We've heard. We've received.	5	5
+	うかる	受かる (U; 受かった)	V	X に受かる pass X	21	7R
+	うきょう	右京	N	[family name]	11	9R

+	うけつけ	受付	N	reception, receptionist	21	7R
+	うけとる	受け取る (-U; 受け取った)	V	take, accept	12	2
+	うける	受ける (-RU; 受けた)	V	receive; catch; be given; Scene 21-1 can work as a joke (slang)	10	6
+	うごかす	動かす (-U; 動かした)	V	move X	23	2
+	うごく	動く (-U; 動いた)	V	move (one's position)	19	6
	うしろ	後ろ	N	back, behind	6	3
+	うすい	薄い	Adj	light colored, thin, dilute, weak (taste, probability)	11	2
	うそ	嘘	N	lie	8	2
	うたう	歌う (-U; 歌った)	V	sing; 歌 song	9	5
+	うち; 〜のもの	うち	N	house, home; Scene 5-3 うちの X our company's X; Scene 5-5 our company/organization; Scene 9-4 inside; X, Y, Z のうちで; 3つのうちで among X, Y, and Z; among three; Scene 17-3 うちの者 someone in our company, someone on our side (of the transaction)	2	5
+	うちあげ	打ち上げ	N	launch, closing reception/party	17	2
+	うちあわせる	打ち合わせる (-RU; 打ち合わせた)	V	arrange, discuss in advance; 打ち合わせ(する) advance meeting	16	3
+	うちだ	内田	N	[family name]	16	8R
+	うつ	打つ (-U; 打った)	V	hit, insert	11	6
+	うっかり	うっかり(する)	N	inadvertently, carelessly	20	6
	うつす	移す (-U; 移した)	V	transmit, move on, infect, transfer	13	5
+	うつす	写す (-U; 写した)	V	copy, duplicate	17	3
+	うつる	写る (-U; 写った)	V	is photographed or copied	17	8R

	うつる	移る (-U; 移った)	V	move (house), transfer (department)	23	4
+	うで	腕	N	arm	11	5
+	うどん	うどん	N	udon (wheat noodles)	2	3
	うまい	上手い・美味い・旨い・うまい	Adj	delicious, skillful	9	6
+	うまれる	生まれる (-RU; 生まれた)	V	be born	20	6
+	うみ	海	N	sea, ocean; Scene 4-4 海の日 Marine Day (BTS 18)	23	1
+	うむ	産む (-U; 産んだ)	V	give birth to	20	6
+	うら	裏	N	back side, undersurface; Scene 24-5 裏日本 the Japan Sea side of Japan	14	3
+	うらがえす	裏返す (-U; 裏返した)	V	turn X over, turn inside out; Scene 14-3 裏返し inside out	14	4
	うらやましい	羨ましい	Adj	enviable	17	6
+	うる	売る (-U; 売った)	V	sell X; Scene 16-9R 売り切れ sold out; Scene 17-4 売り上げ sales	16	6
	うるさい	うるさい	Adj	annoying, loud, noisy, tiresome	8	5
+	うれしい	うれしい / 嬉しい	Adj	happy, glad	7	1
+	うれる	売れる (-RU; 売れた)	V	X sells	16	6
+	うわがき	上書き(する)	N	overwrite (a file)	15	4
	うん	うん	Sp. Exp.	yes (informal)	7	1
	うんざり	うんざり(する)	N	fed up, tedious	23	3
+	うんそう	運送	N	shipping; transportation	15	8R
+	うんちん	運賃	N	(transportation) fare	23	9R
+	うんてん	運転(する)	N	driving (a car)	10	2
+	うんどう	運動(する)	N	exercise; also in Scene 20-5	19	7R
	え	絵	N	drawing, picture	9	5
	え？	え？	Sp. Exp.	What?; Scene 2-3 What (was that)?	2	3

	エアコン	エアコン	N	air conditioner	18	2
+	えいいち	英一	N	[male given name]	10	7R
+	えいが	映画	N	movies; Scene 7-6 映画館 movie theater; Scene 21-9R 映画化 cinematize	10	1
+	えいきょう	影響	N	influence	18	1
	えいぎょうぶ	営業部	N	operations division	11	1
+	えいご	英語	N	English (language)	3	1
+	えいこ・ひでこ	英子	N	[female given name]	10	7R
+	えいこく	英国	N	England	10	7R
+	エイティーエム	ATM	N	ATM	7	1
	えいよう	栄養	N	nutrition; 栄養ドリンク nutritional drink	20	3
+	ええ	ええ	Sp. Exp.	yes (suggesting agreement or indicating understanding; less formal than はい); Scene 2-1 yes (casual)	1	1
	ええと	ええと	Sp. Exp.	uhh (hesitation noise)	2	2
+	えがお	笑顔	N	smiling face	24	7R
+	えき	駅	N	train station; Scene 11-8R 駅前 in front of the station	2	5
+	えて	得手(な)	N	strong point, strength	21	5
+	えらい	偉い	Adj	excellent, distinguished, admirable	9	6
	えらぶ	選ぶ (-U; 選んだ)	V	choose, select	15	4
	えり	恵理	N	[female given name] (Eri is Sasha's housemate)	1	13
	エルディーケー	LDK	N	living room, dining room, kitchen; 2LDK two rooms plus living room, dining room, kitchen	23	4
	えん	〜円	Classifier	yen (Japanese currency)	3	5
+	えんか	演歌	N	*enka* (a popular ballad style of singing)	9	5
	えんき	延期(する)	N	postpone	15	1

+	エンジニア	エンジニア	N	engineer	9	3
+	えんしゅつ	演出	N	(theater, film) direction	19	2
	エンジョイ	エンジョイ(する)	N	enjoy	24	4
+	えんぴつ	鉛筆	N	pencil	3	3
	えんりょ	(ご)遠慮(する)	N	restraint; ご遠慮なく (go ahead) without reservation; Scene 13-1 遠慮しときます。 I'll pass. (lit. 'hold back')	8	3
	お	お	Sp. Exp.	Oh (expression of slight surprise)	20	2
+	オーケー	オーケー(する)	N	okay	22	4
+	オーストラリア	オーストラリア	N	Australia	8	4
	オーバー	オーバー	N	coat	11	3
	おいしい	おいしい	Adj	delicious; おいしそう look(s) delicious	2	3
+	おいつく	Xに追いつく(-U; 追いついた)	V	catch up with X	15	1
+	おいでになる	おいでになる↑(-U; おいでになった)	V	go (honorific)	20	1
	おいわい	お祝い	N	congratulations, celebration, gift	11	4
	おうえん	応援(する)	N	support, cheer on, assistance	23	2
+	おえる	終える (-RU; 終えた)	V	finish X	14	5
+	おおあめ	大雨	N	heavy rain, downpour; Also in 18-1	12	8R
	おおい	多い	Adj	a lot, many, numerous	10	5
+	おおがきしょうかい	大垣商会	N	Ogaki Trading Company, Ltd.	3	1
+	おおがたかでん	大型家電	N	large appliance	21	8R
+	おおきい	大きい	Adj	big; Scene 12-5 大きな large, big	2	7
+	おおさか	大阪	N	Osaka	9	4
+	おおもり	大盛り	N	large serving	17	6
+	おおゆき	大雪	N	heavy snow, snow storm; Also in 18-1	12	8R

	おかえりなさい。	おかえりなさい。	Sp. Exp.	Welcome back.	1	13
	おかげさまで	おかげさまで・お陰様で	Sp. Exp.	thanks to you	7	4
	おかしい	おかしい	Adj	funny, weird, odd, strange	7	6
+	おかね	お金	N	money	9	7R
	おかまいなく	お構いなく	Sp. Exp.	don't go to any bother	8	4
+	おがわ	小川	N	[family name]	12	7R
	おき	INTERVAL おき	Sp. Exp.	after every other INTERVAL	20	5
+	おきなわ	沖縄	N	Okinawa	9	4
	おきる	起きる (-RU; 起きた)	V	wake up, rise	8	1
+	おく	億	Numbers	hundred millions (BTS 4)	4	1
	おく	置く (-U; 置いた)	V	put, place, position	9	1
	おくさま	奥様	N	wife (polite)	11	4
+	おくさん	奥さん	N	wife	7	2
	おくる	送る (-U; 送った)	V	send	12	2
	おくれる	遅れる (-RU; 遅れた)	V	become late, run late; Scene 15-3 遅れるそうです。 They say he will be late.	7	3
+	おこす	起こす (-U; 起こした)	V	wake (someone) up	19	1
+	おこなう	行う (-U; 行った)	V	do, perform, carry out	17	3
	おこのみやき	お好み焼き	N	okonomiyaki (savory pancake containing a variety of ingredients, usually including a choice of meat)	14	2
	おこる	怒る (-U; 怒った)	V	get angry	18	2
+	おこる・おきる	起こる (-U; 起こった)・起きる (-RU; 起きた)	V	occur	20	7R

	おさえる	抑える (-RU; 抑えた)	V	curb, restrain	20	3
+	おさきに	お先に	Sp. Exp.	I'll be X-ing (ahead of you); お先に失礼します。 I'll be leaving (ahead of you).	1	12
+	おじ	伯父/叔父	N	uncle (in-group)	11	4
+	おじいさん・おじいさま	おじいさん/お祖父様	N	uncle (polite)	11	4
+	おしえる	教える (-RU; 教えた)	V	tell, teach	5	5
+	おしゃれ	おしゃれな(な)	N	stylish	11	4
	おす	押す (-U; 押した)	V	push X	14	6
+	おそい	遅い	Adj	late; Scene 12-4 遅く late	3	4
	おそれいります。	恐れ入ります。	Special Ex.	Sorry to impose, excuse me.	17	3
+	おだ	小田	N	[family name]	12	7R
	おだいじに	お大事に	Sp. Exp.	take care	7	4
	おたがいさま	お互い様	Sp. Exp.	we're in this together; we're in the same boat	13	4
+	おたく	お宅	N	home (polite)	2	5
+	おちゃ	お茶	N	tea; Scene 8-4 お茶を淹れる brew or infuse tea	2	3
+	おちる	落ちる (-RU; 落ちた)	V	drop, fall; Scene 23-7R 落ち葉 fallen leaves	14	4
	おつかれさま。	お疲れ様。	Sp. Exp.	Good work, hello. (informal); お疲れ様です。 Good work, hello.; Scene 1-12 お疲れ様でした。 Good work. (formal)	1	11
	オッケー	オッケー	Sp. Exp.	okay	3	4
+	おっしゃる	おっしゃる↑ (-ARU; おっしゃった)	V	say (honorific)	6	2
+	おっと	夫↓	N	husband (humble)	7	2
+	おと	音	N	sound	8	1

+	おとうと	弟↓	N	younger brother (humble); 弟さん younger brother	7	2
+	おとこのひと	男の人	N	man; Scene 7-2 男の子 boy	6	3
	おとす	落とす (-U; 落とした)	V	drop X; Scene 14-4 落とさないように do such that you don't drop it	14	4
+	おととい	おととい	N	the day before yesterday	4	3
+	おとな	おとな・大人	N	adult	7	2
	おとなしい	おとなしい	Adj	laidback, quiet, docile	12	3
	おとめ	乙女	N	little girl, young lady; 乙女チック girlish	21	1
+	おどる	踊る (-U; 踊った)	V	dance	20	5
+	おどろく	驚く (-U; 驚いた)	V	be surprised	20	6
+	おなか	お腹	N	abdomen, stomach; お腹が空く get hungry	8	4
+	おなじ	同じ	N	same; Xと同じ・違う same as/different from X; Scene 7-5 同じ X the same X; Scene 23-3 おんなじ an emphatic form of 同じ	3	6
	おにぎり	おにぎり	N	onigiri (rice formed into a triangular or round shape and often wrapped in nori (seaweed))	21	2
	おねがいします。	お願いします。	Sp. Exp.	please help me with this; よろしくお願いします。よろしくお願いします。 (formal) どうぞよろしくお願いします。 Nice to meet you. (formal)	1	3
	おねがいできる	お願いできる	V	can request; お願いできますか? Can I ask a favor of you?	5	3
+	おば	伯母/叔母	N	aunt (in-group)	11	4
+	おばあさん/おばあさま	おばあさん/お祖母様	N	aunt (polite)	11	4
	おはようございます。	おはようございます。	Day 1 Phrase	Good morning. (formal); Scene 1-6 おはよう。 Good morning. (informal)	0	0
+	おひきだし	お引き出し	N	withdrawal	20	7R
	オフィス	オフィス	N	office	4	5

+	おぼえる	覚える (-RU; 覚えた)	V	remember, memorize	8	2
	みやげ	お土産	N	souvenir, gift	8	4
+	おもい	重い	Adj	heavy, serious	13	6
+	おもいだす	思い出す (-U; 思い出した)	V	remember	9	5
	おもいちがい	思い違い(する)	N	misunderstanding, false impression	20	6
	おもいで	思い出	N	memories, reminiscence	24	1
+	おもいやり	思いやり	N	consideration, thoughtfulness; also in Scene 3-4 BTS 16	18	3
	おもう	思う (-U; 思った)	V	think; Scene 11-4 PERSON 思い thoughtful about PERSON	7	4
	おもしろい	おもしろい	Adj	interesting; おもしろそう look(s) interesting	2	3
+	おもちゃ	おもちゃ	N	toy	14	1
+	おもて	表	N	front side, appearance; Scene 24-5 表日本 the Pacific Ocean side of Japan	14	3
	おや	親	N	parent; Scene 8-6 親孝行 filial piety (a Confucian virtue); dedication to parents; 親不孝 lack of filial piety	8	5
	おやすみなさい。	おやすみなさい。	Sp. Exp.	Good night.	1	14
+	おやま	小山	N	[family name]	12	7R
	およぐ	泳ぐ (-U; 泳いだ)	V	swim	7	2
+	おりる	降・下りる (-RU; 降・下りた)	V	disembark	19	1
	おる	おる↓ (-U; おった)	V	be (humble form of います 'be') The ～て form is rarely used today.	6	4
+	おる	折る (-U; 折った)	V	break X, fold X	20	4
+	おれ	俺	N	I (masculine, informal) (BTS 15)	1	7
	オレゴンしゅう	オレゴン州	N	Oregon	6	1

+	おれる	折れる (-RU; 折れた)	V	get broken, fold	20	4
	オレンジジュース	オレンジジュース	N	orange juice	10	3
+	おろす	下ろす・降ろす (-U; 下ろした・降ろした)	V	take down, drop off (a passenger)	23	2
+	おわび	お詫び(する)	N	apology	16	1
+	おわらせる	終わらせる (-RU; 終わらせた)	V	finish X, close X	10	2
+	おわる	終わる (-U; 終わった)	V	end; 0-0 (Inst. Exp.) 終わります。That's all for today. (used at the end of a class); Scene 9-2 終わり the end (also in Scene 19-7R); Verb Stem + おわる (-U; おわった) finish X-ing	2	2
+	おん	恩	N	benevolence, favor (BTS 1); Scene 24-6R 恩返し repaying kindness; Scene 24-7R 恩師 former/beloved teacher	12	BTS 1
	おんがく	音楽	N	music	9	5
	おんせん	温泉	N	hot spring	9	4
+	おんだんか	温暖化	N	(global) warming	18	1
+	おんど	温度	N	temperature	18	8R
	おんど	音頭	N	leading a group; 音頭を取る take the lead	24	2
	おんなじ	おんなじ	N	same (an emphatic form of 同じ)	23	3
+	おんなのひと	女の人	N	woman; Scene 7-2 女の子 girl	6	3
	おんよみ	音読み	N	Chinese-based readings of kanji	1	BTL 2
	おんれい	御礼	N	gratitude, thanks	24	2
	か	〜か?	S. Particle	[question particle]; Scene 6-6 カレーか今日のランチか curry or today's lunch special; Scene 12-2 食べてるかどうか whether you're eating or not; Scene 12-3 誰か知らない don't know who that is	2	1
+	か	可	N	passable, acceptable (condition)	23	8R
+	が	〜が	Particle	but, and	2	4

	が	〜が	Particle	[phrase particle]	4	3
+	ガーデニング	ガーデニング	N	gardening	20	5
+	かあさん	(お)母さん	N	mother	7	2
+	かい	〜会	N	organization, club, association, group; Scene 11-2 学会 academic conference; Scene 14-9R (お)茶会 tea party; Scene 17-2 食事会 dinner party, dinner/breakfast meeting; 歓迎会 welcome party; 親睦会 informal gathering, meet-and-greet; 送別会 farewell party; X を祝う会 congratulatory celebration for X; Scene 18-4 講演会 lecture (event); Scene 22-4 委員会 committee meeting; 役員会 officers' meeting; 理事会 governing board meeting	3	1
	かい	〜階	Classifier	classifier for naming and counting floors	4	5
	かい	〜回	Classifier	times, instances; 年に２、３回 two or three times a year; １回も not a single time [number + も + neg]; 0-0 (Inst. Exp.) もう１回言ってください。 Please say it again.; Scene 8-1 毎回 every time; Scene 10-5 今回 this time; 次回 next time; 前回 last time	8	6
	かいえん	開演(する)	N	curtain (of a performance)	19	6
+	かいぎ	会議(する)	N	meeting; Scene 4-4 会議室 meeting room	3	2
+	かいけつ	解決(する)	N	resolution, solution, settlement	23	3
+	がいこくじん	外国人	N	foreigner; Scene 10-6 外国語 foreign language	3	1
+	かいさつぐち	改札口	N	ticket gate, wicket	19	1
+	かいし	開始(する)	N	start	19	7R
	かいしゃ	会社	N	office, company; Scene 9-3 会社員 company employee	2	5
+	かいじょう	会場	N	site, the place (for an event); also Scene 19-6 assembly hall, theater	15	7R
	がいしょく	外食	N	dine out	14	2

+	がいじん	外人	N	foreigner (can be derogatory)	3	1
	がいす	害す (-U; 害した)	V	injure, damage	18	5
+	かいぜん	改善(する)	N	improvement	20	3
+	かいそく	快速	N	rapid train	15	2
	かいちょう	会長	N	president of an organization	13	5
+	かいはつ	開発(する)	N	development; Scene 11-1 開発部 development division	6	2
	かいひ	会費	N	participation fee, membership fee	17	2
+	かいふく	回復(する)	N	recovery, improvement	20	4
	がいらいご	外来語	N	borrowed vocabulary, loan words; also in Scene 3-3 BTS 14	21	5
	かいわ	会話	N	conversation	5	6
+	かう	買う (-U; 買った)	V	buy; Scene 5-4 買い物 shopping; Scene 10-1 買っておきますので because/as I'll buy X ahead of time	4	1
+	かう	飼う (-U; 飼った)	V	keep (a pet or other animal)	12	3
	かえす	返す (-U; 返した)	V	flip, return X; 返しながら while turning	14	4
	かえって	かえって	Sp. Exp.	on the contrary, rather	20	2
	かえってくる	返ってくる	V	come back (inanimate)	10	6
+	かえる	帰る (-U; 帰った)	V	return [home]; Scene 1-13 おかえりなさい。 Welcome back.; Scene 14-4 帰れる (-RU: 帰れた) can return; Scene 15-1 帰れたら帰ります。 If I can return I will.; Scene 20-1 お帰りになる↑(-RU; お帰りになった) go/return home (honorific)	3	2
	かえる	変える (-RU; 変えた)	V	change X	8	2
+	かお	顔	N	face; Scene 18-5 顔を潰す cause someone to lose face	11	5
+	かがく	科学	N	science; 科学的 scientific	21	3
	かかす	欠かす (-U; 欠かした)	V	miss, fail	20	5
+	かかり	係	N	(person) in charge; X 係 person in charge of X; 係長 subsection head, assistant manager	23	8R

	かかる	かかる (-U; かかった)	V	take (time/money)	4	6
+	かかん・にちかん	〜日間	Classifier	classifier for counting days	6	2
+	かぎ	鍵	N	key	18	2
+	かきゅうせい	下級生	N	lower-level student	18	6
	かぎる	限る (-U; 限った)	V	limit, restrict; X とは限らない Is not limited to X	21	3
+	かく	書く (-U; 書いた)	V	write; 0-0 (Inst. Exp.) 書いてください。 Please write it.; Scene 5-6 書き writing; 書き取り dictation; Scene 16-5 書き換える・書き変える write over, rewrite, renew; 書き直す (-U; 書き直した) rewrite, revise; 書き直し rewriting	2	2
+	かく	描く (-U; 描いた)	V	draw, paint, sketch	9	5
+	かく	画	N	classifier for naming and counting strokes of a kanji	19	8R
+	かぐ	家具	N	furniture	13	2
+	かくげん	格言	N	saying, proverb	20	2
+	がくしゃ	学者	N	scholar	17	8R
+	がくしゅう	学習(する)	N	learn, study	14	8R
+	かくす	隠す (-U; 隠した)	V	hide X	23	2
	がくせい	学生	N	student; Scene 13-6 学生センター Student Center	3	1
+	がくちょう	学長	N	school president	6	5
	かくにん	確認(する)	N	confirmation, verification	15	4
+	がくひ	学費	N	school expenses, tuition	17	2
+	がくぶ	学部	N	academic division, college	6	1
+	がくれき	学歴	N	educational background	21	9R
+	かくれる	隠れる (-RU; 隠れた)	V	hide, disappear	23	2
	かけ	Verb Stem + かけ	N	catching (a disease), on the verge of X-ing	20	1

	かげつ	〜ヶ月・〜カ月	Classifier	classifier for counting months	4	6
	かける	かける (-RU; かけた)	V	cause (lit. 'hang X'); Scene 11-4 suspend, wear (glasses, buttons); Scene 14-4 put on top (sauce); Scene 18-2 lock; Scene 21-4 multiply	7	4
+	かける	Verb Stem + かける (-RU; 〜かけた)	V	begin (but not finish)	20	1
	かげん	(お)加減	N	personal condition	7	4
	かさ	傘	N	umbrella	3	6
+	カサカサ	カサカサ (する・になる)	N	dry	11	5
	かさなる	重なる (-U; 重なった)	V	pile up, overlap	15	1
	かさねる	重ねる (-RU; 重ねた)	V	put on top; 重ねることにして(い)る usually layer (habit)	11	3
+	かざる	飾る (-U; 飾った)	V	decorate	17	3
	かし	(お)菓子	N	sweets, candy	8	4
+	かしこい	賢い	Adj	clever, smart	12	3
	かしこまりました↓。	かしこまりました↓。	Sp. Exp.	Understood.	10	3
+	カジュアル	カジュアル(な)	N	casual	11	2
	かしら	かしら	Particle	I wonder	22	2
+	かす	貸す (-U; 貸した)	V	lend, rent (to someone)	12	1
+	かずお	和男	N	[male given name]	14	9R
+	かずこ	和子	N	[female given name]	14	9R
+	かぜ	風邪	N	common cold; 風邪気味 feels like a cold; Scene 20-1 風邪っぽい feel like a cold (is coming on); 風邪を引く catch a cold	13	4
+	かぜ	風	N	wind	18	1
+	かぞえる	数える (-RU; 数えた)	V	count X	20	8R

+	かぞく	(ご)家族	N	family; Scene 12-5 X人家族 X number in a family (including oneself)	7	2
+	かた	方(かた)	N	person (honorific)	6	3
+	かた	肩	N	shoulder	11	5
+	かたい	硬・固・堅い	Adj	tough, stiff	14	4
+	かだい	課題	N	subject, issue, matter	18	5
+	ガタガタ	ガタガタ	Sp. Exp.	rattle, rickety	16	2
	カタカナ	片仮名・カタカナ	N	katakana syllabary	1	BTL 1
+	かたち	形	N	shape	16	5
	かたづく	片付く (-U; 片付いた)	V	be in order; be finished; be taken care of	9	2
+	かたづける	片付ける (-RU; 片付けた)	V	clean X up, tidy up; Scene 14-4 片付け clean-up	9	1
	がち	Verb stem + がち(な・の)	N	liable to, apt to	20	5
+	かちょう	課長	N	section chief	6	5
+	かつ	勝つ (-U; 勝った)	V	win	14	5
	がつ	〜月(がつ)	Classifier	classifier for naming the months of the year; Scene 4-6 〜ヶ月・〜カ月 classifier for counting months	4	4
+	がっかい	学会	N	academic conference	11	2
	がっかり	がっかり(な)・(する)	N	feel disappointment, lose heart	10	6
+	がっき	学期	N	school/academic term; classifier for counting and naming school/academic term; 今学期 this term	4	6
+	カッコいい	カッコいい	Adj	good-looking, stylish, cool	11	4
+	がっこう	学校	N	school	2	5
	かって	勝手(な)	N	selfishness, convenience; 勝手に unilaterally, arbitrarily, willfully	18	3
+	かつどう	活動	N	activity; also in Scene 24-1	22	9R
+	かつやく	(ご)活躍(する)	N	activity, thrive	24	2

+	かてい	家庭	N	family, household; Scene 22-2 家庭料理 home cooking	17	4
+	かど	角	N	corner	7	6
	かとう	加藤	N	[family name]	3	9R
	かな	かな	N	syllabary	1	BTL 1
	かなあ	〜かなあ	S. Particle	[sentence particle indicating a shared question]; Scene 9-6 どうかなあ I wonder	2	6
+	かなざわ	金沢	N	Kanazawa	9	4
+	かなしい	悲しい	Adj	sad; Scene 22-6 悲しむ (-U; 悲しんだ) be sad	7	1
+	カナダ	カナダ	N	Canada	6	1
	かならず	必ず	Sp. Exp.	without fail, always, without exception; Scene 21-3 [必ずしも + negative] not always, not necessarily	8	6
	かなり	かなり	Sp. Exp.	quite, considerably	7	3
+	かね	(お)金	N	money	14	1
+	かねだ	金田	N	[family name]	10	8R
+	かのう	可能(な)	N	possibility; 不可能(な) impossibility	21	5
+	かのじょ	彼女	N	she, girlfriend	11	4
+	かばん	かばん	N	bag, briefcase	3	6
+	カフェ	カフェ	N	cafe	4	4
+	カフェテリア	カフェテリア	N	cafeteria	7	1
+	かぶき	歌舞伎	N	kabuki (traditional theater)	10	1
+	かぶる	被る (U; 被った)	V	wear, put on (one's head, such as a hat)	11	4
	かふんしょう	花粉症	N	hay fever	13	5
	かまう	構う (-U; 構った)	V	mind, care, be concerned about (most commonly occurs in the negative)	5	1
+	がまん	我慢(する)	N	endurance, patience, tolerance	17	6
+	かみ	紙	N	paper; Scene 23-7R 紙類 paper things	3	6
	かみ	髪	N	hair	12	3

+	かみむら・うえむら	上村	N	[family name]	9	9R
+	かむ	噛む(-U; 噛んだ)	V	bite, chew	17	1
	かもしれない	あるかもしれません。	Sp. Exp.	There may be.; Scene 14-6 ぶつけてたかも maybe I was hitting it	10	4
+	かゆい	痒い	Adj	itchy	11	5
+	かよう	通う (-U; 通った)	V	commute	7	1
+	かよう(び)	火曜(日)	N	Tuesday	4	6
	から	〜から	Particle	from (starting point); Scene 9-6 Verb 〜てから after Verb-ing	4	4
	から	REASON 〜から	Sentence Particle	because of REASON X; Scene 19-5 〜からいいようなものの good thing that . . .	5	5
+	からい	辛い	Adj	spicy	10	3
+	カラオケ	カラオケ	N	karaoke	7	2
+	からから	からから	N	parched, clattering	20	4
+	からだ	体・身体・からだ	N	body	12	3
+	かりる	借りる (-RU; 借りた)	V	borrow	5	3
	がる	〜がる (-U; 〜がった)	V	show signs of, act as if	18	4
+	かるい	軽い	Adj	light	13	6
+	かれ	彼	N	he, boyfriend	11	4
+	カレーライス	カレーライス	N	curry rice	2	3
+	かれる	枯れる (-RU; 枯れた)	V	wither, wilt	23	1
+	かわ	川	N	river	23	1
	かわいい	かわいい	Adj	cute	3	5
	かわいいこにはたびをさせよ	可愛い子には旅をさせよ	Kotowaza	If you love your child, send them out into the world.	12	0
+	かわいそう	かわいそう(な)	N	pitiful, pathetic	19	3

273

+	かわかす	乾かす (-U; 乾かした)	V	dry X	14	4
+	かわかみ	川上	N	[family name]	9	8R
	かわく	渇く/乾く (-U; かわいた)	V	become dry	8	4
+	かわぐち	川口	N	[family name]	11	8R
+	かわた	川田	N	[family name]	10	8R
+	かわなか	川中	N	[family name]	9	9R
	かわる	Xと代わる (-U; 代わった)	V	switch over to X (on the telephone); Scene 13-5 Xに・と代わる take over for X; take the place of X; Xの代わりに in place of X	11	1
	かわる	変わる (-U; 変わった)	V	change, switch	11	3
	かん	間	N	during the time, meanwhile	24	2
	かん	Amount of time 〜間	Sp. Exp.	number of hours, days, weeks, year; 〜日間 classifier for counting days; 〜年間 classifier for counting years	6	2
+	かんがえる	考える (-RU; 考えた)	V	think about, consider; Scene 11-2 考え過ぎ think too much; Scene 16-5 (お)考え thoughts	4	3
+	カンカン	カンカン	N	fury, intense anger	18	1
	ガンガン	ガンガン	Sp. Exp.	pounding, intense (onomatopoeia); Scene 20-4 pounding (headache)	14	6
+	かんきょう	環境	N	usability, ease of use	23	1
	かんけい	関係(する)	N	relationship	9	3
+	かんげいかい	歓迎会	N	welcome party	17	2
	かんけいの	X関係のY	Sp. Exp.	Y related to X; Scene 24-2 X関係者 associates of X	9	3
	がんこ	頑固(な)	N	stubborn	12	3
+	かんこく	韓国	N	Korea; Scene 3-1 韓国語 Korean (language); 韓国人 Korean (person)	6	1
+	かんごし	看護師	N	nurse	20	3
	かんじ	漢字	N	kanji	1	BTL 1
+	かんじ	Xって感じ	Sp. Exp.	like X	21	9R

+	がんじつ	元日	N	New Year's Day (BTS 18)	4	4
	かんしゃ	感謝(する)	N	appreciation, gratitude	24	1
+	かんじょう	感情	N	emotion; 感情的(な) emotional	22	6
+	かんじる	感じる (-RU; 感じた)	V	feel X	21	9R
	かんしん	感心(する)	N	admiration, being impressed	21	2
+	かんじん	肝心(な)	N	essential, vital	18	5
	かんする	(Xに)関する (-U; 関した)	V	regarding X	23	6
	かんせい	完成(する)	N	complete, bring to perfection	14	4
	かんぜん	完全(な)	N	completion	18	6
+	かんそう	感想	N	impressions, thoughts	17	5
+	かんぞう	肝臓	N	liver	20	4
+	かんだ	神田	Name	Mr/s. Kanda; Scene 1-10 神田さんですか？ Are you Mr./Ms. Kanda?	1	1
	かんたん	簡単(な)	N	simple, easy	15	4
	かんちがい	勘違い(する)	N	mistaken idea, wrong guess	20	6
	かんづめ	缶詰	N	stuck in a confined space; 缶詰状態 backed up, clogged (traffic)	19	6
+	かんどう	感動(する)	N	strong emotion; 感動的(な) emotionally moving	19	2
+	かんとんしょう	広東省	N	Guangdong Province	6	1
+	がんねん	元年	N	first year (of a new era) (BTS 18)	4	4
	かんぱい	乾杯(する)	N	toast; 乾杯！ Cheers!	9	3
	がんばる	頑張る (-U; 頑張った)	V	will one's best; 2-0 頑張りましょう。 Do your best.	2	1
	かんびょう	看病(する)	N	nursing (a patient)	24	1
+	かんぺき	完璧(な)	N	perfect	22	4
	かんり	管理(する)	N	manage, control	21	2
+	かんりょう	完了(する)	N	completion	22	7R
+	き	木	N	wood, tree	9	7R

	き	気	N	Scene 13-4 BTS 13 spirit, mood, care, attention, energy flow; Scene 7-1 気持ち feeling, sensation; 気持ちがいい good feeling; Scene 11-5 気持ちが悪い feel unwell; sickening, unpleasant, revolting; Scene 13-4 気を遣う pay attention (to someone's needs); Scene 9-5 X に気がつく (-U; 気がついた) notice X; Scene 10-5 気にする care about, be bothered, worry; Scene 14-4 気をつける (-RU; 気をつけた) take care, be careful; Scene 16-3 乗り気 enthusiasm; 強気 confident; 弱気 timid, faint-hearted; その気 what one has in mind, with that in mind; Scene 18-5 気分を害す offend, hurt someone's feelings; Scene 20-5 気に入る like, be pleased with; Scene 22-6 気が立つ get worked up, get excited; 気を入れる set your mind to; 気を落とす get discouraged, become disheartened; 気を落とさなくたって even if you don't get discouraged; やる気を出す become enthusiastic	13	4
	キー	キー	N	key (on a keyboard)	14	5
	キーボード	キーボード	N	keyboard	14	5
	きいてください。	聞いてください。	Inst. Exp	Please listen.; Scene 2-0 PERSON に聞いてください。 Please ask PERSON.	0	0
+	きいろ	黄色	N	yellow	6	3
+	ぎいん	議員	N	member of the Diet, parliament, or congress	18	6
+	きえる	消える (-RU; 消えた)	V	go off, turn off	14	6
+	きおん	気温	N	(atmospheric) temperature	18	1
	きかい	機会	N	opportunity, chance	18	4
+	きかく	企画(する)	N	plan, project, design; Scene 11-1 企画部 planning division; 企画書 proposal	6	2

	きく	聞く (-U; 聞いた)	V	hear; listen; Scene 5-6 聞き取り listening; Scene 6-6 X に聞く ask X; Scene 9-5 聞くの専門 listening is my specialty; Scene 16-3 聞いたところ just heard; Scene 16-5 聞かせる (-RU; 聞かせた) inform, let know; 聞かせてください。 Let us know.	4	4
+	にきく		Sp. Exp.		6	6
+	きく	(X に)効く (-U; 効いた)	V	be effective for X	20	3
	きくはいっときのはじ、きかぬはいっしょうのはじ	聞くは一時の恥、聞かぬは一生の恥	Kotowaza	To ask may lead to shame for a moment, but not to ask leads to shame for a lifetime.; also in Scene 20-2	5	0
+	きげん	期限	N	term, time frame	23	4
+	きこえる	聞こえる (-RU; 聞こえた)	V	be audible	8	1
	きこく	(ご)帰国(する)	N	return to the home country	24	3
+	きごこち	着心地	N	comfort when wearing something	23	1
	きじ	記事	N	news story, article	17	4
+	きずつける	傷つける (-RU; 傷つけた)	V	injure, hurt someone's feelings	18	5
+	ぎせいご	擬声語	N	onomatopoeia (words that are evocative of sound by convention) (see Act 11)	16	2
	きせつ	季節	N	season; 季節によって depending on the season	11	3
	きそく	規則	N	rules, regulations	23	1
+	きた	北	N	north; Scene 15-9R 北口 north exit/entrance; Scene 18-1 北風 north wind	15	2
+	きたい	(ご)期待(する)	N	expectation	24	2
+	ぎたいご	擬態語	N	onomatopoeia (words that sound like what they are)	16	2
+	きたない	汚い	Adj	dirty	23	1
+	きたの	北野	N	[family name]	15	9R

	きちんと	きちんと	Sp. Exp.	precisely, neatly, accurately, as it should be	10	5
	きつい	きつい	Adj	severe, intense	7	1
	キッチン	キッチン	N	kitchen	14	2
	きっと	きっと	Sp. Exp.	surely, undoubtedly	12	2
	きっぷ	切符	N	ticket(s); Scene 19-1 切符売り場 ticket window	8	2
+	きのう	きのう	N	yesterday	4	3
+	きのした	木下	N	[family name]	9	8R
	きびしい	厳しい	Adj	strict, severe, intense	7	3
	きぶんをがいす	気分を害す	Sp. Exp.	offend, hurt someone's feelings; 気分を害さないかが問題 the problem is not to hurt her feelings	18	5
	きほん	基本	N	foundation, basis	16	5
+	きまる	決まる (-U; 決まった)	V	get decided; Scene 10-3 お決まりでしょうか。 Have you decided?; Scene 14-9R 決まり rule	14	1
+	きむら	木村	N	[family name]	9	9R
	きめる	決める (-RU; 決めた)	V	decide X	5	1
+	きもち	気持ち	N	feeling, sensation; 気持ちがいい good feeling; Scene 11-5 気持ちが悪い feel unwell; sickening, unpleasant, revolting	7	1
+	きもの	着物	N	kimono	15	7R
	きゃく	(お)客(様)	N	guest, customer, client	8	5
	キャベツ	キャベツ	N	cabbage	14	2
+	キャラ(クター)	キャラ(クター)	N	(fictional) character	12	1
+	キャンセル	キャンセル(する)	N	cancel	15	1
	キャンパス	キャンパス	N	campus	7	1
	きゅう	急(な)	N	sudden; 急に suddenly	11	5
	きゅう、く	九・9	Numbers	nine	3	2
+	きゅうか	休暇	N	break, holiday	8	6

	きゅうけい	(ご)休憩(する)	N	break, rest, intermission; 休憩時間 rest time, intermission	13	1
+	きゅうこう	急行	N	express	15	1
+	きゅうしゅう	九州	N	Kyushu	9	4
+	きゅうりょう	給料	N	salary	23	3
+	きょう	きょう・今日	N	today	2	2
+	きょういく	教育(する)	N	education	9	3
+	きょうかい	教会	N	church	12	7R
+	きょうかしょ	教科書	N	textbook; Scene 17-2 教科書代 cost of textbooks	2	2
	ぎょうぎ	行儀	N	manners; 行儀(が)いい・悪い good/bad manners	17	1
+	きょうこ	今日子	N	[female given name]	9	7R
	きょうし	教師	N	instructor, teacher	6	2
+	きょうしつ	教室	N	classroom	4	4
+	きょうじゅ	教授	N	professor (academic rank)	12	5
+	きょうそう	競争(する)	N	competition	17	5
+	きょうだい	(ご)兄弟	N	brothers, siblings; Scene 12-5 X 人兄弟 X number of siblings (including oneself)	7	2
+	きょうと	京都	N	Kyoto	9	4
	きょうまでだったでしょう？	今日までだったでしょう？	Sp. Exp.	It was until today, wasn't it?	5	2
	きょうみ	興味	N	interest; X に興味がある have an interest in X	9	3
+	きょうゆう	共有(する)	N	co-ownership, sharing	16	3
+	きょか	許可(する)	N	permission	22	4
+	きょねん	去年	N	last year	4	3
	きょり	距離	N	distance	14	4
	キリ	キリ	N	end; キリがいい good place to end or make a cut; キリがない endless, boundless; キリをつける put an end to (the matter); 1人きり on one's own, by oneself; Past sentence + きり doing X and ending there	23	4

+	ぎり	義理	N	obligation (BTS 1)	12	BTS 1
+	ギリギリ	ギリギリ	Sp. Exp.	just barely	19	5
	きる	着る (-RU; 着た)	V	wear, put on; 面接に着る wear to an interview	11	2
	きる	切る (-U; 切った)	V	cut; Scene 17-6 Verb Stem + きる do completely	14	3
+	きれい	きれい(な)	N	pretty, clean	2	3
	きれる	切れる (-RU; 切れた)	V	expire, wear off, break	23	4
	キロ(メートル)	〜キロ(メートル)	Classifier	kilometers	14	5
	ぎんこう	銀行	N	bank	5	4
+	きんし	禁止(する)	N	prohibition	23	7R
+	きんじょ	近所	N	neighborhood	15	9R
	きんちょう	緊張(する)	N	tension, nervousness	10	5
+	きんトレ	筋トレ	N	weight training	14	6
+	きんにく	筋肉	N	muscle	20	4
	きんよう(び)	金曜(日)	N	Friday	4	6
+	きんろうかんしゃのひ	勤労感謝の日	N	Labor/Thanksgiving Day (BTS 18)	4	4
+	ぐあい	具合	N	condition; 具合がいい・悪い be in a good/bad condition	7	4
+	くうき	空気	N	air	15	8R
+	くうこう	空港	N	airport	15	2
+	くうちょう	空調	N	air conditioning	18	2
+	くさい	臭い	Adj	smelly	23	1
+	くじょう	苦情	N	complaint, grievance	18	2
+	くすり	(お)薬	N	medicine	2	3
	くずれる	崩れる (-RU; 崩れた)	V	fall apart	16	2
	くせ	くせ	N	habit, tendency	19	3
	くせに	〜くせに	Sp. Exp.	even though, in spite of	19	3

+	クタクタ	クタクタ	N	exhausted, tedious	18	1
+	くださる	くださる↑ (-ARU; くださった)	V	give (to in-group) (honorific); Scene 5-3 任せてください。 Leave it to me. Let someone do it. Scene 5-5 X くださって↑ありがとう(ございます)。 Thank you for doing X.; Scene 17-4 X させて いただく・もらう・ください let me X	12	1
+	くだもの	果物	N	fruit	10	3
+	くだる	下る (-U; 下った)	V	come/go down from	7	2
+	くち	口	N	mouth; Scene 19-3 口だけ(です) just words, just talk	11	5
	グチャグチャ	グチャグチャになる	Sp. Exp.	become sloppy, messy	16	2
+	くつ	靴	N	shoes	11	4
	クッキー	クッキー	N	cookie	2	3
	くてん	句点	N	phrase point, comma	2	BTL 2
	くとうてん	句読点	N	punctuation	2	BTL 2
+	くに	国	N	the nation; Scene 24-2 国々 countries	9	4
+	くび	首	N	neck	11	5
	くみあわせる	組み合わせる (-RU; 組み合わせた)	V	combine, join together	21	5
+	くもる	曇る (-U; 曇った)	V	get cloudy	8	2
	くやしい	悔しい	Adj	frustrating, annoying	10	6
+	くよくよ(する)	くよくよ(する)	N	fret, worry	23	2
	くらい	暗い	Adj	dark	7	1
	ぐらい・くらい	X ぐらい・くらい	Sp. Exp.	about X; Scene 14-5 どのぐらいだっけ about how much is it?	4	1
	クラシック	クラシック	N	classical (music)	9	5
+	クラスメート	クラスメート	N	classmate	3	6

281

	クラブ	クラブ	N	club; Scene 24-2 クラブ活動 club activities	3	1
	グラフ	グラフ	N	graph	17	4
+	くらべる	比べる (-RU; 比べた)	V	compare	19	2
	クリエイティブ	クリエイティブ(な)	N	creative	21	5
+	くりかえす	繰り返す(-U; 繰り返した)	V	repeat, do over	23	3
	クリニック	クリニック	N	clinic	11	5
	クリントンだいがく	クリントン大学	N	Clinton University	10	4
+	くる	来る (IRR; 来た)	V	come; Scene 12-4 来ていただいて getting you to come; 来てくださってありがとうございます。 Thank you for coming.; 来てくれてありがとう（ございます）。 Thanks for coming.	2	1
+	くるしい	苦しい	Adj	painful, distressing	20	5
	くるま	車	N	car	5	4
	グルメ	グルメ	N	gourmet, connoisseur	6	6
+	グレー	グレー	N	gray	6	3
	くれる	くれる (-RU; くれた)	V	give (to in-group)	12	1
+	くろい	黒い	Adj	black; Scene 6-3 黒 black (N)	3	5
+	くろう	（ご）苦労(する)	N	hardship	23	6
+	くわしい	詳しい	Adj	well-informed, detailed; Scene 22-7R X に詳しい be familiar with X	16	5
	くん	NAME 〜君	Sp. Exp.	[informal title]	6	1
	くんよみ	訓読み	N	Japanese-based readings of kanji	1	BTL 2
+	け	毛	N	fur	12	3
+	ケーキ	ケーキ	N	cake	2	3
+	ゲーム	ゲーム	N	game(s)	9	5
+	けい	X 系		X system, X lineage	17	1
+	けいかくしょ	計画書	N	plan, program	13	3

+	けいけん	(ご)経験(する)	N	experience	21	7R
+	けいこ	(お)稽古(する)	N	practice, training	20	5
+	けいご	敬語	N	politeness, polite language (BTS 10)	5	5
+	けいざい(がく)	経済(学)	N	economics; Scene 21-3 経済的(な) economical	4	2
+	けいさん	計算(する)	N	calculate	22	5
	けいさんき	計算機	N	calculator	22	5
+	けいたい	携帯/ケータイ	N	cell phone, mobile phone; 0-0 (Inst. Exp.) 携帯を見ないでください。 Please don't look at your phone.	2	2
	けいやく	(ご)契約(する)	N	contract	23	4
+	けいろうのひ	敬老の日	N	Respect for the Aged Day (BTS 18)	4	4
+	けがにん	けが人・怪我人	N	injured person	19	9R
	けさ	今朝	N	this morning	4	4
+	けしゴム	消しゴム	N	(pencil) eraser	3	6
	けす	消す(-U; 消した)	V	extinguish X	14	4
	けつい	決意(する)	N	determination	24	5
	けっか	結果	N	result	11	6
+	けっかん	血管	N	blood vessel, vein	20	4
	けっきょく	結局	N	in the end, ultimately	17	6
	けっこう	けっこう	Sp. Exp.	a fair amount	4	2
	けっこう	結構(な)	N	nice, wonderful, quite, enough, sufficient (often by implication 'no thank you')	8	5
+	けっこん	(ご)結婚(する)	N	wedding, marriage; Scene 24-7R 結婚式 marriage ceremony	8	1
+	けっせき	欠席	N	absence, non-attendance	17	2
+	げつようび	月曜(日)	N	Monday	4	6
	けど	～けど	Particle	but; ～け(れ)ど(も) but	2	4
+	ケニヤ	ケニヤ	N	Kenya	6	1
+	げり	下痢	N	diarrhea; 下痢気味 diarrhetic	13	5

+	けん	～軒	Classifier	[classifier for buildings]	23	5
+	けん	件	N	matter, case	23	9R
+	げんいん	原因	N	cause, origin	19	4
+	げんかん	玄関	N	entry way	9	5
+	げんき	元気(な)	N	healthy, energetic; 元気そう(な) looks healthy, energetic; Scene 10-6 元気ない have no energy	8	5
+	けんきゅう	研究(する)	N	research; Scene 9-3 研究所 research institute; Scene 21-8R 研究室 research office, university faculty office; 研究費 cost of research	10	2
+	げんきん	現金	N	cash	22	8R
	けんこうかんり	健康(な)	N	health; Scene 20-5 健康にいい good for one's health; Scene 21-2 健康管理 health management	20	5
	げんこうようし	原稿用紙	N	Japanese writing paper	1	BTL 5
+	げんごがく	言語学	N	linguistics	4	2
+	けんこくきねんび	建国記念日	N	Foundation Day (BTS 18)	4	4
+	けんさ	検査(する)	N	(medical) examination	20	3
+	げんざい	現在	N	current, present	24	6R
+	けんさく	検索(する)	N	search for, retrieve	15	4
+	けんしゅう	研修(する)	N	training; Scene 23-8R 研修生 intern	10	4
+	げんじゅうしょ	現住所	N	current address	22	8R
+	けんじょうご	謙譲語	N	humble language (BTS 10)	5	5
+	げんだい	現代	N	the present day	22	8R
	げんち	現地	N	the place, destination	3	4
+	けんちく	建築	N	architecture	9	3
+	けんちょう	県庁	N	prefectural office	24	2
+	げんてい	限定	N	limitation	22	7R
+	けんとう	検討(する)	N	consider, investigate, examine	22	4
+	けんどう	剣道	N	kendo	9	5

+	げんば	現場	N	the scene (of a crime/an accident)	22	8R
+	けんばいき	券売機	N	ticket machine	19	1
+	けんぽうきねんび	憲法記念日	N	Constitution Day (BTS 18)	4	4
+	けんめい	件名	N	subject	23	9R
+	けんりつだいがく	県立大学	N	prefectural university	10	4
	こ	～個	Classifier	classifier for counting small objects	3	5
	ご	五・5	Numbers	five	3	2
	ゴーサイン	ゴーサイン	N	"go" signal	22	4
	コード	コード	N	code	22	3
+	コーヒー	コーヒー	N	coffee	2	3
+	コーラ	コーラ	N	cola	10	3
+	こい	濃い	Adj	dark colored, thick, strong (flavor, possibility)	11	2
+	ごい	語彙	N	vocabulary	5	6
+	こいぬ	子犬	N	puppy	20	9R
+	ごう	～号	Classifier	issue (or a periodical), number	16	8R
+	こうえん	公園	N	park	4	4
+	こうえん	(ご)講演	N	speech, lecture; 講演会 lecture (event)	18	4
+	こうか	効果	N	effect; 効果的(な) effective	17	5
+	こうがく	工学	N	engineering	4	2
	こうかん	交換	N	exchange	6	4
+	こうぎ	(ご)講義	N	lecture	18	4
+	こうこう	高校	N	high school; Scene 9-8R 高校生 high school student	3	1
+	こうさいひ	交際費	N	socializing expenses	17	2
	こうさてん	交差点	N	intersection	7	6
	こうじ	工事	N	construction; 工事中 under construction	19	1
+	ごうしつ	～号室	Classifier	classifier for naming a room number	4	5
+	こうしょう	交渉(する)	N	negotiation	23	5

285

Appendix A

+	こうじょう	工場	N	factory, workshop	5	4
+	こうせい	構成	N	organization, composition	19	2
+	こうちゃ	紅茶	N	black tea	2	3
	こうつう	交通	N	traffic; 交通の便 transportation facilities; Scene 17-2 交通費 travel fees, commuting expense(s)	23	5
+	こうどう	行動(する)	N	behavior, conduct	19	3
+	こうとうがっこう	高等学校	N	high school	22	8R
	ごうにいってはごうにしたがえ	郷に入っては郷に従え	Kotowaza	When in Rome, do as the Romans do.	16	0
+	こうねつひ	光熱費	N	utility costs, heat and electricity	23	6
+	こうはい	後輩	N	junior (BTS 30)	2	8
+	こうばん	交番	N	police box	7	6
+	こうふん	興奮(する)	N	excitement	22	6
+	こうへい	公平(な)	N	objectivity, fairness; 不公平(な) partiality, unfairness	21	5
+	こうむいん	公務員	N	public servant, government worker	9	3
+	こうりつ	効率	N	performance, efficiency; Scene 22-4 効率的(な) efficiently	16	6
+	こうりつ	公立	N	public	20	9R
	こうれい	高齢	N	old age; Scene 17-4 高齢者 older person, senior citizens	20	4
	こえ	声	N	voice	8	1
	ごえんりょなく	ご遠慮なく	Sp. Exp.	without reservation	8	3
+	こおり	氷	N	ice	14	3
+	こおる	凍る(-U; 凍った)	V	freeze	18	1
+	ごかい	誤解(する)	N	misunderstanding	20	6
+	こがたかでん	小型家電	N	small appliances	21	8R
	こくご	国語	N	Japanese (lit. 'national') language	10	6
+	こくさい	国際	N	international	24	3
+	こくりつだいがく	国立大学	N	national university	10	4

	ここ	ここ	N	here		2	7
+	ここ	個々	N	one by one, individually		24	2
+	ごご	午後	N	afternoon, p.m.		3	4
	ここち	心地	N	feeling, sensation; 心地がいい・悪い good/bad feeling		23	1
+	こころ	心	N	heart, mind		18	5
	ございます	ございます+ (-ARU)	V	exists (polite form of あります) The 〜て form and the informal forms are rarely used today.		5	5
+	こさめ	小雨	N	light rain, drizzle		18	1
+	こし	腰	N	(lower) back		11	5
	ごしどう、ごべんたつのほど	ご指導、ご鞭撻のほど	Sp. Exp.	your guidance and encouragement		24	5
	ごじゅうおんひょう	五十音表	N	Chart of Fifty Sounds		2	BTL 1
+	ごしゅじんさま	ご主人様	N	husband (polite)		11	4
+	コショウ	コショウ	N	pepper		14	3
+	こしょう	故障(する)	N	(be) out of order		14	6
+	ごしんせき	ご親戚	N	relative, family (polite)		11	4
+	こじんてき	個人的(な)	N	personal		19	9R
	コスト	コスト	N	cost		16	6
	ごぜん	午前	N	morning, a.m.; Scene 15-1 午前中 within the morning		3	4
	こそ	Noun ＋こそ	Sp. Exp.	[emphasizes preceding word]		17	5
	ごぞんじだ↑	ご存知だ↑	Sp. Exp.	know (honorific)		6	6
+	こたえる	答える(-RU; 答えた)	V	answer, respond; 0-0 (Inst. Exp.) 答えてください。 Please answer.; 2-0 (Inst. Exp.) PERSON に答えてください。 Please answer PERSON.; Scene 21-4 答え合わせ(する) check answers		11	6
+	こたえる	応える (-RU; 応えた)	V	answer, meet (expectations or demands), respond		24	2
	こだわる	(X に)こだわる (-U; こだわった)	V	be particular about X, have one's mind set on X		23	4

ごちそうさま。	ごちそうさま。	Sp. Exp.	Thank you. (lit. 'It was a feast.'); ごちそうさまでした。 Thank you. (lit. 'It was a feast,' formal)	1	6
こちら	こちら	N	here, this, in this general area, in this direction, this alternative (of two), the speaker's side of a telephone conversation, this person (polite); Scene 14-3 こちら側 this side	2	4
こちらこそ	こちらこそ	Sp. Exp.	(the pleasure/fault/etc.) is mine	1	10
こっち	こっち	N	here, in this general area, in this direction, this alternative (of two); Scene 14-3 こっち側・こちら側 this side	2	7
こと	こと	N	matter; Scene 2-8 すること something to do; Scene 3-1 X のこと it's a matter of X; it means X; Scene 7-2 ということは that is to say; Scene 8-4 いらしたこと have gone; the experience of having gone; Scene 9-6 そんなことない no such thing; Scene 10-5 分からないこと things/matters one doesn't understand; Scene 10-6 そういうこと a thing like that; that kind of thing; Scene 11-3 重ねることにして(い)る usually layer (habit); Scene 12-6 行くことになりました。 It has been decided I will go.; Scene 13-4 大したことない it's nothing; it's trivial; Scene 14-2 できることはできる it is indeed possible; Scene 14-6 どういうこと what does that mean; Scene 15-3 7時過ぎとのことです。 The report is that it will be after 7:00.; Scene 16-6 下げられないかということ that is to say, can we lower it; Scene 17-4 何てことない it's nothing; it's no big deal; Scene 18-6 言っていいことと悪いことがある there are things that are okay to say and things that are not okay to say; Scene 20-4 何のこと？ What do you mean? What is it? Scene 21-1 X、つまりYっていうこと X, in other words Y; Scene 24-3 Sentence + ことができる can do X	4	4

+	ことし	今年	N	this year	4	4
+	ことば	言葉・ことば	N	language, word(s); Scene 22-6 言葉遣い language use; 言葉遣いまで even the choice of words	10	6
+	こども	こども・子供	N	child; Scene 4-4 BTS 18 こどもの日 Children's Day	7	2
	ことわざ	ことわざ	N	words of wisdom, proverb; also in Scene 20-2	1	0
+	ことわる	断る (-U; 断った)	V	refuse, decline	16	1
	こな	粉	N	powder, flour	14	3
	この	この+N	Sp. Exp.	this N; Scene 7-4 このあいだ the other day, recently; Scene 10-2 このごろ lately, these days; Scene 12-5 このまま as it is; without change	3	5
	こばやし	小林	N	[family name]	3	9R
+	ごはん	ご飯	N	cooked rice or a meal; Scene 2-3 朝ごはん breakfast; (お)昼ごはん lunch; 晩ごはん dinner; Scene 14-4 ご飯茶碗 rice bowl	2	3
	コピー	コピー(する)	N	copy; コピーしたり、整理したり doing things like making copies and sorting; Scene 22-3 コピー機 copy machine	13	6
+	コピペ	コピペ(する)	N	copy and paste	15	4
+	こぼす	こぼす (-U; こぼした)	V	spill something	22	1
	こまかい	細かい	Adj	small, fine, detailed	16	5
	こまったときはおたがいさま	困った時はお互い様	Kotowaza	When in need, we're all in the same boat.; also in Scene 20-2	13	0
+	こまる	困る (-U; 困った)	V	be troubled; be bothered; be embarrassed	6	6
	ゴミ	ゴミ	N	trash, garbage; Scene 23-1 燃えるゴミ burnable garbage	9	1
+	こむ	込む(-U; 込んだ)	V	become crowded	15	3
+	こめ	米	N	(uncooked) rice	14	3

+	コメディ	コメディ	N	comedy	19	2
	ごめん	ごめん	Sp. Exp.	sorry (casual); ごめんなさい sorry	16	4
+	こやま	小山	N	[family name]	12	7R
	ごらんになる	ご覧になる↑ (-RU; ご覧になった)	V	look (honorific)	20	1
+	こる	こる (-U; こった)	V	become stiff	11	5
+	ゴルフ	ゴルフ	N	golf	3	4
+	これ	これ	N	this (thing); Scene 2-2 これから from now; Scene 10-3 これで being this; Scene 15-5 これくらい about this much	2	1
	ごろ	TIME +ごろ	Sp. Exp.	about [time]	3	2
+	ごろごろ	ごろごろ	N	grumbling (stomach), thundering	20	4
+	ころぶ	転ぶ (-U; 転んだ)	V	fall down	23	2
+	こわい	恐い・怖い	Adj	scary, frightening	8	5
	こわす	壊す (-U; 壊した)	V	break X	14	6
	こわれる	壊れる (-RU; 壊れた)	V	X breaks, splits	14	6
+	こんかい	今回	N	this time; Scene 3-4 今度 this time, next time; Scene 4-4 今月 this month; 今週 this week; 今晩 this evening; Scene 4-6 今学期 this term; Scene 21-8R 今夜 tonight; Scene 24-3 今月末 end of this month; 今週末 end of this week; 今年度末 end of this school year, end of this fiscal year	10	5
+	こんかつ	婚活	N	searching for a (marriage) partner	24	1
+	こんげつ	今月	N	this month; Scene 24-3 今月末 end of this month	4	4
+	コンサート	コンサート	N	concert	4	4
+	こんしゅう	今週	N	this week; Scene 24-3 今週末 end of this week	4	4

	コンセプト	コンセプト	N	concept	16	6
+	こんど	今度	N	this time, next time	3	4
	こんな	こんな	Sp. Exp.	this kind; こんなの this kind (of thing); Scene 9-6 こんなに to this extent	8	1
	こんにちは。	こんにちは。	Day 1 Phrase	Hello.	0	0
+	こんねんどまつ	今年度末		end of this school year, end of this fiscal year	24	3
+	コンパ	コンパ	N	get-together, party	17	2
+	こんばん	今晩	N	this evening	4	4
	こんばんは。	こんばんは。	Day 1 Phrase	Good evening.	0	0
+	コンビニ	コンビニ	N	convenience store; Scene 22-2 コンビニ弁当 bento from a convenience store	2	5
+	こんや	今夜	N	tonight	21	8R
+	こんやく	婚約(する)	N	wedding engagement	24	6R
	さ	～さ	Particle		12	3
	さ、さあ	さ、さあ	Sp. Exp.	well, well now, so, go on	9	2
	サークル	サークル	N	club	3	1
	ザーザー	ザーザー	N	sound of heavy rainfall, gushing water	18	1
+	サーシャ	サーシャ	Name	Sasha [given name]	1	1
	さい	～歳・才	Classifier	classifier for naming age	7	2
	さいあく	最悪(な・の)	N	the worst	21	2
	サイエンスフィクション	サイエンスフィクション	N	science fiction	19	2
	さいきん	最近	N	lately	16	4
	さいご	最後	N	last; 最後に lastly; Scene 24-1 最後になりましたが、 lastly	15	4
+	さいこう	最高	N	highest, supreme; Scene 20-2 greatest (often used as an exclamation of approval)	16	6
+	さいしょ	最初	N	first; 最初に firstly	15	4

+	さいしょう	最小	N	smallest, least	21	2
+	さいじょうかい	最上階	N	top floor	23	9R
+	さいしん	最新	N	newest	21	2
+	さいぜん	最善	N	the best	21	2
+	サイダー	サイダー	N	soda	10	3
+	さいだい	最大	N	biggest, largest	21	2
+	さいてい	最低	N	lowest, worst; 21-8R 最低の人 horrible/worst person (character attribute); 最低な人 worst person (on a test, for example), horrible/worst person (character attribute)	21	2
+	さいてん	採点(する)	N	scoring, grading	21	4
	さいとう	斎藤	N	[family name]	3	9R
+	サイフ	サイフ(財布)	N	wallet	3	5
+	ざいらいせん	在来線	N	conventional train (as opposed to *shinkansen*)	19	1
+	ざいりょう	材料	N	ingredients	14	3
	さえ	さえ	Particle	[particle indicating if and only if]; [Noun さえ + Provisional Sentence] if and only if X; Scene 22-4 [Verb stem + さえ + 〜れば・たら] if and only if X; Scene 22-6 X 〜てさえいれば as long as you keep doing X, as long as it keeps doing X	22	3
+	さかい	酒井	N	[family name]	14	9R
+	さがす	探す(-U;探した)	V	look for X	22	5
+	さかな	(お)魚	N	fish	10	3
+	さかもと	坂本	Name	Sakamoto [family name]; 坂本先生 Prof./Dr. Sakamoto	1	1
+	さがる	下がる (-U; 下がった)	V	go down, drop; Scene 19-1 come down, dangle, step back	13	5
+	さき	(お)先	N	ahead, previous; Scene 1-12 お先に I'll be x-ing (ahead of you); お先に失礼します。I'll be leaving (ahead of you). Scene 11-5 先ほど a while ago, just now	4	3

+	さきょう	左京	N	[family name]	11	9R
+	さく	咲く (-U; 咲いた)	V	bloom	23	1
+	さくじょ	削除(する)	N	cancel, delete	13	2
+	さくぶん	作文	N	composition, essay, formal writing	10	2
+	さくや	昨夜	N	last night	21	8R
+	さけ	(お)酒	N	sake, alcohol	10	3
+	さける	避ける (-RU; 避けた)	V	avoid	17	6
	さげる	下げる (-RU; 下げた)	V	lower X; 下げられないかということ that is to say, can we lower it	16	6
+	ささえる	支える(-RU; 支えた)	V	support, prop; 支え合う (-U; 支え合った) support each other	17	5
	ささき	佐々木	N	[family name]	3	9R
+	さしあげる	差し上げる↓ (-RU; 差し上た)	V	give (to out-group) (humble)	12	6
+	さしみ	刺身	N	sashimi (raw sliced fish and other seafood)	17	6
	さすが	さすが (Noun)	Sp. Exp.	true to (your reputation), what I expected, etc.; Scene 19-4 さすがに still, even so	6	6
+	ざせつ	挫折(する)	N	setback	23	3
	させていただく	X させていただく・もらう・ください	Sp. Exp.	let me X	17	4
	さそう	誘う (-U; 誘った)	V	invite	16	1
+	さつ	〜冊	Classifier	classifier for counting bound volumes	3	5
+	サッカー	サッカー	N	soccer	3	4
+	さっき	さっき	N	a while ago	4	4
	さっぱり	さっぱり	N	refreshing, clean	20	3
+	さっぽろ	札幌	N	Sapporo	9	4
	さとう	佐藤	N	[family name]	3	9R
+	さとう	(お)砂糖	N	sugar	14	3

293

Appendix A

+	さどう	茶道	N	tea ceremony	14	9R
+	さびしい・さみしい	寂しい	Adj	lonely	7	1
	サボる	サボる (-U; サボった)	V	skip (school), skip out	20	5
	さま	～様	N	[honorific title]	10	3
+	さます	冷ます (-U; 冷ました)	V	let cool	14	3
	さむい	寒い	Adj	cold (climate); 寒さ the cold; 寒さには慣れました。 I got used to the cold.	7	1
	さめる	冷める (-RU; 冷めた)	V	get cold	17	6
+	さよ(う)なら	さよ(う)なら	Sp. Exp.	goodbye (BTS 11)	1	5
+	さら	(お)皿	N	dish, plate	14	4
	さら	さら・更(な)	N	further, even more	24	2
+	さらいげつ	再来月	N	month after next	10	2
	さらいしゅう	再来週	N	week after next	10	2
+	さらいねん	再来年	N	year after next	10	2
	さらに	さらに・更に	Sp. Exp.	even more, moreover; Scene 24-2 さらなる・更なる furthermore, even more	21	5
	サラリーマン	サラリーマン	N	salaried worker	15	1
+	さわがしい	騒がしい	Adj	noisy	23	1
	さん	NAME さん	Title	Mr/s. NAME	1	1
	さん	三・3	Numbers	three	3	2
+	ざんぎょう	残業	N	overtime work	21	9R
+	さんこう	参考	N	reference	16	9R
+	さんせい	3世		third generation	17	1
+	さんせい	賛成(する)	N	agreement	17	5
	ざんねん	残念(な)	N	too bad, regrettable; Scene 16-2 残念ながら unfortunately	10	6
	さんぶんのいち	3分の1	Sp. Exp.	one-third	9	2

294

+	さんぽ	散歩(する)	N	walk (for pleasure)	20	5
	さんもん	3文	N	three mon (coins) (old unit of currency)	21	3
+	し	市	N	city	24	2
	じ	～時	Classifier	classifier for naming hours on the clock; X 時半 half past (hour X) (2:30)	3	2
	し、よん	四・4	Numbers	four	3	2
+	シージー	CG	N	computer graphics	19	2
	しあい	試合(する)	N	match, contest, game	10	1
	しあげる	仕上げる (-RU; 仕上げた)	V	finish up, complete	10	2
	ジェーアール	JR	N	Japan Railway	19	1
	ジェーエルシー	JLC	N	Japanese Language Club	3	1
	ジェシカ	ジェシカ	N	Jessica	12	3
	しえん	(ご)支援(する)	N	support	24	2
	しお	(お)塩	N	salt	14	3
	じかい	次回	N	next time	10	5
	しか	しか + negative	Particle	nothing but; 4時間しか寝てない I haven't slept but for four hours; Scene 18-3 やるしかない have no choice but to do X	13	1
	しかし	しかし	Sp. Exp.	but	19	5
	しかた	しかた・仕方	N	way of doing; 仕方がない・しょうがない there's nothing to be done; 勉強の仕方 way of studying	10	6
+	しかる	叱る (-U; 叱った)	V	scold	18	2
	じかん	時間	N	time; Scene 5-6 お時間 your time; Scene 4-6 ～時間 classifier for counting hours; Scene 13-4 時間通り on time; Scene 21-4 時間です。Time's up.; Scene 22-4 時間が過ぎる time passes	3	4
+	しきし	色紙	N	square poetry card	16	7R

+	しきじょう	式場	N	ceremonial hall	24	6R
+	じきゅう	時給	N	hourly wage	23	3
	しく	敷く (-U; 敷いた)	V	spread out (a cloth, sheet, etc.)	14	3
+	シクシク	シクシク(する・痛む)	N	dull continuous pain	11	5
	しけん	試験	N	test	7	3
+	じけん	事件	N	matter, case, incident	23	9R
	しご	死語	N	obsolete word, extinct language	21	5
+	じこ	事故	N	accident	15	3
	しこく	四国	N	Shikoku	9	4
	じこしょうかい	自己紹介(する)	N	self-introduction	6	1
+	しごと	(お)仕事(する)	N	work, job	2	2
+	じしゅう	自習	N	self study	14	8R
+	しじりつ	支持率	N	approval rating	17	4
+	じしん	地震	N	earthquake	18	1
+	じすい	自炊	N	cooking for oneself	14	2
+	しずか	静か(な)	N	quiet	7	1
+	しぜん	自然	N	nature	23	1
+	した	下	N	bottom, under	6	2
+	した	舌	N	tongue	11	5
	しだい	X 次第	Sp. Exp.	depending on X	22	4
+	したがき	下書き(する)	N	rough draft	15	4
+	したぎ	下着	N	underwear	15	7R
	したしい	親しい	Adj	close, familiar, intimate	24	4
	しち	七・7	Numbers	seven; also なな	3	2
	じつ	実は	Sp. Exp.	actually, in fact; Scene 19-9R 実に truly; 実を言うと to tell the truth	8	5
+	じっか	(ご)実家	N	home (where one grew up)	23	4
+	しつがいい	質がいい・良い	N	of good quality	22	7R
	しっかり	しっかり	Sp. Exp.	thoroughly	14	3

+	しつける	躾ける (-RU; 躾けた)	V	discipline, train	18	2
+	じっけん	実験(する)	N	experiment	10	2
	じっこう	実行(する)	N	performance, practice; 実行に移す put into practice, put into effect	19	3
	しっている	知っている (-RU; 知っていた)	V	know	6	6
	じっと	じっと	Sp. Exp.	without moving, patiently	14	3
+	しっぱい	失敗(する)	N	failure; 大失敗 big failure; 失敗談 a story about failure	16	2
	しっぱいはせいこうのもと	失敗は成功のもと	Kotowaza	Failure is the foundation of success.	14	0
	しつもん	質問(する)	N	(ask a) question	5	2
	じつようてき	実用的(な)	N	practical	11	3
+	じつりょく	実力	N	ability, strength	24	5
	しつれい	失礼(な)	N	rude, impolite; Scene 1-5 失礼します。 Excuse me.	10	4
+	じてんしゃ	自転車	N	bicycle	4	5
	しどう	(ご)指導(する)	N	guidance, leadership	24	5
+	じどううんてん	自動運転	N	automated driving	20	7R
+	シトシト	シトシト	N	drizzling	18	1
	しぬ	死ぬ (-U; 死んだ)	V	die	14	5
	しばらく	しばらく	N	a while, a moment	11	5
	じぶん	自分	N	oneself; 自分で(は) on one's own, by oneself (without help); Scene 11-4 自分的(な) like oneself; Scene 18-3 自分勝手(な) one's own convenience	9	5
+	しほうはっぽう	四方八方	N	all directions	13	7R
+	しまい	姉妹	N	sisters; X人姉妹 X number of sisters (including oneself)	12	5
+	しまう	しまう (-U; しまった)	V	put away	12	2
+	しまる	閉まる (-U; 閉まった)	V	X closes	19	5

	しみず	清水	N	[family name]	3	9R
+	じむしょ	事務所	N	(business) office; Scene 15-1 事務員 office employee; Scene 22-5 事務室 office	9	3
+	しめる	締める (-RU; 締めた)	V	wear, put on, fasten (a necktie) (lit. 'tie, tighten'); Scene 15-5 締め切り deadline	11	4
+	しめる	閉める (-RU; 閉めた)	V	close X	13	2
+	じもと	地元	N	local	23	9R
	じゃ。	じゃ(あ)。	Sp. Exp.	So. (informal leave taking); Scene 2-8 じゃあ well then,; Scene 1-5 では、Well then,; Scene 4-7R written equivalent of じゃ	1	9
+	シャーペン	シャーペン	N	mechanical pencil	3	3
+	ジャイアンツ	ジャイアンツ	N	Giants	10	1
	しゃいん	社員	N	company employee; 社員旅行 company trip; Scene 21-8R 正社員 full-time employee	14	6
+	しゃかいがく	社会学	N	sociology; Scene 10-9R 社会人 a (working) member of society, an employed adult; Scene 11-4 社会的(な) social	4	2
+	ジャケット	ジャケット	N	jacket	11	3
+	しゃざい	謝罪(する)	N	apology	16	1
	しゃしん	写真	N	photo	6	3
+	ジャズ	ジャズ	N	jazz	9	5
+	しゃちょう	社長	N	company president; Scene 22-5 社長室 president's office	6	5
+	シャツ	シャツ	N	shirt	11	3
+	しゃっきん	借金(する)	N	debt, loan	22	8R
	じゃない	Xじゃない	Sp. Exp.	X, isn't it?; X, for sure	10	6
	じゃね。	じゃ(あ)ね。	Sp. Exp.	See you later. (informal)	1	9
	じゃま	(お)邪魔(する)	N	a bother, a nuisance, an obstacle	8	3
	じゃまた。	じゃまた。	Sp. Exp.	See you again. (informal); じゃまたね。See you again. (informal)	1	9

+	シャワー	シャワー	N	shower	9	5
	じゃん	Sentence じゃん	Sp. Exp.	slang equivalent of [Sentence じゃない]	15	5
	しゅう	週	N	week; 先週 last week; Scene 3-4 週末 weekend; Scene 4-4 今週 this week; Scene 8-1 毎週 every week; Scene 10-2 再来週 week after next; Scene 24-3 今週末 end of this week	4	3
+	しゅう	州	N	state, as in the U.S.	6	1
+	ジュース	ジュース	N	juice	2	3
	じゅう	十・１０	Numbers	ten	3	2
+	じゆう	自由(な)	N	freedom	17	5
	じゅういち	十一・１１	Numbers	eleven	3	2
	しゅうかつ	就活	N	job-hunting	24	1
+	しゅうかつ	終活	N	making preparations to die	24	1
+	しゅうかん	～週間	Classifier	classifier for counting weeks	4	6
	しゅうきょう(がく)	宗教(学)	N	religion, religious studies	4	2
+	しゅうごう	集合	N	gathering	16	8R
+	しゅうじ	(お)習字	N	calligraphy	14	8R
	じゅうじつ	充実(する)	N	completion, fullness	24	3
+	じゅうしょ	住所	N	address; also in Scene 23-6; Scene 23-6 住所変更(する) change of address	22	8R
+	しゅうしょく	(ご)就職(する)	N	employment, getting a job	8	1
+	じゅうたい	渋滞(する)	N	(traffic) congestion	19	6
+	しゅうちゅう	集中(する)	N	concentrate	14	8R
	じゅうに	十二・１２	Numbers	twelve	3	2
	じゆうに	自由に	Sp. Exp.	freely	17	5
+	しゅうぶんのひ	秋分の日	N	Autumnal Equinox (BTS 18)	4	4
+	しゅうまつ	週末	N	weekend	3	4
+	しゅうり	修理(する)	N	repair	23	8R
	しゅうりつだいがく	州立大学	N	state or public university	10	4

+	しゅうりょう	終了(する)	N	termination, end	22	7R
	しゅうりょうしき	修了式	N	closing ceremony	24	2
+	しゅぎょう	修行(する)	N	training	23	8R
+	じゅぎょう	授業(する)	N	instructional class; Scene 17-2 授業料 tuition	3	2
+	しゅくす	祝す (-U; 祝した)	V	celebrate, congratulate	24	2
+	しゅくだい	宿題(する)	N	homework	2	2
+	じゅけん	受験(する)	N	examination	21	7R
+	しゅじゅつ	手術(する)	N	surgery	20	6
+	しゅしょう	首相	N	prime minister, chancellor	18	6
+	しゅじん	(ご)主人	N	husband	7	2
	しゅっしん	(ご)出身	N	birthplace	8	4
	しゅっせき	出席	N	attendance	17	2
+	しゅっちょう	出張	N	business trip	8	6
+	しゅっぱつ	(ご)出発(する)	N	departure [time/place]	15	7R
+	しゅっぴ	出費	N	expense	17	7R
	しゅみ	趣味	N	hobby	9	5
+	しゅるい	種類	N	type, variety	20	2
+	じゅんちょう	順調(な)	N	doing well, favorable, okay	22	6
+	じゅんばん	順番	N	sequential order	15	3
	じゅんび	準備(する)	N	preparation	10	5
	しゅんぶんのひ	春分の日	N	Vernal Equinox (BTS 18)	4	4
+	しょう	省	N	provinces in China	6	1
+	しょう〜はい・ぱい	X 勝 Y 敗	Sp. Exp.	X wins and Y losses	22	9R
+	しょうかい	紹介(する)	N	introduction	13	6
+	しょうがつ	(お)正月	N	New Year's Day/Month (BTS 18)	4	4
+	しょうがっこう	小学校	N	elementary school; Scene 12-7R 小学生 elementary school student	9	6

+	しょうがない	しょうがない	Sp. Exp.	there's nothing to be done	10	6
+	じょうきゃく	乗客	N	passenger	15	9R
	じょうきゅうせい	上級生	N	upper-level student	18	6
+	じょうきょう	状況	N	circumstances	19	4
+	しょうきょくてき	消極的(な)	N	passive, unmotivated, pessimistic	11	4
	じょうけん	条件	N	condition, terms, set-up	23	3
+	しょうさい	詳細	N	detail	22	7R
+	じょうし	上司	N	superior, boss	18	6
	しょうじき	正直	N	honest, frank, candid	18	5
+	じょうしき	常識	N	common sense; 常識的 common sensical	21	3
+	じょうしゃ	(ご)乗車(する)	N	ride on a vehicle	15	7R
	しょうしょう	少々	Sp. Exp.	a little (polite)	10	3
+	しょうじょう	症状	N	symptoms	20	3
	じょうず	上手	N	skillful, good at	6	1
+	しょうせつ	小説	N	novel, fiction	20	7R
	しょうたい	(ご)招待	N	invitation	18	4
	じょうたい	状態	N	status, circumstances	19	6
+	しょうだく	承諾(する)	N	consent, agree	22	4
	じょうたつ	上達(する)	N	improve	24	5
	じょうだん	(ご)冗談	N	joke	8	2
	しょうち	(ご)承知(する)	N	acceptance, consent	11	1
+	しょうテスト	小テスト	N	small test, quiz	12	7R
+	しょうはい	勝敗	N	winning and losing, result	22	9R
+	しょうぶ	勝負(する)	N	match, contest	20	9R
+	じょうぶ	丈夫(な)	N	strong	20	4
	じょうほう	情報	N	information, data	16	6
+	しょうゆ	醤油	N	soy sauce	14	4
+	しょうろんぶん	小論文	N	short formal paper	21	8R

+	しょうわ	昭和	N	Showa era (1926–1989); 昭和の日 Showa Day (BTS 18)	4	4
	ジョギング	ジョギング	N	jogging; Scene 14-6 ジョギングでも even jogging or something	14	6
+	しょくいん	職員	N	staff; Scene 22-5 職員室 staff room	22	8R
+	しょくぎょう	職業	N	job, occupation	22	8R
	しょくじ	(お)食事	N	a meal; お食事の方 the food part of your order; Scene 17-2 食事会 dinner party, dinner/breakfast meeting; 食事代 cost of food	10	3
+	しょくちゅうどく	食中毒	N	food poisoning	20	4
+	しょくどう	食堂	N	dining hall, cafeteria	7	1
	しょくば	職場	N	workplace	24	3
	しょくひ	食費	N	food expense(s)	17	2
+	しょくれき	職歴	N	work experience	22	8R
+	じょし	女子	N	young woman	9	7R
+	じょしゅ	助手	N	assistant	17	7R
	しょしん	初心	N	original intention, basics; 初心にかえって returning to the basics, returning to the original intention	24	3
	しょしんわするべからず	初心忘るべからず	Kotowaza	Do not forget the spirit of your original intention.	24	0
	じょせい	女性	N	woman, girl	12	3
	しょだん	初段	N	first or lowest rank black belt in martial arts, calligraphy, shogi, igo, etc.	6	2
+	しょちょう	所長	N	head of a laboratory, research center	6	5
	しょっちゅう	しょっちゅう	Sp. Exp.	frequent, often	10	4
+	しょっぱい	しょっぱい	Adj	salty	10	3
+	しょどう	書道	N	calligraphy	19	8R
+	しょるい	書類	N	documents, papers	13	3
+	しらい	白井	Name	Mr/s. Shirai	1	1
	しらせる	知らせる	V	notify; let known; Scene 12-7R お知らせ announcement, notice (lit. 'letting know')	17	2

+	しらべる	調べる (-RU; 調べた)	V	investigate, inquire, search	10	5
+	しり	(お)尻	N	buttocks, behind	11	5
+	しりつだいがく	私立大学	N	private university	10	4
+	しる	知る (-U; 知った)	V	find out, know; Scene 7-2 知り合い acquaintance	6	6
+	しろい	白い	Adj	white; Scene 6-3 白 white (N)	3	5
+	しんかんせん	新幹線	N	bullet train, high speed rail	15	1
+	しんきょ	(ご)新居	N	new home, new place	23	6
+	しんけい	神経	N	nerves	20	4
+	しんけん	真剣(な)	N	seriousness	16	1
+	しんごう	信号	N	traffic light	7	6
+	しんじゅうしょ	新住所	N	new address	23	6
	しんじょうほう	新情報	N	news, new information	23	6
	しんじる	信じる (-RU; 信じた)	V	believe	17	4
+	しんじん	新人	N	new person	23	6
+	しんせき	親戚	N	relative, family (in-group)	11	4
+	しんせつ	親切(な)	N	kind, gentle; 親切そう(な) looks kind	8	5
+	しんぞう	心臓	N	heart	20	4
+	じんぞう	腎臓	N	kidney	20	4
+	しんだん	診断(する)	N	diagnosis	20	3
	しんぱい	(ご)心配(な)・(する)	N	worry; Scene 11-5 心配をかける make (someone) worry; Scene 20-3 ご心配かけてすみません。 I'm sorry to make you worry.	11	5
+	しんぽ	進歩(する)	N	progress	24	5
	しんぼくかい	親睦会	N	informal gathering, meet-and-greet	17	2
	ず(に)	Verb～ず(に)	Sp. Exp.	without X-ing, not X-ing	20	1
+	スーツ	スーツ	N	suit	11	2
+	スーツケース	スーツケース	N	suitcase	14	1

+	スーパー	スーパー	N	supermarket	5	4
+	スイッチ	スイッチ	N	switch	14	6
	ずいぶん	ずいぶん・随分(な)	N	extremely, very	18	3
+	すいみん	睡眠	N	sleep; 睡眠時間 sleep time; 睡眠不足 lack of sleep time	13	1
+	すいよう(び)	水曜(日)	N	Wednesday	4	6
	すうがく	数学	N	mathematics	4	2
+	すうじ	数字	N	numeral, figure	20	1
+	スカート	スカート	N	skirt	11	2
	すき	(お)好き(な)	N	liking, fondness, love; 大好き(な) very likeable, like very much	2	3
	すきこそもののじょうずなれ	好きこそものの上手なれ	Kotowaza	What one likes, one does well.; also in Scene 20-2	9	0
	ズキズキ	ズキズキ(する・痛む)	N	throbbing	11	5
	すぎたるはおよばざるがごとし	過ぎたるは及ばざるが如し	Kotowaza	Too much of a good thing.; also in Scene 20-2	20	0
+	スキャン	スキャン(する)	N	scan	17	4
+	すぎる	過ぎる (RU; 過ぎた)	V	exceed, go beyond; Scene 3-2 過ぎ after, past [time]; Scene 11-2 〜過ぎ(る) over- (overeat, overdo, etc.); 食べ過ぎ eat too much	11	2
+	すく	空く (-U; 空いた)	V	become empty	8	4
	すぐ	すぐ	N	soon, immediately, right away	5	1
+	すくない	少ない	Adj	few, scarce	10	5
	すごい	すごい	Adj	amazing; Scene 9-6 すっごい really, really	2	1
	すこし	少し	N	a little, a few	5	1
	すごす	過ごす (-U; 過ごした)	V	pass time	24	2
+	すし	(お)すし・寿司	N	sushi	2	3

+	すじ	筋	N	plot	19	2
	すずき	鈴木	N	[family name]	3	9R
+	すずしい	涼しい	Adj	cool (climate)	7	1
+	すすむ	進む (-U; 進んだ)	V	go forward, improve	19	1
	すすめる	Xに勧める・薦める (-RU; 勧めた・薦めた)	V	recommend to X, advise X, encourage X; (お)勧め recommendation, suggestion	6	6
+	すすめる	進める (-RU; 進めた)	V	move X forward	16	5
	ずつう	頭痛	N	headache; 頭痛がする have/get a headache	13	5
	すっかり	すっかり	N	completely	12	6
	ずっと	ずっと	Sp. Exp.	continuously, by far, the whole time	6	5
+	すっぱい	すっぱい	Adj	sour	10	3
+	ステーキ	ステーキ	N		17	6
	すてき	素敵(な)	N	sharp, nice, good-looking	11	4
	すでに	すでに	Sp. Exp.	already	22	4
	すてる	捨てる (-RU; 捨てた)	V	throw away	9	1
	ステレオタイプ	ステレオタイプ	N	stereotype	21	1
+	ストーブ	ストーブ	N	room heater	14	6
	ストーリー	ストーリー	N	story	19	2
	ストレス	ストレス	N	stress	14	6
	すなお	素直(な)	N	cooperative, accommodating	18	3
	すばらしい	すばらしい・素晴らしい	Adj	wonderful, splendid	15	4
+	スペインご	スペイン語	N	Spanish (language); スペイン人 Spanish (person)	3	1
	スポーツ	スポーツ	N	sport(s); Scene 4-4 (BTS 18) スポーツの日 Sports Day	9	5
+	すまい	(お)住まい	N	dwelling, housing	23	1

+	すませる	済ませる (-RU; 済ませた)	V	finish, get through	10	2
	スマホ	スマホ	N	smartphone	3	3
+	すむ	住む (-U; 住んだ)	V	reside; Scene 23-1 (お)住まい dwelling, housing; 住み心地 feeling of living (in a place)	8	4
+	すむ	済む (-U; 済んだ)	V	is finished; Scene 1-3 すみません・すいません。 Excuse me./I'm sorry./Thank you.; Scene 2-2 すみませんでした・すいませんでした。 Sorry/thank you (for what has happened).	21	7R
	すめばみやこ	住めば都	Kotowaza	Home is where you make it.	7	0
+	すらすら	すらすら	N	smoothly, easily	20	4
+	する	する (IRR; した)	V	do, play (a game or sport); Scene 2-8 すること something to do; Scene 4-3 しました did; Scene 4-5 そうしましょう。 Let's do it that way.; Scene 6-6 X にする decide on X; Scene 11-4 wear, put on (jewelry, accessories, make-up); Scene 12-3 茶色の目をしている has brown eyes; Scene 13-1 される do (honorific)	2	1
+	すわる	座る(-U; 座った)	V	sit; Scene 23-1 座り心地 comfort when sitting	6	3
	せ	背	N	back, spine, rear side; 背が高い人 tall person/people	6	3
	ぜ	ぜ	Particle	[particle for emphasis or force, blunt]	23	2
	セーター	セーター	N	sweater	11	3
+	セーフ	セーフ	N	safe (from baseball)	19	5
+	セールス	セールス	N	sales	6	2
	せいかい	正解	N	correct (answer or solution); 不正解 incorrect	21	4
+	せいかつ	生活(する)	N	(everyday) life	22	9R
+	せいこう	成功(する)	N	success	16	2
+	せいさん	精算(する)	N	calculation adjustment	19	1
+	せいじ	政治	N	politics; Scene 18-6 政治家 politician	21	7R

+	せいしゃいん	正社員	N	full-time employee	21	8R
+	せいしん	精神	N	mind, spirit	20	4
+	せいじんのひ	成人の日	N	Coming of Age Day (BTS 18)	4	4
+	せいせき	成績	N	results, grades	17	4
	せいちょう	(ご)成長(する)	N	growth, development	24	2
+	せいひん	製品	N	product, manufactured good	16	6
	せいぶつ	生物	N	biology	6	2
+	せいり	整理(する)	N	sorting, putting in order	9	1
+	せかい	世界	N	the world	9	4
	せき	(お)席	N	seat, (seated) occasion; Scene 17-9R 席を外す leave one's seat	10	3
+	せき	咳	N	cough; 咳が出る have/get) a cough	13	5
+	せき	関	N	[family name]	23	8R
+	せきにん	責任(が ある・ない)	N	responsibility, liability; 責任を取る take responsibility; 責任を持つ assume responsibility 責任感 sense of responsibility	18	3
+	セクハラ	セクハラ	N	sexual harassment	21	1
	せだい	X 世代	N	X generation	17	1
+	せつ	説	N	theory	20	7R
	せっかく	せっかく	Sp. Exp.	with trouble, at great pains	13	1
	せっきょくてき	積極的(な)	N	active, positive, optimistic	11	4
	せっさたくま	切磋琢磨	Kotowaza	Learn from experience.	23	0
	ぜったい	絶対(に)	N	absolutely	10	2
+	せつめい	説明(する)	N	explanation	9	3
+	ぜつめつ	絶滅(する)	N	extinction	21	5
+	せなか	背中	N	back	11	5
+	ぜひ	是非	Sp. Exp.	by all means	5	5
+	せまい	狭い	Adj	narrow, confined	7	1
	ゼロ・まる・れい	ゼロ・まる・零	Numbers	zero	3	5

Appendix A

	せわ	(お)世話(する)	N	help, aid, assistance (for someone); Scene 11-7R お世話様 your kindness	6	4
	せん	千(１０００〜９０００)	Numbers	thousands (1,000 ~ 9,000)	4	1
+	せん	先 TIME	N	先学期 last semester; 先月 last month; 先日 the other day; 先週 last week	4	3
+	せん	X 線	N	X-(bus/train) line	15	2
	ぜんいん	全員	N	everyone, all members of a group	17	2
+	ぜんかい	前回	N	last time	10	5
+	せんきょ	選挙(する)	N	election	22	4
	せんこう	(ご)専攻(する)	N	major field of study	4	2
+	せんざい	洗剤	N	detergent	23	1
+	ぜんじつ	前日	N	the previous day	9	8R
	せんせい	NAME 先生	Title	Prof./Dr. NAME	1	1
	ぜんぜん	全然	N	not at all, entirely	4	2
+	せんだい	仙台	N	Sendai	9	4
+	ぜんたい	全体	N	whole, entirety; Scene 20-1 X 全体 whole, all over X	16	5
+	せんたく	洗濯(する)	N	laundry; also in Scene 23-1; Scene 23-1 洗濯物 laundry	9	1
+	セント	〜セント	Classifier	cent	3	5
	セントルイス	セントルイス	N	St. Louis	8	4
+	せんぱい	先輩	N	senior (BTS 30); Scene 7-2	2	8
	ぜんぶ	全部	N	all, everything; Scene 3-5 全部でX X for everything, X all together	5	3
+	せんめんじょ	洗面所	N	washroom	9	5
+	せんもん	(ご)専門	N	specialization, major; Scene 10-5 専門的(な) specialized	4	2
	せんやく	先約	N	prior engagement	16	1
	せんりのみちもいっぽから	千里の道も一歩から	Kotowaza	A journey of a thousand miles begins with a single step.; also in Scene 20-2	2	0
	せんりょく	戦力	N	asset	24	5
	ぞ	〜ぞ	Particle	[particle adding force or emphasis]; いいぞ！ Way to go! Nice going!	21	4

	ソース	ソース	N	sauce	14	4
	そう	そう	N	that way, so; Scene 2-7 そうですね(え) (hesitation); Scene 5-3 (to express consideration) let's see Scene 3-3 そう、そう。 Right, right.; Yes, yes.; Scene 4-4 そうか。 Is that so? (expression of awareness); そうしましょう。 Let's do it that way.; Scene 5-6 そうしていただけますか？ Can I have you do that?; Scene 7-2 そうなんだ。 So that's it.; I get it now.; Scene 7-3 そうか。 I see.; Scene 10-6 そういうこと a thing like that; that kind of thing; Scene 22-5 そう言えば speaking of that . . ., come to think of it,	2	5
	そう	～そう	Sp. Exp.	できるそう I hear you can; they say you can	14	2
+	そうきん	送金(する)	N	sending money	15	8R
	そうじ	掃除(する)	N	cleaning; 掃除したの誰？ Who is it that cleaned up?	9	1
+	そうたい	早退(する)	N	leaving early	19	3
+	そうだん	(ご)相談(する)	N	consultation; Scene 6-6 X に・と相談する consult with X	6	5
+	そうべつかい	送別会	N	farewell party	17	2
+	そこ	そこ	N	there (near you), that place just mentioned	2	7
+	そだつ	育つ (-U; 育った)	V	be raised, be brought up	18	2
+	そだてる	育てる (-RU; 育てた)	V	raise (someone or something), bring up	18	2
+	そちら	そちら	N	there (near you), that (near you), in that general area, in that direction (in your direction), that alternative (of two near you), the other side of a telephone conversation, that person (polite)	2	4
+	そつぎょう	(ご)卒業(する)	N	graduation; Scene 22-8R 卒業生 students who graduated; Scene 24-6R 卒業式 graduation ceremony	8	1

	そっくり	そっくり	N	exactly like, completely; X にそっくり look exactly like X	12	5
+	そっち	そっち	N	there (near you), in that general area, in that direction (in your direction), that alternative (of two near you)	2	7
	そっちょく	率直(な)	N	candor, frankness	16	5
+	そと	外	N	outside	6	2
+	その	その + N	Sp. Exp.	that N; Scene 11-4 その上 what's more, in addition, plus; Scene 13-2 その通り that's true; Scene 15-2 その時間なら if that's the timing; Scene 16-3 その気 what one has in mind, with that in mind; Scene 20-2 そのくらい about that much; Scene 23-6 その他 besides that	3	5
+	そのむら	園村	N	[family name]	20	9R
+	そば	そば	N	soba (buckwheat noodles)	2	3
+	そふ	祖父	N	grandfather (in-group)	11	4
+	そぼ	祖母	N	grandmother (in-group)	11	4
	そりゃそうだ	そりゃそうだ	Sp. Exp.	that's right	19	6
	それ	それ	N	that (thing near you); Scene 7-1 それより leaving that aside, apart from that, more importantly; Scene 7-5 それに what's more, besides; Scene 9-5 それとも or (else); Scene 11-2 それにしたら? If you did that? (how would it be); Scene 11-6 それで、 then, following that; Scene 12-3 それで、 because of that; Scene 16-4 それが、 that's (just it); well, in fact; それにしても anyway, at any rate, be that as it may; Scene 16-6 それなら if that's the case; Scene 21-2 それどころか on the contrary, in fact; Scene 22-5 それはそうと by the way	2	1
	それぞれ	それぞれ	N	each, respectively	24	2
+	そろう	揃う (-U; 揃った)	V	be a full set, become complete	22	3
+	そろえる	揃える (-RU; 揃えた)	V	arrange, complete	22	3

	そろそろ	そろそろ	Sp. Exp.	soon, gradually, slowly	14	4
+	そんけいご	尊敬語	N	honorific language (BTS 10)	5	5
+	そんざい	存在(する)	N	existence, presence	24	6R
+	ぞんじる	存じる↓ (-RU; 存じた)	V	know, find out (humble)	6	6
	そんなことない	そんなことない	Sp. Exp.	no such thing	9	6
	そんなに	そんなに	Sp. Exp.	to that extent; so/such a X	8	2
	だ	だ	Sp. Exp.	Informal form of です; Sentence だけど but; Scene 8-2 Sentence + だから、so of course, so; Scene 9-3 教えるの好きだし I like teaching, and; Scene 10-6 だけど but, however (Also in Scene 19-8R); Scene 14-5 どのぐらいだっけ about how much is it?; Scene 15-5 だったら in that case; Scene 17-6 X だって even X, but X; Scene 19-3 だからと言って nevertheless, while it may be true that; Scene 21-6 だから as a discourse connector; Scene 21-8R だが however, nevertheless	3	4
+	ターミナル	ターミナル	N	terminal	15	2
	たい	Verb 〜たい	Adj	want to Verb	6	5
	だい	X 代	Sp. Exp.	decade of X year-olds; 10代 teens; Scene 17-2 cost; 飲み物代 cost of drinks; 食事代 cost of food; 教科書代 cost of textbooks	17	4
+	だいがく	大学	N	university, college; X 大学 X University, X College; Scene 8-9R 大学生 university student	3	1
+	だいがくいん	大学院	N	graduate school	3	1
+	たいぐう	待遇	N	treatment, working conditions	23	3
+	たいけん	(ご)体験(する)	N	(personal) experience	20	9R
+	タイご	タイ語	N	Thai (language)	8	8R
	だいじ	(お)大事(な)	N	important, valuable; お大事に take care	7	4
	たいしたことない	大したことない	Sp. Exp.	it's nothing; it's trivial	13	4

	だいしっぱい	大失敗	N	big failure	16	2
+	たいしょう	大正	N	Taisho era (1912–1926)	4	4
	だいじょうぶ	大丈夫	N	fine, safe, all right	2	1
+	だいすき	大好き	N	very likeable, like very much	2	3
+	たいせつ	大切(な)	N	important, necessary	8	5
+	だいそつ	大卒	N	college graduates	22	8R
+	だいたい	だいたい	N	generally, approximately	15	5
+	たいち	太一	N	[male given name]	16	9R
+	たいてい	大抵	Sp. Exp.	usually, as a rule	8	6
+	だいとうりょう	大統領	N	president (of a country)	18	6
+	だいどころ	台所	N	kitchen	9	5
+	だいにげんご	第2言語	N	second language	22	9R
	だいひょう	代表(する)	N	representative; X を代表して as a representative of X	24	2
+	だいぶ	だいぶ	Sp. Exp.	a fair amount	9	2
+	たいふう	台風	N	typhoon	18	1
	たいへん	大変(な)	N	tough (to do), awful, terrible	4	3
	タイム	タイム	N	time, timing	14	4
+	たいよう	太陽	N	sun	18	1
	タウンシネマ	タウンシネマ	N	Town Cinema	7	6
+	たおす	倒す (-U; 倒した)	V	throw down, knock down, defeat	19	1
+	たおれる	倒れる (-RU; 倒れた)	V	fall over, collapse	14	5
+	だが	だが	N	however, nevertheless	21	8R
	たかい	高い	Adj	expensive; Scene 6-3 tall (in stature); Scene 10-6 high, tall; Scene 16-6 高すぎるように思います。I think it's too expensive.	2	7
	たがい	(お)互い	N	mutual, each other	13	4
	たかはし	高橋	N	[family name]	3	9R
	だから	だから、	N	so of course, so, as a discourse connector; Scene 8-2 Sentence + だから	21	6

+	たがわ	田川	N	[family name]	10	8R
+	だきょう	妥協(する)	N	compromise	23	5
	だくおん	濁音	N	voiced consonant	5	BTL9
+	たくさん	たくさん	N	a lot, many	3	5
+	たぐち	田口	N	[family name]	11	8R
	だくてん	濁点	N	[diacritical marks]	2	BTL 4
	だけ	～だけ	Particle	just, only; Scene 13-4 できるだけ as much as one can; Scene 19-3 口だけ(です) just words, just talk	4	2
	だけど	だけど	Sp. Exp.	but, however	19	8R
+	だしあう	出し合う (-U; 出し合った)	V	contribute jointly	17	5
	たしか	確か(な)	N	sure, certain; 確かに for sure, certainly	8	5
+	たしかめる	確かめる (-RU; 確かめた)	V	make sure	19	1
+	たす	足す (-U; 足した)	V	add (numbers)	21	4
	だす	出す (-U; 出した)	V	submit, take out (of a container), send out (mail); Scene 22-6 やる気を出す become enthusiastic	5	2
	だす	Stem + だす (-U; だした)	V	begin X-ing; 降りだしたなんてもんじゃない it's not just that it started raining	18	1
	たすかる	助かる (-U; 助かった)	V	be helped, be saved, be rescued	5	4
+	たすける	助ける (-RU; 助けた)	V	help (someone); Scene 175 助け合う (-U; 助け合った) help each other, cooperate	13	4
+	たずねる	尋ねる (-RU; 尋ねた)	V	inquire	17	3
+	たずねる	訪ねる (-RU; 訪ねた)	V	visit, call on	18	4
	たた	多々	N	very much, very many, more and more	24	3
	ただ	ただ	N	simply; free of charge; Scene 23-1 only, just, but	12	4

	ただいま。	ただいま。	Sp. Exp.	I'm home; I'm back.	1	13
+	たたえる	讃える (-RU; 讃えた)	V	extol, praise	24	2
+	たたく	叩く (-U; 叩いた)	V	strike, hit	23	2
+	ただしい	正しい	Adj	correct	21	3
	ただちに	直ちに	Sp. Exp.	immediately, right away	22	1
+	たちかわ	立川	N	[place name in Tokyo]	9	9R
	たつ	立つ・建つ (-U; 立った・建った)	V	stand; Scene 23-2 立ち上がる (-U; 立ち上がった) get up, stand up; 立ち直る (-U; 立ち直った) recover (one's footing); Scene 23-7R立(ち)入(り)禁止 no entry, no trespassing	6	3
+	たつ	発つ (-U; 発った)	V	depart	15	2
+	たっきゅうびん	宅急便	N	express delivery service	14	1
	ダッシュ	ダッシュ(する)	N	dash, run	19	6
	たったいま	たった今	Sp. Exp.	just now	22	1
	だったら	だったら	Sp. Exp.	in that case	15	5
	だって	Xだって	Sp. Exp.	even X, but X	17	6
+	たて	縦	N	vertical; Act 1 BTL 3 縦書き vertical writing	11	5
+	たてる	建てる・立てる (-RU; 建てた・立てた)	V	build X, erect X	23	6
	たとえ	たとえ	N	even if, supposing that; たとえ上級生でも even for an upper-level student	18	6
	たとえば	例えば・たとえば	Sp. Exp.	for example	13	6
+	たな	棚	N	shelf; Scene 14-1 本棚 book shelf	12	1
+	たなか	田中	N	[family name]	10	8R
+	たにん	他人	N	others, outsider; also in 20-6; 他人事 other person's affairs	19	9R
	たのしい	楽しい	Adj	fun	7	4

+	たのしむ	楽しむ (-U; 楽しんだ)	V	enjoy X; Scene 7-2 (お)楽しみ(な) enjoyment, pleasure	19	8R
	たのむ	頼む (-U; 頼んだ)	V	order (at a restaurant, online, etc.), request	6	6
+	たぶん	多分	Sp. Exp.	probably	14	6
	たべる	食べる (-RU; 食べた)	V	eat; 食べ物 food; Scene 9-2 食べに行く go to eat; Scene 11-2 食べ過ぎ eat too much; Scene 12-2 食べてるかどうか whether you're eating or not; Scene 14-4 食べた後で after eating	2	3
	タマ	タマ	N	[a common name for cats]	20	4
	たまご	卵	N	egg	14	3
	だます	騙す (-U; 騙した)	V	trick, cheat; 騙されたと思って。trust me; lit. 'assume that you've been conned'	20	3
+	たまたま	たまたま	Sp. Exp.	accidentally	13	3
+	たまに	たまに	Sp. Exp.	once in a while	8	6
+	たまねぎ	玉ねぎ	N	bulb onion	14	2
	だまる	黙る (-U; 黙った)	V	stay quiet, be silent	18	6
	たまわる	賜る↓ (-U; 賜った)	V	be given, be granted (humble)	24	2
+	たむら	田村	N	[family name]	10	8R
	ため	ため(に)	N	benefit, sake, purpose; Scene 13-2 念のため(に) just in case	16	5
+	だめ	だめ(な)	N	bad, useless, problematic	3	4
	ためす	試す (-U; 試した)	V	attempt, try out	20	3
+	たよる	頼る (-U; 頼った)	V	depend on, count on	19	3
	たら	それにしたら?	Sp. Exp.	If you did that? (how would it be); Scene 2-3 よかったら if it's all right; Scene 12-1 使ってくれたら if you would use it (for me); Scene 15-4 1度使えるようになったら once you become able to use it; Scene 15-5 だったら in that case	11	2

	だらけ	Nounだらけ	Sp. Exp.	full of X	24	4
+	だらだら	だらだら	N	sluggishly, slowly	20	4
+	たりる	足りる (-RU; 足りない)	V	be enough, suffice	12	4
	だるい	だるい	Adj	sluggish, dull	20	1
	だれ	だれ・誰	N	who; Scene 12-3 誰か知らない don't know who that is	2	6
+	だんし	男子	N	young man; also in Scene 17-4	9	7R
	たんじゅん	単純(な)	N	simple	13	6
	たんじょうび	(お)誕生日	N	birthday; お誕生日おめでとう(ございます)。 Happy birthday. (lit. 'Congratulations on your birthday.')	8	1
+	ダンス	ダンス	N	dance	20	5
+	だんせい	男性	N	man, boy	12	3
	チーズ	チーズ	N	cheese; チーズ！ Cheese!	6	3
	チーム	チーム	N	team	19	3
	ちいき	地域	N	region, area	24	2
	ちいさい	小さい	Adj	small; Scene 12-5 小さな small, little	2	7
+	ちか	地下	N	basement, underground; Scene 5-4 地下鉄 subway; Scene 23-9R 地下室 basement room	4	5
+	ちかい	近い	Adj	close; Scene 6-2 近く near-by, vicinity, neighborhood	2	7
	ちがう	違う (-U; 違った)	V	different from X; (Xと)違う・同じ different from/same as X; Scene 6-6 Xと違わない not different from X; Scene 21-8R 違い difference	3	6
+	ちから	(お)力	N	power	24	5
+	ちきゅう	地球	N	earth	18	1
+	チケット	チケット	N	ticket	3	5
	ちこく	遅刻(する)	N	delay, lateness	19	3
+	ちじん	知人	N	acquaintance	20	6
+	ちち	父↓	N	father (humble); Scene 8-5 父親 father	7	2
+	ちちゅうかい	地中海	N	Mediterranean Sea	18	5

	ちっとも	ちっとも	Sp. Exp.	not a bit, not at all	19	3
	ちなみに	ちなみに	Sp. Exp.	by the way, incidentally	16	3
+	チャージ	チャージ(する)	N	charge	19	1
+	ちゃいろ	茶色	N	brown; Scene 12-3 茶色の目をしている has brown eyes	6	3
+	ちゃかい	(お)茶会	N	tea party	14	9R
	ちゃく	[time/place] 着	Sp. Exp.	arrival [time/place]; Scene 15-7R X 着 Xth place goal-in (in a competition); classifier for counting outfit	15	2
+	ちゃくしん	着信(する)	N	arriving signal, an incoming call/signal	17	8R
+	ちゃやま	茶山	N	[family name]	14	9R
+	ちゃわん	(お)茶碗	N	tea cup; ご飯茶碗 rice bowl	14	4
+	ちゃん	〜ちゃん	Title	[suffix for familiar person]	13	5
	チャンス	チャンス	N	chance	24	5
	ちゃんと	ちゃんと	Sp. Exp.	properly, reliably, satisfactorily	8	1
	チューインガム	(チューイン)ガム	N	chewing gum	17	1
	ちゅう・じゅう	X 中	N	while X-ing; in the middle of X-ing; within X; 1 日中 all day	10	2
+	ちゅう	注	N	note	18	8R
+	ちゅうい	注意(する)	N	caution	18	1
+	ちゅうがっこう	中学校	N	middle school	9	6
+	ちゅうかりょうり	中華料理	N	Chinese food	10	3
+	ちゅうこ	中古	N	used	13	8R
+	ちゅうこく	忠告(する)	N	advice	20	2
+	ちゅうごく	中国	N	China; Scene 3-1 中国語 Chinese (language); 中国人 Chinese (person)	6	1
+	ちゅうし	中止(する)	N	cancellation	19	7R
+	ちゅうせいぶ	中西部	N	the Midwest	24	5
+	ちゅうもく	X に注目(する)	N	attention, pay attention to X	18	8R
	ちゅうもん	(ご)注文	N	order, request	17	6

+	チョー	チョー・超	Sp. Exp.	extremely (casual); Scene 22-3 超特急 super fast	13	1
+	ちょう	兆	Numbers	trillions (BTS 4)	4	1
+	ちょう・ジャン	張	N	Zhang or Cho [Chinese family name]	3	1
+	ちょうさ	調査(する)	N	investigation, survey	10	2
	ちょうし	調子	N	condition, rhythm; Scene 21-6 調子に乗る get caught up, get carried away	16	3
	ちょうだい	頂戴(する)↓	N	receive (humble)	22	3
	ちょうど	ちょうど	Sp. Exp.	exactly, precisely, just	9	2
	ちょうとっきゅう	超特急	N	super fast; Scene 15-1 特急 limited express	22	1
+	ちょっき	直帰(する)	N	going directly home	19	3
	ちょっと	ちょっと	Sp. Exp.	a little	2	2
+	チン	チン(する)	N	ding (finishing sound of a microwave)	14	3
+	ちんたい	賃貸	N	rental	23	9R
	つ	～つ	Classifier	classifier for counting items	5	3
	つい	つい	Sp. Exp.	just; Scene 22-5 つい３０分 just 30 minutes	14	2
	ついたち	ついたち～３１日	Numbers	the first ~ the 31st	4	4
	ついて	Nについて	Sp. Exp.	with regard to N	6	5
+	つうがく	通学(する)	N	commuting to school	19	4
+	つうきん	通勤(する)	N	commuting to work	19	4
+	つうじる	通じる (-RU; 通じた)	V	get through, be understood	16	6
	つうやく	通訳(する)	N	interpretation	10	5
	つかう	使う (-U; 使った)	V	use; Scene 4-5 使いやすい easy to use; 使いにくい hard to use; Scene 12-1 使ってくれたら if you would use it (for me); Scene 15-4 １度使えるようになったら once you become able to use it; Scene 23-1 使い勝手 comfort when wearing something	4	2

	にくい	〜にくい	Adj	hard to X; 使いにくい hard to use	4	5
+	つかれる	疲れる (-RU; 疲れた)	V	get tired; (お)疲れ tiredness, fatigue	13	1
+	つき	月	N	moon, month; Scene 21-8R 月夜 moonlit night	7	8R
+	つぎ	次	N	next, following; Scene 10-6 次、頑張ろう！Do your best next time.; Scene 15-4 次に next	3	4
+	つきあう	付き合う (-U; 付き合った)	V	go out with; 付き合い socializing (especially among co-workers)	16	1
+	つきあたり	突き当たり	N	end (of a street, hallway, etc.)	7	6
+	つく	着く (-U; 着いた)	V	arrive	7	6
+	つく	付く・つく (-U; 付いた)	V	X is attached; Scene 14-6 X turns on	14	1
+	つくえ	机	N	desk	12	1
+	つくる	作る (-U; 作った)	V	make	4	1
+	つける	付ける・つける (-RU; 付けた)	V	attach, apply; Scene 14-4 turn X on; attach X	11	4
	つごう	(ご)都合	N	circumstances, condition; 都合がいい・悪い convenient/inconvenient; 都合がある there are circumstances to consider	15	1
+	つたえる	伝える (-RU; 伝えた)	V	convey a message	11	1
+	つたわる	伝わる (-U; 伝わった)	V	X is told/spread	16	7R
+	つちや	土屋	N	[family name]	13	8R
+	つづく	続く (-U; 続いた)	V	continue, go on; 続き continuation, succession	15	5
+	つづける	続ける (-RU; 続けた)	V	keep on, continue X	10	6
+	つつむ	包む (-U; 包んだ)	V	wrap	17	3
	って	〜って	Particle	[topic particle]	3	1

	って・と	QUOTATION + って・と	Particle	[Quotation]	7	3
+	つとめる	勤める (-RU; 勤めた)	V		9	3
+	つぶす	潰す (-U; 潰した)	V	smash, wreck	18	5
+	つま	妻↓	N	wife (humble)	7	2
+	つまらない	つまらない	Adj	boring; Scene 19-2 つまんない	2	7
	つまり	つまり	Sp. Exp.	that is to say, in other words; Scene 21-1 X、つまりYっていうこと X, in other words Y	14	5
+	つめたい	冷たい	Adj	cold (to the touch), cold (personality)	7	1
+	つめる	詰める (-RU; 詰めた)	V	pack, cram X	14	1
	つもり	つもり	N	plan, intention; そのつもり that's the plan, that's the intention; 乗るつもり plan to get on board; Scene 15-5 X に頼んだつもり I thought I asked X; Scene 15-6 そのつもりでいる I'll be planning it like that; Scene 16-3 諦めるつもりはない don't plan to give up	15	2
+	つもる	積もる(-U; 積もった)	V	pile up, accumulate	18	1
	つゆ	梅雨	N	rainy season; 梅雨にしても even for *tsuyu*	18	1
+	つよい	強い	Adj	strong	5	6
+	つよき	強気	N	confident	16	3
+	つらい	辛い・つらい	Adj	tough, bitter (experience), painful	7	1
	づらい	Verb stem + づらい	Adj	difficult to X	21	5
	つれていく	連れて行く	V	take (a person) along; 連れて来る bring (a person) along	5	4
+	て	手	N	hand	11	5
	で	PLACE で	Particle	location of activity	3	4
	で	〜で	Particle	by means of X	5	4

	で	〜で	Sp. Exp.	the 〜て form of です・だ; X でも Y でも whether it's X or Y; X でも X じゃなくても whether it's X or not X;; Scene 8-1 1人で by oneself, alone (lit. 'as one person'); Scene 10-3 Noun でいらっしゃいます↑ It's [Noun] (honorific); Noun でございます+ It's [Noun] (polite); Scene 14-1 でないと otherwise; Scene 14-6 ジョギングでも even jogging or something; Scene 15-4 どこからでも from wherever, from anywhere	5	1
	で、	で、	Sp. Exp.	and . . . ; Scene 14-3 then, next; Scene 19-6 so then, and then	12	3
+	てあし	手足	N	arms and legs	20	8R
+	ディーケー	1 DK	N	one room plus living room, dining room, kitchen	23	4
+	ティーシャツ	ティーシャツ	N	T-shirt	3	5
+	ていじ	提示(する)	N	presentation, suggestion	23	3
+	ていしょく	定食	N	set meal; Scene 17-6 X 定食 X set menu	6	6
+	ていど	程度	N	about (following a number), degree	22	2
	ていねい	(ご)丁寧	N	Polite; Scene 5-5 BTS 10 丁寧語 formal language	11	1
+	でかける	出かける (-RU; 出かけた)	V	go out	10	2
	てから	Verb 〜てから	Sp. Exp.	after Verb-ing	9	6
+	てきとう	適当	N	perfunctory, irresponsible; appropriate, suitable	18	3
+	できる	できる (-RU; できた)	V	can do, become complete; Scene 13-4 できるだけ as much as one can; Scene 14-2 できることはできる it is indeed possible; できるそう I hear you can; they say you can	2	1
+	でぐち	出口	N	exit	6	3
+	デザート	デザート	N	dessert	10	3
+	デザイン	デザイン(する)	N	design	6	2
	てじゅん	手順	N	process, protocol	15	3

	です	X です。	Sp. Exp.	It's X; NAME です。My name is NAME.; Scene 10-3 Noun でいらっしゃいます↑ It's [Noun] (honorific); Noun でございます+ It's [Noun] (polite)	1	4
+	テスト	テスト	N	test	2	2
	てっきり	てっきり	Sp. Exp.	surely	20	4
+	てつだう	手伝う (-U; 手伝った)	V	Help X; Scene 16-2 手伝ってもらえばよかった I should have had you help me	4	3
+	てつづき	手続き	N	paperwork process	20	1
+	てつや	徹夜(する)	N	stay up all night	13	1
+	てにしょく	手に職	N	marketable skill in hand	22	8R
	テニス	テニス	N	tennis	3	4
	では	では	Sp. Exp.	Well then, Scene 4-7R written equivalent of じゃ; Scene 1-9 じゃ(あ)。So. (informal leave taking); Scene 2-8 じゃあ well then	1	5
+	てぶくろ	手袋	N	gloves	11	4
+	てまえ	手前	N	this side (of a location); a little before reaching (a location, a situation)	19	1
	でも	でも	Sp. Exp.	but, however, and yet; X でも Y でも whether it's X or Y; X でも X じゃなくても whether it's X or not X; Scene 14-6 ジョギングでも even jogging or something	5	1
	てりょうり	手料理	N	home cooking	22	2
	でる	出る (-RU; 出た)	V	go out, leave, attend (an event), appear, answer (the phone); Scene 16-4 出ようとしたところに just as I was about to leave	5	4
	てん	点(、)	N	point, dot; Act 2 BTL 4 点々 [diacritical marks]; Scene 10-6 classifier for counting and naming points	2	BTL 2
+	てんいん	店員	N	shopkeeper	15	1
	てんかい	展開	N	expansion, development	19	6

+	てんき	天気	N	weather; 天気がいい weather is good; Scene 18-1 天気予報 weather forecast	7	1
+	でんき	電気	N	electricity, light; also in Scene 14-6	12	8R
+	てんけいてき	典型	N	pattern, model; 典型的(な) typical	21	3
+	でんごん	(ご)伝言(する)	N	square poetry card	16	7R
	でんしゃ	電車	N	train	5	4
+	てんじょうがひくい	天井が低い	Sp. Exp.	low ceiling	21	7R
+	てんしょく	転職(する)	N	job change	22	8R
+	でんしレンジ	電子レンジ	N	microwave	14	3
+	てんそう	転送(する)	N	transfer	20	7R
+	てんちょう	店長	N	store owner	14	8R
+	てんのうへいか	天皇陛下	N	emperor (honorific) (BTS 18); 天皇誕生日 Emperor's Birthday	4	4
+	てんぷら	天ぷら	N	tempura	10	3
	でんわ	電話(する)	N	telephone; Scene 6-4 (お)電話番号 telephone number (your telephone number)	2	2
	と	〜と	Particle	XとY X and Y; Scene 12-4 Sentenceと Sentence; 2時を過ぎると when it gets past 2:00; Scene 12-4 どちらかと言うと if I have to say which; Scene 14-1 でないと otherwise; Scene 24-4 Non-past Sentence + とともに along with X	3	2
	と	〜と	Particle	Xと言います/申します↓/おっしゃいます↑ say X; Scene 7-2 ということは that is to say; Scene 12-4 どちらかと言うと if I have to say which; Scene 18-3 と言うか何と言うか should I say . . . ; Scene 19-2 というより、rather than; Scene 19-9R 実を言うと to tell the truth Scene 21-2 Xというと？ What do you mean, (by) X?	6	2
	ど	〜度	Classifier	times, degrees	8	4
+	とい	問い	N	question	19	7R

+	といあわせる	問い合わせる (-RU; 問い合わせた)	V	inquire (for information); Scene 19-7R 問い合わせ inquiry	19	1
	ということは	ということは	Sp. Exp.	that is to say	7	2
	というと	(X)というと？	Sp. Exp.	What do you mean, (by) X?	21	2
	というより、	というより、	Sp. Exp.	rather than	19	2
+	ドイツ	ドイツ	N	Germany	6	1
+	トイレ	トイレ	N	toilet	2	5
	どう	どう	N	how; Scene 9-6 どうやって (doing) how; どうかなあ I wonder; Scene 11-4 どういう意味 what do you mean? what does that mean?; Scene 14-6 どういうこと what does that mean	2	7
+	どうが	動画	N	motion picture, movie	19	8R
+	どうきゅうせい	同級生	N	same-level student	18	6
+	どうぐ	道具	N	tool, utensil	14	1
+	とうざい	東西	N	east-west	15	2
+	とうさん	(お)父さん	N	father	7	2
	とうじつ	当日	N	the day of	23	1
	どうして	どうして	Sp. Exp.	why	7	3
+	とうじょうぐち	搭乗口	N	boarding area (for flight)	15	3
	とうぜん	当然	N	of course, naturally	14	1
	どうぞ。	どうぞ。	Sp. Exp.	Go ahead.; Scene 1-4 どうぞよろしく。 Nice to meet you.; どうぞよろしくお願いします。 Nice to meet you. (formal)	1	2
+	とうだい	東大	N	University of Tokyo	11	8R
+	とうちゃく	(ご)到着(する)	N	arrival	24	3
	とうてん	読点	N	point, dot	2	BTL 2
+	とうひょう	投票(する)	N	vote	22	4
+	どうぶつ	動物	N	animal	19	7R

+	とうほく	東北	N	northeast	24	5
	どうも	どうも	Sp. Exp.	Hello.	1	7
+	どうりょう	同僚	N	co-worker, colleague	3	6
	とうろく	登録(する)	N	registration	15	3
+	とおい	遠い	Adj	far; Scene 7-1 遠く distant; Scene 20-8R 耳が遠い poor hearing	2	7
+	とおす	通す (-U; 通した)	V	diffuse, let X pass	14	1
+	とおの	遠野	N	[family name]	17	7R
+	とおる	通る (-U; 通った)	V	go along (a road), go through, go via; Scene 7-6 通り way, road, street	14	1
	とか	〜とか	Particle	(things) like, such as; 〜とかも also (things) like, such as	4	2
+	とかい	都会	N	city	23	4
	とき	時・とき		time; Scene 8-6 時々 sometimes; Scene 13-4 Sentence + とき(に) when Sentence	7	9R
+	ドキドキ	ドキドキ	N	thump-thump	20	4
	ときはかねなり	時は金なり	Kotowaza	Time is money.; also in Scene 20-2	4	0
	とく	徳	N	virtue, benevolence	21	3
+	とく	(お)得(な)	N	profitable; 得(を)する benefit	22	9R
	とくい	得意(な)	N	strong point, specialty	10	6
+	どくしょ	読書	N	reading	9	5
+	どくしん	独身	N	single; unmarried	12	5
	とくに	特に	Sp. Exp.	especially	10	2
+	とくべつ	特別	N	special	22	8R
+	とける	溶ける(-RU; 溶けた)	V	melt, dissolve	18	1
	どこ	どこ	N	where; Scene 15-4 どこからでも from wherever, from anywhere	2	5
	ところ	ところ・所	N	place; Scene 15-7R 所々 here and there; Scene 16-3 聞いたところ just heard; Scene 16-4 出ようとしたところに just as I was about to leave	4	4

	ところが、	ところが、	Sp. Exp.	as a matter of fact	23	3
+	ところで	ところで	Sp. Exp.	by the way, incidentally	22	5
	として	Xとして	Sp. Exp.	as/in one's capacity as X	13	5
	としても	Xとしても	Sp. Exp.	even for X; Xとしては for an X	19	1
+	としょかん	図書館	N	library	3	4
+	としより	(お)年寄	N	old person	17	4
+	とじる	閉じる (-RU; 閉じた)	V	(someone) closes X	14	7R
	とちゅう	途中	N	on the way, in the middle of	19	6
+	どちら	どちら	N	where, which, which direction, which (of two), which person/who (polite); Scene 12-4 どちらかと言うと if I have to say which	2	4
	とっきゅう	特急	N	limited express; Scene 22-3 超特急 super fast	15	1
+	とつぜん	突然	N	suddenly	18	3
+	どっち	どっち	N	where, which direction, which (of two)	2	7
+	とても	とても	Sp. Exp.	very; Scene 17-5 とても + [negative sentence] (not) at all, by no means	2	7
+	とどうふけん	都道府県	N	prefectures (BTS 11)	9	4
+	とどく	届く (-U; 届いた)	V	reach, get delivered	14	1
+	とどける	届ける (-RU; 届けた)	V	deliver X; Scene 22-7R (お)届け先 shipping address	14	1
	どなた	どなた	N	who (polite)	2	6
+	となり	隣	N	next door, beside	6	2
	とにかく	とにかく	Sp. Exp.	anyway, at any rate	13	3
+	どの	どの + N	Sp. Exp.	which N; Scene 14-5 どのぐらいだっけ about how much is it?; Scene 16-5 どのように in what way	3	5
+	とばす	飛ばす (-U; 飛ばした)	V	skip X	21	2

	とびこむ	飛び込む (-U; 飛び込んだ)	V	rush in	19	6
	とびだす	飛び出す (-U; 飛び出した)	V	rush out	19	6
+	トマト	トマト	N	tomato	14	3
+	とまる	泊まる (-U; 泊まった)	V	stop, come to a halt	15	2
	とまる	止まる (-U; 止まった)	V	come to a halt, stop	19	6
+	とめる	止める (-RU; 止めた)	V	stop X	19	7R
	とも	Non-past Sentence + とともに	Sp. Exp.	along with X	24	4
+	ともこ・ゆうこ	友子	N	[female given name]	13	8R
+	ともだち	ともだち	N	friend	3	6
+	どよう(び)	土曜(日)	N	Saturday	4	6
	とりあえず	とりあえず	Sp. Exp.	for now, first of all	10	3
+	とりいそぎ	取り急ぎ	N	in haste	19	8R
+	とりかえる	取り替える (-RU; 取り替えた)	V	exchange, replace	17	3
+	どりょく	努力(する)	N	effort, exertion	16	1
	ドリンク	ドリンク	N	drink	17	2
	とる	取る (-U; 取った)	V	take (a class)	4	2
+	とる	撮る (-U; 撮った)	V	take (a photo)	6	3
+	ドル	〜ドル	Classifier	dollar(s) (U.S. currency)	3	5
+	どれ	どれ	N	which (thing)	2	1
+	トレーニング	トレーニング	N	training	20	5
+	ドレス	ドレス	N	dress	11	2

+	とれる	取れる (-RU; 取れた)	V	X comes off, disappear (as a fever)	14	6
+	どん	X 丼	N	X bowl	17	6
+	とんかつ	豚カツ	N	pork cutlet	17	6
	とんだ	とんだ X	Sp. Exp.	unthinkable X, awful X	20	6
	とんでもない	とんでもない	Sp. Exp.	not at all	7	4
	どんどん	どんどん	Sp. Exp.	rapidly, steadily; Scene 20-4 drumming	9	2
	ドンマイ	ドンマイ	Sp. Exp.	never mind, don't worry	23	2
+	な	名	N	name	9	8R
	なあ	～なあ	S. Particle	[sentence particle indicating shared agreement]; Scene 9-6 どうかなあ I wonder	2	6
	ないよう	内容	N	content	10	5
+	なおす	直す・治す (-U; 直した・治した)	V	fix, repair X; Scene 20-3 cure, heal	14	1
	なおす	～なおす	V	re-, do over	16	3
	なおる	直る・治る (-U; 直った・治った)	V	get better, get fixed; restore (itself)	7	6
+	なか	中	N	inside; Scene 9-4 CATEGORY の中で一番行ってみたいの within/among [category] the one I want to go to most; Scene 24-2 [Sentence] + 中 in the midst of X	6	2
+	ながい	長い	Adj	long; Scene 11-3 長袖 long sleeves; Scene 12-3 長さ length; Scene 24-1 長生き(する) long life, longevity	5	5
+	なかた・なかだ	中田	N	[family name]	10	8R
	なかてん	中点(・)	N	raised period	2	BTL 2
	なかなか	なかなか + negative	Sp. Exp.	quite, considerably, rather; Scene 11-2 [なかなか + affirmative] rather, more than expected	8	1

	なかむら	中村	N	[family name]	3	9R
+	なかやま	中山	N	[family name]	9	9R
+	なく	泣く (-U; 泣いた)	V	cry, weep; Scene 21-9R 泣き声 tearful voice, crying sound; Scene 24-7R 泣き顔 crying face	8	2
+	なぐさめる	慰める (-RU; 慰めた)	V	console, comfort (someone)	22	6
+	なくなる	亡くなる (-U; 亡くなった)	V	pass away	14	5
	なげる	投げる (-RU; 投げた)	V	throw	23	2
+	なごや	名古屋	N	Nagoya	13	8R
+	なさけない	情けない	Adj	pathetic, miserable	22	6
	なさる	なさる↑ (-ARU; なさった)	V	do (honorific)	7	4
+	なぜ	何故・なぜ	N	why	7	3
+	なだめる	宥める (-RU; 宥めた)	V	soothe, calm	23	3
+	なつ	夏	N	summer; 夏休み summer vacation/holiday; 夏休みの間 during summer vacation	8	6
+	なつかしい	懐かしい	Adj	nostalgic, remembered fondly	24	1
+	なっとう	納豆	N	natto, fermented soy beans (BTS 4 FN)	12	2
	なつめそうせき	夏目漱石	N	Natsume Soseki (author, 1867–1916)	9	4
	など	〜など	Particle	and the like, et cetera	22	2
	なな	七・7	Numbers	seven; also しち	3	2
+	なな	七菜	N	[female given name]	14	9R
	ななころびやおき	七転び八起き	Kotowaza	Fall down seven times, get up eight.; also in Scene 20-2	10	0
+	ななめ	斜め	N	diagonal	11	5

+	なに	何(なに)	N	what (See also なん); Scene 2-8 なにか・何か something; also in Scene 6-5; Scene 3-1 何語 which language?; 何人・なに人 what nationality; Scene 6-1 何も nothing; Scene 6-3 何色 what color; Scene 21-1 so-and-so, such-and such	2	3
+	なは	那覇	N	Naha	9	4
	ナビ	ナビ	N	GPS, navigator	7	6
+	なまえ	(お)名前	N	name (your name)	6	4
+	なまける	怠ける (-RU; 怠けた)	V	neglect a job or task	19	3
+	なやむ	悩む (-U; 悩んだ)	V	worry about	19	3
	なら	X なら	Sp. Exp.	if that's the X; 16-6 それなら if that's the case; Scene 15-2 その時間なら if that's the timing; Scene 23-5 払わせられるくらいなら if one is to be made to pay	16	6
+	ならう	習う (-U; 習った)	V	learn	9	5
	ならぶ	並ぶ (-U; 並んだ)	V	stand alongside; line up; X と・に並ぶ stand/line up alongside X; 並んでいると似てる look alike standing next to each other	12	5
+	ならべる	並べる (-RU; 並べた)	V	line up X	13	2
	なり	X なり(に)	N	X for instance (though there may be other options); X なりの Y Y in X's own way	21	2
+	なりたくうこう	成田空港	N	Narita Airport	24	6R
	なる	なる (-U; なった)	V	become; 難しくなりました。It became difficult.; Scene 6-2 初段になりました I became a black belt.	5	6
	なるべく	なるべく	Sp. Exp.	as . . . as possible	5	1
	なるほど	なるほど	Sp. Exp.	Oh, now I see.	3	1

	なれる	(X に) 慣れる (-RU; 慣れた)	V	get used/accustomed (to X)	7	1
	なん	何 (なん)	N	what (See also なに); Scene 3-2 何時 what time; Scene 3-5 何百 how many hundreds; Scene 4-6 何曜(日) what day (of the week)?; Scene 5-3 何でしょう。 What? What could it be?; Scene 7-3 なんで why; Scene 7-6 何とかスーパー so-and-so/such-and-such/something-or-other supermarket; Scene 9-6 何倍も上手 many times better at; Scene 12-6 なんとなく somehow or other; Scene 13-1 〜なんか for example (casual), something/anything like that; Scene 17-4 何てことない it's nothing; it's no big deal; Scene 19-5 何とか・なんとか something-or-other; Scene 20-4 何のこと？ What do you mean? What is it?; 何だ・なあんだ。 Oh, so that's it!; Scene 22-2 何と言っても no matter what people say, in the end	2	3
+	なんせいぶ	南西部	N	the Southwest	24	5
	ナンバーワン・トップ	○○ナンバーワン・トップ	Sp. Exp.	number one/top	17	4
+	なんぶ	南部	N	the South	24	5
+	なんぼく	南北	N	north-south	15	2
	に	二・2	Numbers	two	3	2
	に	TIME に	Particle	point of time	3	4
	に	〜に	Particle	[inanimate location particle]	3	6
	に	〜に	Particle	to, towards X; Scene 9-2 食べに行く go to eat	5	4
	に、に	X に Y に	Sp. Exp.	X, Y, and . . . (BTS)	24	2
	にあう	似合う (U; 似合った)	V	looks good on; X が Y に似合う X looks good on Y	11	2
+	にいさん	(お)兄さん	N	older brother	7	2
+	におう	臭う・匂う (-U; 臭った・匂った)	V	smell; Scene 14-4 匂い smell, scent	23	1

+	にがい	苦い	Adj	bitter	10	3
	にがて	苦手(な)	N	weak point, weakness	10	6
+	にく	(お)肉	N	meat	10	3
	にくい	〜にくい	Adj	hard to X; 使いにくい hard to use	4	5
+	にげる	逃げる (-RU; 逃げた)	V	escape	23	2
+	にこにこ	にこにこ	N	smiling	20	4
	にごりてん	濁り点	N	[diacritical marks]	2	BTL 4
+	にし	西	N	west; Scene 15-9R 西口 west exit/entrance; Scene 24-5 西海岸 west coast	15	2
+	にしかわ	西川	N	[family name]	15	9R
	にしても	X にしても	Sp. Exp.	even for X; X にしては for an X; 梅雨にしても even for *tsuyu*; Scene 16-4 それにしても anyway, at any rate, be that as it may	18	1
	にする	X にする	Sp. Exp.	decide on X	6	6
+	にせい	二世		second generation	17	1
	にち・か	〜日	Classifier	classifier for naming the day of the month; Scene 4-6 counting; Scene 6-2 〜日間 classifier for counting days	4	4
+	にちじ	日時	N	date and time	7	9R
+	にちよう(び)	日曜(日)	N	Sunday	4	6
	について	N について	Sp. Exp.	with regard to N	6	5
+	にっけいじん	日系人	N	person of Japanese heritage	3	1
+	にっすう	日数	N	number of days	20	8R
+	にった	新田	N	[family name]	10	7R
+	にほん	日本(にほん・にっぽん)	N	Japan; Scene 3-1 日本語 Japanese (language); 日本人 Japanese (person); 日本語クラブ Japanese Language Club; Scene 4-2 日本学 Japanese studies; Scene 21-9R 日本史 Japanese history; Scene 23-9R 日本海 Sea of Japan; Scene 24-5 表日本 the Pacific Ocean side of Japan; 裏日本 the Japan Sea side of Japan	6	1

	にほんごではなしましょう。	日本語で話しましょう。	Inst. Exp	Let's speak in Japanese.	2	0
+	にもつ	荷物	N	baggage, package	14	1
+	ニュース	ニュース	N	news	3	3
+	にゅうがくしき	入学式	N	school entrance ceremony	24	6R
+	にゅうきょ	入居(する)	N	moving in; 入居者 tenant	23	7R
+	にゅうしゃしき	入社式	N	company's welcoming ceremony	24	6R
	によると	Xによると	Sp. Exp.	according to X	17	4
	にる	似る (-RU; 似た)	V	resemble; Xと・に似る look like X; resemble X	12	5
+	にわ	庭	N	garden	9	5
	にん・り	～人	Classifier	classifier for people	6	2
	にんき	人気(がある)	N	popularity	17	4
+	にんげん	人間	N	human, human being; 人間関係 human relationships	18	6
+	にんじん	人参	N	carrot	14	3
	ぬく	抜く (-U; 抜いた)	V	omit, extract	21	2
+	ぬすむ	盗む (-U; 盗んだ)	V	steal	18	6
+	ぬる	塗る (-U; 塗った)	V	apply (paint)	17	3
+	ぬれる	濡れる (-RU; 濡れた)	V	get wet	18	1
	ね	～ね	S. Particle	[sentence particle indicating agreement]	2	1
	ね?	～ね?	S. Particle	[sentence particle checking on whether the other person is following]	2	1
	ねえ	～ねえ	S. Particle	[sentence particle assuming shared attitude/opinion]	2	3
+	ねえさん	(お)姉さん	N	older sister	7	2

+	ねかす	寝かす (-U; 寝かした)	V	put to sleep; lay X on its side	20	8R
	ネクタイ	ネクタイ	N	necktie	11	4
+	ねこ	猫	N	cat	12	3
+	ねすごす	寝過ごす (-U; 寝過ごした)	V	sleep through	20	8R
+	ねだん	値段	N	price	16	6
	ねつ	熱	N	fever; 熱がある have a fever 熱が出る get a fever 熱が上がる a fever goes up/goes down 熱が下がる a fever goes down; Scene 20-1 熱っぽい feverish	13	5
+	ねっちゅうしょう	熱中症	N	heatstroke	18	1
	ねぶそく	寝不足	N	lack of sleep	12	4
	ねむい	眠い	Adj	sleepy	12	4
+	ねむる	眠る (-U; 眠った)	V	sleep	17	1
+	ねる	寝る (-RU; 寝た)	V	sleep, go to bed, lie down; Scene 12-4 寝不足 lack of sleep; Scene 20-8R 寝過ごす (-U; 寝過ごした) sleep through	8	1
	ねるこはそだつ	寝る子は育つ	Kotowaza	A child who sleeps well grows up well.; also in Scene 20-2	19	0
	ねん	～年	Classifier	classifier for naming the years; Scene 4-6 counting; Scene 6-2 ～年間 classifier for counting years; Scene 8-6 年に２、３回 two or three times a year; Scene 9-6 ３年で in three years	4	4
+	ねんじゅうむきゅう	年中無休	N	open all year round	23	8R
+	ねんせい	～年生	Classifier	classifier for naming grade, class in school	6	1
+	ねんど	年度	N	fiscal year	24	3
	ねんのため(に)	念のため(に)	Sp. Exp.	just in case	13	2
	の	の	N	one(s); 赤いの the red one; Scene 3-6 私のです。It's mine.; Scene 9-1 掃除したの誰？ Who is it that cleaned up? Scene 9-5 聞くの専門 listening is my specialty	3	5

	の	の	Particle	Scene 3-1 X のこと it's a matter of X; it means X; Scene 8-6 休みの時 during one's vacation; when one is on vacation	3	1
+	ノート	ノート	N	notebook	3	5
+	のう	(お)能	N	noh (traditional theater)	10	1
+	のう	脳	N	brain	20	4
+	のうりょく	能力	N	ability	22	4
+	のぐち	野口	N	[family name]	14	9R
+	のこす	残す	V	leave X	18	9R
+	のこる	残る (-U; 残った)	V	remain, be left; 残り what's left, remainder	15	5
	のせる	載せる・乗せる (-RU; 載せた・乗せた)	V	put X on top	14	3
+	のぞく	除く (-U; 除いた)	V	exclude, eliminate	19	3
+	のだ	野田	N	[family name]	14	9R
+	のちほど	後ほど	N	later	10	8R
	のど	喉	N	throat; 喉が渇く get thirsty	8	4
	のに	Sentence のに	Sp. Exp.	even though Sentence; しようと思ったのに even though I thought about doing it	16	1
	のには	〜のには	Sp. Exp.	in order to . . .	19	1
	のぼる	登る (-U; 登った)	V	climb	7	2
+	のむ	飲む・呑む (-U; 飲・呑んだ)	V	drink, swallow (i.e., medicine); 飲み物 drink, beverage; Scene 11-2 飲み過ぎ drink too much; Scene 17-2 飲み物代 cost of drinks	2	3
+	のりかえる	(X に)乗り換える (-RU; 乗り換えた)	V	transfer (to X)	15	2
+	のりつぐ	乗り継ぐ (-U; 乗り継いだ)	V	connect (with a different flight, train, etc.)	15	2

+	のる	乗る (-U; 乗った)	V	ride, get onboard; Scene 15-1 乗れる (-RU: 乗れた) can ride; Scene 15-2 乗り場 boarding area (for ground transportation); Scene 16-3 乗り気 enthusiasm	5	4
	は	〜は	Phr. particle	(for contrast)	2	6
	は	Xは	Particle	as for X	3	2
+	は	歯	N	tooth	11	5
+	ば	場	N	place; Xの場 place for X; Scene 15-2 乗り場 boarding area (for ground transportation);	15	7R
	ば	〜ば	Sp. Exp.	[provisional ending] 手伝ってもらえばよかった。 I should have had you help me.; 呼んでくれれば行った。 I'd have come to help you if you'd called.	16	2
+	パーセント	パーセント	N	percent	9	2
+	パートナー	パートナー	N	(romantic) partner	11	4
	ハーフマラソン	ハーフマラソン	N	half marathon	14	4
	はあ	はあ	Sp. Exp.	yes (formal); [in this context, unconvinced]	18	3
	バアーっと	バアーっと	Sp. Exp.	[expression of dismay], all over and rapidly	22	6
+	ばあい	場合	N	situation; case	16	8R
	はい	肺	N	lungs	20	4
	ばい	倍	N	double, -fold; 〜倍 classifier for multiples	9	6
	はい・ぱい・ばい	〜杯	Classifier	classifier for counting cupfuls, glassfuls	24	2
	はい、	はい、	Inst. Exp	okay; Scene 1-1 はい。 Present. (in roll call); Scene 1-2 Here you are. (handing something over); はい、どうぞ。 Here you go (take it, do it); Scene 1-3 Got it. (accepting something); Scene 2-1 Yes.	0	0

	バイ。	バイ。	Sp. Exp.	Bye. (informal); バイバイ。 Bye-bye. (informal)	1	9
	はいけん	拝見(する)↓	N	look (humble)	22	3
	はいしゃく	拝借(する)↓	N	borrow (humble)	22	3
+	はいしん	配信(する)	N	deliver information	20	8R
+	ばいてん	売店	N	shop, stand, kiosk	7	1
+	バイト	バイト(する)	N	part-time job	13	6
	はいる	入る (-U; 入った)	V	go in, enter	9	6
+	ばえ	X映え	N	X-worthy	19	8R
	ばかり・ばっかり	ばかり・ばっかり	Sp. Exp.	just; Scene 22-1 Past sentence + ばかり・ばっかり just X-ed; Scene 22-2 Noun + ばかり・ばっかり just, only X; Scene 22-4 Non-past sentence + ばかり all it does is X	22	1
+	はかる	計る・測る (-U; 計った・測った)	V	measure	14	3
+	はく	履く (-U; 履いた)	V	put on, wear (on the legs, such as slacks); Scene 23-1 履き心地 comfort when wearing something	11	2
	はげます	励ます (-U; 励ました)	V	encourage	24	3
	はげむ	励む (-U; 励んだ)	V	strive; Xに励む strive to X	24	5
	はこ	箱	N	box	14	1
+	はこぶ	運ぶ (-U; 運んだ)	V	carry, move	17	3
+	はさむ	挟む(-U; 挟んだ)	V	hold between, insert	14	3
+	はし	(お)箸	N	chopsticks	14	4
+	はじ	恥	N	shame, embarrassment	20	2
+	はじまる	始まる (-U; 始まった)	V	X begins; Scene 19-7R 始まり beginning, origin; Scene 23-6 Xに始まって、Y、Z、 starting with X, then Y, Z	15	1

+	はじめる	始める (-RU; 始めた)	V	begin X; 0-0 (Insr. Exp.) 始めましょう。 Let's begin.; Scene 6-4 はじめまして。 How do you do.; Scene 8-5 初めて first time; Scene 9-2 Verb Stem + はじめる (-RU; はじめた) begin X-ing; Scene 19-7R 始め beginning; Scene 24-3 X始めY beginning from X to Y	2	2
	ばしょ	場所	N	place	4	4
+	はしる	走る (-U; 走った)	V	run	7	2
	はず	はずです	Sp. Exp.	it's expected; Sentence + はずです it's expected that Sentence	17	2
+	バス	バス	N	bus; Scene 7-1 バスがある there's a bus; 15-2 バス停 bus stop	5	4
	はずかしい	恥ずかしい	Adj	embarrassing	20	6
	はずす	外す (-U; 外した)	V	take off, remove, unfasten	19	3
+	パソコン	パソコン	N	personal computer, laptop	3	6
	パターン	パターン	N	(behavioral) pattern	16	4
	はたち	二十歳(はたち)	classifier	20 years old	7	2
	はたらく	働く (-U; 働いた)	V	work	11	6
	はち	八・8	Numbers	eight	3	2
+	はつ	TIME/PLACE 発	Sp. Exp.	departure TIME/PLACE	15	2
+	ばつ	ばつ	N	x-mark, wrong	21	4
	はつおん	発音	N	pronunciation	9	6
	はつか	２０日	N	the 20th day of the month	4	4
	はっきり	はっきり(と)	N	clear(ly), definite(ly)	15	6
+	はっしん	発信(する)	N	signal transmission, an outgoing call/signal	17	8R
+	はっそう	発送(する)	N	shipping; sending	15	8R
	バッチリ	バッチリ	Sp. Exp.	perfectly, properly, sure thing (informal)	8	1

	はってん	(ご)発展(する)	N	development	24	2
+	はってん	(ご)発展(する)	N	development	24	2
	はっとりスーパー	服部スーパー	N	Hattori Supermarket	7	6
+	はっぱ	葉(っぱ)	N	leaf	23	7R
+	はっぴょう	発表	N	presentation	5	5
+	はな	鼻	N	nose	11	5
+	はな	花	N	flower	14	0
	ぱなし	Verb stem + っぱなし	Sp. Exp.	keep X-ing, leave X in that (usually bad) condition	18	2
+	はなす	話す (-U; 話した)	V	talk; Scene 6-5 (お)話 talk お話しする↓talk(humble); Scene 16-5話し合う (-U; 話し合った) discuss (お)話し合い discussion; Scene 17-5 話し合っているうちに while we were brainstorming	3	4
+	はなす	離す (-U; 離した)	V	divide X, separate, put distance between two things	19	1
	はなみず	鼻水	N	runny nose 鼻水が出る have/get a runny nose	13	5
	はなれる	離れる (-RU; 離れた)	V	be away, separate; X から/と離れる be away, separate from X	12	2
	はは	母↓	N	mother (humble); Scene 8-5 母親 mother	7	2
	ハヤ！	ハヤ！	Sp. Exp.	Already? So fast? (informal)	9	6
	はやい	早い	Adj	early; Scene 12-4 早く	3	4
	はやい	速い	Adj	speedy	9	6
	はやおき	早起き	N	get up early	21	3
	はやおきはさんもんのとく	早起きは三文の徳	Kotowaza	The early bird catches the worm.	21	0
	はやし	林	N	[family name]; Scene 23-1 woods	3	9R
	はやす	生やす (-U; 生やした)	V	grow (a beard); ひげを生やす grow a beard	12	5
	はやね	早寝	N	go to bed early; 早寝早起き Early to bed and early to rise.	21	3
	はやめ	早目	Sp. Exp.	on the early side	13	4

	はやる	流行る (-U; 流行った)	V	become popular; become prevalent	13	5
+	はらう	払う (-U; 払った)	V	pay; 23-5 払わせられるくらいなら if one is to be made to pay	17	2
+	はらはら	はらはら	N	heart beating rapidly	20	4
+	バラバラ	バラバラ	Sp. Exp.	separately, scattered, in drops	16	2
+	はる	春	N	spring	8	6
	はれる	晴れる (-RU; 晴れた)	V	clear up (of weather); Scene 18-1 晴れ時々曇り clear, sometimes cloudy; 晴れたり曇ったり clearing up and clouding up	8	2
+	パワハラ	パワハラ	N	harassment of underlings (those over whom one has power)	21	1
+	ばん	晩	N	evening; Scene 2-3 晩ごはん dinner	3	4
	ばん	〜番	Classifier	classifier for naming a numbers (in a series)	4	4
+	パン	パン	N	bread	14	3
	ばんきょうしつ	〜番教室	Classifier	classifier for naming a classroom number	4	5
	ばんごう	番号	N	number	6	4
+	はんせい	反省(する)	N	reflection, introspection	16	1
	はんそで	半袖	N	short sleeves	11	3
+	はんたい	反対(する)	N	opposite, oppose; Scene 14-3 反対側 opposite side	17	5
+	パンツ	パンツ	N	slacks, pants	11	2
	はんぶん	半分	N	half (of something)	9	2
	ひ	火	N	fire	14	4
+	ビール	ビール	N	beer	2	3
	ひあたり	日当たり	N	sunlight, sunny place	23	4
+	ひえる	冷える (-RU; 冷えた)	V	X cools down, chills	14	4
+	ひかえる	控える (-RU; 控えた)	V	hold back; Scene 21-2 refrain; Scene 23-7R 控えめ(な) modest, reserved	17	6
+	ひがし	東	N	east; Scene 24-5 東海岸 east coast	15	2

+	ひき	〜匹	Classifier	classifier for counting small animals	12	3
+	ひきうける	引き受ける (-RU; 引き受けた)	V	take on, undertake	19	3
+	ひきおこす	引き起こす (-U; 引き起こした)	V	trigger X	20	7R
+	ひきざん	引き算	N	subtraction	20	7R
+	ひきだす	引き出す (-U; 引き出した)	V	draw; Scene 14-1 引き出し drawer	20	7R
	ひく	弾く (-U; 弾いた)	V	play (a stringed instrument)	9	5
	ひく	引く (-U; 引いた)	V	pull, subtract; Scene 14-3 油を引く coat the surface with oil; Scene 20-1 catch (a cold)	14	3
	ひくい	低い	Adj	low; Scene 6-3 (背が)低い short (in stature)	10	6
	ひげ	ひげ	N	beard; ひげを生やす grow a beard	12	5
+	ひこうき	飛行機	N	airplane	15	3
	ひごろ	日頃	N	normal, daily	14	6
+	ひざし	日差し	N	sunlight	18	1
	ひさしぶり	久しぶり	N	a while (since the last time); 久しぶりに for the first time in a while	10	1
+	ひしょ	秘書	N	secretary; 秘書室 secretary's office	22	5
+	ひじょう	非常(に)	N	extraordinary; emergency	22	4
	ビショビショ	ビショビショ	N	soaked, drenched	18	1
+	ひだり	左	N	left; Scene 14-3 左側 left side	6	2
	ひっくりかえす	ひっくり返す (-U; ひっくり返した)	V	turn X over; flip over	16	2
	びっくりする	Xに・Adjective-くてびっくりする (IRR)	V	be surprised (at X)	7	1
+	ひづけ	日付	N	date	16	7R

	ひっこす	引っ越す (-U; 引っ越した)	V	move (houses), change residence; 引っ越し(する) move (residence)	23	5
	ピッタリ	ピッタリ・ピッタシ	N	perfectly, exactly	11	4
	ヒット	ヒット	N	hit; Scene 17-4 ヒット数 number of hits	23	2
+	ひっぱる	引っ張る (-U; 引っ張った)	V	drag, pull	23	2
	ひつよう	(ご)必要	N	necessary; 必要でしたら if (it's) needed; Scene 13-2 必要ない unnecessary	11	1
	ひと	人(ひと)	N	person; Scene 17-5 人によって depending on the person; Scene 24-2 人々 people, persons	6	3
+	ひどい	ひどい	Adj	cruel, harsh, severe	9	6
	ひとこと	ひとこと	N	something (to say)	6	1
	ひとやすみ	一休み(する)	N	breather, short rest	13	1
+	ひとり	(お)1人	N	one (person); alone; single; Scene 6-2 1人ずつ one (person) at a time; 1人ずつ言ってください。Please say it one at a time. Scene 8-1 1人で by oneself, alone (lit. 'as one person'); Scene 12-5 一人っ子 only child	12	5
+	ひはん	批判(する)	N	criticism	19	2
	ひび	日々	N	days	24	2
+	ひま	暇(な)	N	free (time)	8	6
	ひゃく	百 (１００～９００)	Numbers	hundreds (100 through 900)	3	5
	ひやく	飛躍(する)	N	great progress, great strides, leap	24	2
	ひゃくぶんはいっけんにしかず	百聞は一見にしかず	Kotowaza	Seeing is believing.	15	0
+	ひやす	冷やす (-U; 冷やした)	V	cool, chill X	14	3
+	びょういん	病院	N	hospital	5	4
+	ひょうか	評価(する)	N	assessment, evaluation	19	2

+	びょうき	病気	N	sick	3	2
+	ひょうげん	表現	N	(linguistic) expression	17	5
+	ひらい	平井	N	[family name]	21	7R
	ひらがな	平仮名・ひらがな	N	hiragana syllabary	1	BTL 1
+	ひらく	開く (-U; 開いた)	V	(someone) opens X	14	7R
+	ヒリヒリ	ヒリヒリ(する・痛む)	N	tender (as a rash); Scene 20-4 stinging, prickling (pain)	11	5
	ひる	(お)昼	N	noon, lunch time; lunch; Scene 2-3 (お)昼ごはん lunch; Scene 12-9R 昼休み lunch break; Scene 13-1 (お)昼寝(する)nap	9	2
+	ビル	ビル	N	building	19	6
+	ひろあき	広明	N	[male given name]	16	9R
	ひろい	広い	Adj	spacious, wide	7	1
	ひろう	拾う (-U; 拾った)	V	pick up, gather	23	2
+	ひろげる	広げる (-RU; 広げた)	V	spread, expand X	16	6
+	びん	便	N	flight	15	3
+	ピンク	ピンク	N	pink	6	3
	ピンピン	ピンピン	N	healthy, lively	20	4
+	プール	プール	N	pool	7	2
	ふぁあ	ふぁあ	Sp. Exp.	[onomatopoeia for sound of a yawn]	13	1
	ファイル	ファイル(する)	N	file	13	6
+	ふあん	不安	N	uneasy, suspicious	14	6
	ふう	風	N	manner, style, way	18	5
	ふうん	ふうん	Sp. Exp.	hmm	4	2
+	ふえて	不得手(な)	N	weak point, weakness	21	5
+	ふえる	増える (-RU; 増えた)	V	X increases	15	5
	フォーマル	フォーマル(な)	N	formal	11	2

	フォント	フォント	N	font	4	5
+	ふか	不可	N	not acceptable	23	8R
+	ぶか	部下	N	subordinate (at work)	18	6
+	ふかのう	不可能(な)	N	impossibility; 可能(な) possibility	21	5
	ふく	服	N	clothing, outfit	11	2
+	ふく	拭く (-U; 拭いた)	V	wipe, dry X	14	4
+	ふくおか	福岡	N	Fukuoka	9	4
+	ふくざつ	複雑(な)	N	complicated	15	4
	ふくざわだいがく	福沢大学	N	Fukuzawa University	3	1
+	ふくしゅう	復習(する)	N	review	5	6
	ふくつう	腹痛	N	stomachache 腹痛がする have/get a stomachache	13	5
	ふくろ	袋	N	bag	9	1
+	ふこうへい	不公平(な)	N	partiality, unfairness; 公平(な) objectivity, fairness	21	5
+	ふざいとどけ	不在届	N	undeliverable notice	24	6R
+	ぶじ	無事(に)	N	without incidents, safety	24	3
	ふじさん	富士山	N	Mount Fuji	7	2
+	ぶしゅ	部首	N	(major) radical of a kanji	20	8R
+	ふせいかい	不正解	N	incorrect; 正解 correct (answer or solution)	21	4
+	ふそく	不足(する)	N	insufficiency; 寝不足 lack of sleep; 勉強不足 lack of study	12	4
+	ふたご	双子	N	twins	12	5
+	ぶちょう	部長	N	division chief	3	6
+	ふつう	普通	N	ordinary	15	2
+	ぶつかる	ぶつかる (-U; ぶつかった)	V	X collides, bumps into	14	6
	ぶつける	ぶつける (-RU; ぶつけた)	V	hit X, crash into; ぶつけてたかも maybe I was hitting it	14	6
+	ぶっけん	物件	N	estate, investment	23	9R

+	ぶつり(がく)	物理(学)	N	physics	4	2
+	ふとい	太い	Adj	thick, fat	14	3
+	ふとる	太る(-U; 太った)	V	gain fat, become broad (fat)	16	9R
+	ふね	船	N	boat, ship	15	3
+	ふぶき	吹雪	N	snowstorm, blizzard	18	1
+	ぶぶん	部分	N	part, section	16	5
+	ふへい	不平	N	dissatisfaction, discontent	18	2
+	ふべん	不便(な)	N	inconvenient; 便利(な) convenient	7	1
+	ふまん	不満	N	unsatisfied, not content; Scene 19-3 満足(な) satisfaction	14	6
+	ふむ	踏む (-U; 踏んだ)	V	step on, tread on	22	6
+	ふやす	増やす (-U; 増やした)	V	increase X, add to	14	2
+	ふゆ	冬	N	winter	8	6
	ブライアン・ワン	ブライアン・ワン	Name	Brian Wang; Scene 1-7 ブライアン？ (Is it/Are you) Brian?	1	1
	フライパン	フライパン	N	frying pan	14	3
+	ブラウス	ブラウス	N	blouse	11	2
+	ブラジル	ブラジル	N	Brazil	6	1
+	フラフラ	フラフラ(する)	N	dizzy; Scene 20-4 wandering	11	5
+	ぶらぶら	ぶらぶら	N	swinging, rambling, leisurely	20	4
+	フランスご	フランス語	N	French (language); フランス人 French (person)	3	1
	ぶり	DURATION ぶり	Sp. Exp.	after (a period of time); Scene 10-1 久しぶり a while (since the last time); 久しぶりに for the first time in a while	24	1
+	フリーター	フリーター	N	non-permanent worker	9	3
+	フリーランス	フリーランス	N	freelance, freelancer	9	3
	ふりかえる	振り返る (-U; 振り返った)	V	look back, reflect, reminisce; 振り返り reflection, reminiscence	24	4
	ふりがな	振り仮名	N	phonetic guide to reading	1	BTL 4

	ふる	降る (-U; 降った)	V	precipitate, fall (i.e., rain); Scene 18-1 降られる (-RU; 降られた) get rained on; 降りだしたなんてもんじゃない it's not just that it started raining	7	5
	ふる	振る (-U; 振った)	V	sprinkle, shake, swing; Scene 18-5 (Xに)振る wave, pass along to X, shake (out, as salt)	14	3
+	ふるい	古い	Adj	old	4	1
+	ふるさと	ふるさと	N	hometown	23	4
+	ふるた	古田	N	[family name]	13	8R
	プレゼン	プレゼン	N	presentation	5	5
	ふろ	(お)風呂	N	bath	9	5
	フロア	フロア	N	floor	14	2
+	プログラム	プログラム	N	program, computer program, software	13	2
	プロジェクト	プロジェクト	N	project	22	6
	ふん	～分 (ふん・ぷん)	Classifier	classifier for naming and counting minutes; Scene 6-2 ～分間 classifier for counting minutes	3	4
+	ぶん	分	N	portion	9	8R
+	ふんがい	憤慨(する)	N	indignation	21	5
+	ぶんがく	文学	N	literature; Scene 6-1 文学部 faculty of arts and humanities; Scene 11-4 文学的(な) literary	4	2
+	ぶんかのひ	文化の日	N	Culture Day (BTS 18)	4	4
+	ぶんけい	文系	N	literature type	18	8R
+	ぶんしょ	文書	N	document	13	2
+	ぶんせき	分析(する)	N	analysis	9	3
+	ぶんべつ	分別(する)	N	separate	22	8R
+	ぶんぽう	文法	N	grammar	5	6
+	ぶんぼうぐ	文房具	N	stationery	12	1
+	へ	～へ	Particle	to, towards X	5	4
	ページ	～ページ	Classifier	pages	5	2
+	ヘアスタイル	ヘアスタイル	N	hairstyle	11	4

+	へいき	平気	N	calm, unconcerned, all right	2	1
	へいきん	平均	N	average	10	6
+	べいこく	米国	N	U.S.A.	14	7R
+	へいじつ	平日	N	weekday	21	7R
+	へいせい	平成	N	Heisei era (1989–2019)	4	4
+	へいわ	平和(な)	N	peace, peaceful	21	7R
	へえ	へえ	Sp. Exp.	oh, yes? really?	3	5
	べき	べき	N	should, must, ought	16	1
+	ぺけ	ぺけ	N	x-mark, wrong	21	4
+	ぺこぺこ	ぺこぺこ	N	famished, hungry	20	4
	へた	下手	N	unskillful, bad at	6	1
+	べつ	別	N	different, separate, distinct; Scene 2-8 別に (not) particularly	6	6
+	ペット	ペット	N	pet	12	3
+	ベトナムご	ベトナム語	N	Vietnamese (language)	8	8R
	へや	部屋	N	room	4	5
+	へらす	減らす (-U; 減らした)	V	decrease X	14	2
+	ぺらぺら	ぺらぺら	N	fluent, frivolous	20	4
+	ベランダ	ベランダ	N	veranda	23	1
+	へる	減る (-U; 減った)	V	X decreases	15	5
+	へん	辺	N	area, vicinity; この・その・あの辺 this/that/that area	7	6
	へん	変(な)	N	weird, odd, strange	7	6
+	ペン	ペン	N	pen	3	3
+	へんかん	変換(する)	N	change, conversion	15	4
+	べんきょう	勉強(する)	N	study; Scene 10-6 勉強の仕方 way of studying; Scene 12-4 勉強不足 lack of study; Scene 16-3 勉強になる learn from, take a lesson from	2	2
+	へんこう	変更(する)	N	modification, alteration	15	4
+	べんごし	弁護士	N	lawyer, attorney	9	3

	へんじ	返事(する)	N	answer, reply	19	3
+	へんしゅう	編集(する)	N	edit	15	4
+	へんそう	(ご)返送(する)	N	return, sending back	19	8R
	べんたつ	(ご)鞭撻	N	encouragement	24	5
+	べんとう	(お)弁当	N	meal in a box	2	3
+	べんぴ	便秘	N	constipation; 便秘気味 get constipated	13	5
	べんり	便利(な)	N	convenient; 不便(な) inconvenient	7	1
+	ぽ	〜歩	N	classifier for counting steps	20	2
+	ホーム	ホーム	N	platform	19	1
	ホームステイ	ホームステイ	N	homestay	6	1
+	ホームラン	ホームラン	N	home run	23	2
	ぽい	〜っぽい	Adj	-ish, -like; 熱っぽい feverish	20	1
+	ポイすて	ポイ捨て	N	littering	23	7R
	ほう	方	N	way, alternative (of two)	6	3
	ぼうえき	貿易	N	trade	24	3
+	ほうげん	方言	N	dialect	13	7R
+	ほうこう	方向	N	direction, district	19	1
+	ほうこく	(ご)報告(する)	N	report; Scene 6-6 X に報告する make a report to X; Scene 13-3 報告書 (written) report	6	5
+	ぼうし	帽子	N	hat	11	4
	ぼうせん	棒線	N	long vowel symbol	5	BTL2
+	ほうめん	PLACE/DESTINATION 方面	Sp. Exp.	in the direction of PLACE/DESTINATION	15	2
+	ほうもん	(ご)訪問(する)	N	visit, call on	18	4
+	ほうりつ	法律	N	law	9	3
	ほか	他・外	N	other, else, besides; Scene 7-5 ほかに in addition, besides	6	6
	ぼく	僕	N	I (masculine); 僕、一郎。I'm Ichiro. (casual)	1	7
	ほけんしつ	保健室	N	infirmary, clinic	11	5

	ほしい	欲しい (欲しくて)	Adj	want; Scene 12-5 〜て ほしい・欲しい want (someone) to X	8	1
+	ほす	干す (-U; 干した)	V	air out, dry	23	1
+	ポスター	ポスター	N	poster	4	1
	ほそい	細い	Adj	thin, slender	14	3
+	ほそかわ	細川	N	[family name]	16	9R
+	ほぞん	保存(する)	N	preserve, store, save	13	2
	ボタン	ボタン	N	button	14	6
+	ほっかいどう	北海道	N	Hokkaido	9	4
	ぼっちゃん	『坊ちゃん』	N	*Botchan* (novel by Natsume Soseki)	9	4
	ホッとする	ホッとする	Sp. Exp.	feel relieved	19	6
+	ホテル	ホテル	N	hotel	4	4
	ほど	ほど	Particle	as much as (particle for comparison); カレーほどすごくない not as awesome as curry; Scene 4-1 それほど that much; to that extent; Scene 10-6 思ったほど more (less) than I thought	6	6
	ほど	[quantity] + ほど	Particle	about, as many as; Scene 20-5 やればやるほど the more I do it, the more . . .	19	6
	ほとんど	ほとんど	N	almost; barely (plus negative)	4	6
+	ほね	骨	N	bone	20	4
+	ほめる	褒める (-RU; 褒めた)	V	praise	18	2
	ボランティア	ボランティア(する)	N	volunteer	13	6
	ボリューム	ボリューム	N	volume	17	6
+	ボロボロ	ボロボロ	Sp. Exp.	worn out, tattered, scruffy (onomatopoeia)	13	1
+	ほん	本	N	book; 0-0 (Inst. Exp.) 本を見ないでください。 Please don't look at the book.	3	5
+	ほん	〜本	Classifier	classifier for counting long objects	3	5
+	ほんじつ	本日	N	today (formal); also in Scene 24-2	8	7R

349

+	ほんしゅう	本州	N	Honshu	9	4
+	ほんだ	本田	N	[family name]	10	8R
+	ほんだな	本棚	N	book shelf	14	1
	ほんとう	本当	N	True; Scene 7-6 ほんと short, informal form of ほんとう; Scene 10-5 本当に really, truly	4	3
	ほんにん	本人	N	the person in question, said person	20	6
+	ほんや	本屋	N	bookstore	5	4
+	ほんやく	翻訳(する)	N	translation	10	5
+	マーケティング	マーケティング	N	marketing	6	2
	まあ	ま(あ)	Sp. Exp.	I guess [non-committal opinion]	3	1
	まあ！	まあ！	Sp. Exp.	oh!	8	4
	まあまあ	まあまあ	Sp. Exp.	so-so	4	1
+	まい	毎 TIME	N	every TIME; 毎朝 every morning; 毎回 every time; 毎学期 every academic term, semester; 毎時間 every hour; 毎週 every week; 毎月 every month; 毎年 every year; 毎日 every day; 毎晩 every evening	8	1
+	まい	〜枚	Classifier	classifier for counting thin, flat things	3	5
	まいる	参る↓ (-U; 参った)	V	go, come (humble); Scene 18-3 give up	5	5
	マイル	〜マイル	Classifier	miles	14	5
+	まえ	前	N	before [time]; Scene 6-3 front; Scene 14-3 水を入れる前(に) before putting water in; Scene 16-1 前もって in advance, beforehand	3	2
+	まえだ	前田	N	[family name]	10	8R
	まかせる	任せる (-RU; 任せた)	V	leave it to someone else, let someone else do it; 任せてください。 Leave it to me. Let someone do it.	5	3
	まがる	曲がる (-U; 曲がった)	N	turn, make a turn	7	6
+	まける	負ける (-RU; 負けた)	V	lose (a game or competition)	14	5

+	まげる	曲げる (-RU; 曲げた)	V	bend X	14	6
	まさか	まさか	Sp. Exp.	no way, never (interjection)	7	6
+	まざる・まじる	混ざる・混じる (-U; 混ざった・混じった)	V	X mixes, blends	14	4
	まじ	まじ	N	really, truly, honestly (very informal)	9	6
+	まじめ	真面目(な)	N	diligent, serious; 真面目そう(な) looks diligent, serious	8	5
	まず	まず	Sp. Exp.	first of all, to start with	15	4
+	まずい	まずい	Adj	awkward, unappetizing, unpleasant	9	5
	ますます	ますます	Sp. Exp.	more and more, less and less	9	4
	まぜる	混ぜる (-RU; 混ぜた)	V	mix, stir X; 混ぜて(い)る間(に) while mixing it in	14	3
	また	また	Sp. Exp.	again; Scene 3-4 またあとで again later	1	9
	まだ	まだ	Sp. Exp.	still, yet	6	1
	またせる	待たせる (-RU; 待たせた)	V	make someone wait; Scene 6-6 お待たせしました。 Sorry to make you wait.; Scene 10-3 お待たせする ↓make someone wait; お待たせいたしました↓。 Sorry to make you wait. (humble)	10	3
	または	X または Y	Sp. Exp.	X or Y	24	4
+	マタハラ	マタハラ	N	harassment of pregnant women (*mata* from "maternity")	21	1
+	まち	町	N	town	24	2
+	まちがう	間違う (-U; 間違った)	V	make a mistake; 間違い mistake, blunder	21	4
	まちがえる	間違える (-RU; 間違えた)	V	mistake X, make a mistake or error (on something)	10	4
+	まつ	待つ (-U; 待った)	V	wait; Scene 10-3 お待ちください。 Please wait.	3	2
	まつ	～末	Sp. Exp.	the end of	24	3
+	まっか	真っ赤(な)	N	bright red (as in flushed face)	17	8R

#	まっくら	真っ暗	N	pitch dark, bleak future	17	8R
+	まっくろ	真っ黒(な)	N	pitch black	17	8R
+	まっさお	真っ青(な)	N	deep/bright blue; pale	17	8R
+	まっさき	真っ先	N	the very first, the foremost	17	8R
+	まっしろ	真っ白(な)	N	pure white; complete blank	17	8R
	まっすぐ	まっすぐ	N	straight	7	6
	まったく	まったく	Sp. Exp.	good grief (expression of exasperation); Scene 19-2 completely, entirely	9	1
	まつもと	松本	N	[family name]	3	9R
	まつやま	松山	N	Matsuyama (a city in Ehime Prefecture)	9	4
	まで	〜まで	Particle	up to, until; Scene 5-5 TIME 〜までに by TIME X; Scene 14-3 焼けるまで until it browns	4	4
+	まど	窓	N	window; Scene 19-1 窓口 ticket window	6	3
	まとまる	まとまる (-U; まとまった)	V	get put into order, get collected	17	5
	まとめる	まとめる (-RU; まとめた)	V	put into order, summarize	17	5
	まなぶ	学ぶ(U; 学んだ)	V	learn	24	3
	まにあう	X に間に合う	Sp. Exp.	be on time for X	15	5
+	マネージャー	マネージャー	N	manager	6	2
	まま	まま	N	as is, condition	12	5
+	まもる	守る(守った)	V	guard, watch over	19	3
	まよう	迷う (-U; 迷った)	V	become confused, lost	6	6
	マヨネーズ	マヨネーズ	N	mayonnaise	14	4
+	マラソン	マラソン	N	marathon	7	2
	まる	丸(。)	N	circle, period; Scene 21-4 丸・まる circle (used to indicate an item is correct); Noun に丸(を)つける put a circle around Noun; ○○・マルマル [placeholder when content is unclear], certain, unnamed	2	BTL 2

	まるで	まるで	Sp. Exp.	just like, as though	18	6
+	まわす	回す (-U; 回した)	V	turn, circulate X	14	3
+	まわる	回る (-U; 回った)	V	X turns, revolves, visit several places (intrans.)	14	4
	まん	万	Numbers	10,000s; 何万 how many ten thousands	4	1
+	まんが	漫画・マンガ	N	comics, manga; Scene 21-1 マンガチック manga-tic, cartoonish	12	1
+	マンション	マンション	N	condominium	7	6
+	まんぞく	満足(な)・(する)	N	satisfaction; Scene 14-6 不満 unsatisfied, not content	19	3
+	まんてん	満点	N	full score	21	4
+	まんなか	真ん中	N	middle, center	6	3
+	ミーティング	ミーティング	N	meeting	2	2
	ミールプラン	ミールプラン	N	meal plan	14	2
+	みえる	見える (-RU; 見えた)	V	appear, be visible	6	3
+	みおくる	見送る (-U; 見送った)	V	send (someone) off	15	8R
+	みがく	磨く (-U; 磨いた)	V	polish	24	5
	みぎ	右	N	right; 右からでいい from the right is good; Scene 6-3 右、じゃなく左 right, I mean left; Scene 14-3 右側 right side	6	2
	みじかい	短い	Adj	short	5	5
+	みず	(お)水	N	water; Scene 14-3 水を入れる前(に) before putting water in	2	3
	ミズーリ	ミズーリ	N	Missouri	8	4
+	みずうみ	湖	N	lake	23	1
+	みずた	水田	N	[family name]	10	8R
+	ミステリー	ミステリー	N	mystery	19	2
+	みせ	店	N	store, shop	6	2

+	みせる	見せる (-RU; 見せた)	V	show; Scene 15-4 見せてもらえますか? Can I have you show it?; Scene 16-5 見せ合う (-U; 見せ合った) show one another	5	5
	みたい	みたい(な)	N	similar to, resembling, like; Sentence + みたい it seems that	16	3
	みち	道	N	street	7	6
+	みつかる	見つかる (-U; 見つかった)	V	X is found	22	5
+	みつける	見つける (-RU; 見つけた)	V	find X	22	5
	みどり	緑・みどり	N	green; Scene 4-4 BTS 18 緑の日 Green Day; Scene 14-9R 緑色 green color; Scene 19-1 みどりの窓口 JR ticket office (lit. 'green window')	6	3
	みなさま	皆様・みなさま	N	everyone	24	2
	みなさん	みなさん	N	everyone (out-group)	3	7R
+	みなみ	南	N	south; Scene 15-9R 南口 south exit/entrance	15	2
+	みみ	耳	N	ear; Scene 20-8R 耳が遠い poor hearing	11	5
+	みる	見る (-RU; 見た)	V	look, watch; Scene 2-1 (Inst. Exp.) 見てください。 Please look at it.; Scene 13-3 見に来られる come to see (honorific); Scene 10-6 夢を見る have (see) a dream	3	4
+	みる	診る (-RU; 診た)	V	look over, assess	20	3
+	ミルク	ミルク	N	milk	2	3
+	みんしゅく	民宿	N	guesthouse	15	2
+	みんな	みんな	N	everyone, all; みんなで all together; 0-0 (Inst. Exp.) みんなで言ってください。 Please say it all together.	3	4
+	むかう	向かう (-U; 向かった)	V	head towards	23	2
	むかえる	迎える (-RU; 迎えた)	V	go to meet; welcome; 迎え greeting, welcome	12	4

	むかし	昔	N	long ago	21	3
+	ムカムカ	ムカムカ(する)	N	nauseated; queasy	11	5
+	むく	向く (-U; 向いた)	V	turn toward, suitable for; Xに向く turn toward X, suitable for X; X向き facing X, suitable for X	23	4
+	むけ	X 向け	N	intended for X	23	9R
+	むこう	向こう	N	opposite side, other side, over there; Scene 14-3 向こう側 that side, other side	6	2
+	むしあつい	蒸し暑い	Adj	hot and humid	18	1
	むしろ	むしろ	Sp. Exp.	rather, on the contrary	22	2
+	むずかしい	難しい	Adj	hard, difficult; Scene 5-6 難しくなりました。 It became difficult.	2	7
+	むすこ	息子↓	N	son (humble); 息子さん son	7	2
+	むすめ	娘↓	N	daughter (humble); 娘さん daughter	7	2
	むだ	無駄(な)	N	waste, futility	19	6
+	むね	胸	N	chest	11	5
+	むら	村	N	village	24	2
+	むらかみ	村上	N	[family name]	9	9R
+	むらさき	紫	N	purple	6	3
+	むらた	村田	N	[family name]	10	8R
	むり	無理(な)	N	impossible, unreasonable; Scene 11-5 無理する try/work too hard, overdo	9	5
+	むりょう	無料	N	free of charge	23	8R
	め	〜目	Classifier	classifier for naming numbers in a series	5	6
+	め	目	N	eye; Scene 16-7R 目が覚める (-RU; 覚めた) become awake; 目を覚ます (-U: 覚ました) someone wakes up	11	5
	め	Adjective + 目	Sp. Exp.	-sh, on the X side; 早目 on the early side	13	4
+	メートル	〜メートル	Classifier	meters	14	5
+	メール	メール	N	email	6	4
	めい	〜名	Classifier	classifier for counting people (formal)	10	3

355

	めいさま	～名様	Classifier	classifier for counting people (polite)	10	3
	めいし	名刺	N	business card	6	4
+	めいじ	明治	N	Meiji era (1868–1912)	4	4
	めいわく	(ご)迷惑(な)・(する)	N	trouble, bother; (ご)迷惑になる become an annoyance; (ご)迷惑をかける cause someone trouble	7	4
+	めうえ	目上	N	superior, senior, elder	9	8R
+	メガネ	メガネ	N	eyeglasses	11	4
+	メキシコ	メキシコ	N	Mexico	6	1
+	めざす	目指す (-U; 目指した)	V	look for, search	23	4
	めざまし(どけい)	目覚まし(時計)	N	alarm (clock)	8	1
	めしあがる	召し上がる↑ (-U; 召し上がった)	V	eat (honorific)	13	1
+	めした	目下	N	subordinate, junior, younger	9	8R
	めずらしい	珍しい	Adj	unusual, rare	7	3
	メチャ	メチャ	Sp. Exp.	absurd, really, extreme (slang)	9	6
	めちゃくちゃ	めちゃくちゃ	Sp. Exp.	disorder, confusion, extreme	13	1
+	メチャメチャ	メチャメチャ	Sp. Exp.	messy, absurd	16	2
	メニュー	メニュー	N	menu	10	3
	めはくちほどにものをいい	目は口ほどに物を言い	Kotowaza	Eyes say as much as words.; also in Scene 20-2	11	0
+	めん	麺	N	noodles	10	3
	めんせつ	面接(する)	N	interview (for a job); 面接に着る wear to an interview	11	2
+	めんどう	面倒(な)	N	trouble(some), care, attention; 面倒そう(な) looks troublesome; めんどくさい bothersome, tiresome; Scene 24-1 面倒(を)かける trouble someone; 面倒(を)見る take care of someone	8	5
	メンバー	メンバー	N	member	6	1
	も	～も	Particle	[also, too]	3	6

	もう	もう	Sp. Exp.	already; Scene 8-2 Really!	6	1
	もう	もう QUANTITY	Sp. Exp.	further, additionally; もう1枚 one more sheet; もうちょっと a little more; 0-0 (Inst. Exp.) もう1回言ってください。 Please say it again.; Scene 2-0 (Inst. Exp.) PERSON にもう1度聞いてください。 Please ask PERSON again.	6	3
+	もうしあげる	申し上げる (-RU; 申し上げた)	V	say, tell	11	1
	もうしつたえる	申し伝える (-RU; 申し伝えた)	V	convey a message	11	1
	もうしわけない	申し訳ない	Sp. Exp.	I'm very sorry (informal); Scene 5-3 申し訳 ありません・ないです。 I'm sorry.; 申し訳 ありませんでした・なかったです。 I'm sorry (for what happened).; Scene 6-4 申し訳ございません↓。 I am terribly sorry. (lit. 'I have no excuse,' humble)	12	4
+	もうす	申す↓ (-U; 申した)	V	say (humble)	6	2
+	もえる	燃える (-RU; 燃えた)	V	burn; 燃えるゴミ burnable garbage	23	1
+	もくてき	目的	N	purpose	19	9R
+	もくよう(び)	木曜(日)	N	Thursday	4	6
	もし	もし	Sp. Exp.	if, supposing	11	1
+	もじ	文字	N	letter, symbol	18	8R
	もしかしたら	もしかしたら	Sp. Exp.	by some chance; maybe; also もしかすると; Scene 19-4 もしかして maybe, by some chance	12	6
	もちろん	もちろん	Sp. Exp.	of course	5	1
	もつ	持つ (-U; 持った)	V	hold, have, carry; 持っていく take (a thing); 持ってくる bring (a thing); 持ってきていただけますか？ Can I have you bring it?; Scene 14-8R 持ち物 things to bring	5	3

357

+	もったいない	もったいない	Adj	wasteful, too good to waste	17	6
	もっと	もっと	Sp. Exp.	more; 0-0 (Inst. Exp.) もっと大きな声で話してください。 Please talk louder.	6	3
+	もどす	戻す (-U; 戻した)	V	return, put X back	14	3
	もとより	X はもとより、Y	Sp. Exp.	of course X, but also Y (BTS)	24	2
+	もどる	戻る (-U; 戻った)	V	go back	7	6
	もの	もの	N	thing (tangible)	6	6
	もの	者	N	person, someone	17	3
	もらう	もらう (-U; もらった)	V	get, receive; Scene 12-2 もらっちゃって take, get; Scene 15-4 見せてもらえますか？ Can I have you show it?; Scene 17-4 X させて いただく・もらう・ください let me X	11	5
+	もり	森	N	forest	23	1
+	もりあわせ	盛り合わせ	N	assortment, combination platter	17	6
+	モリス	モリス	Name	Morris [family name]	1	1
+	もんく	文句	N	troubles, grumbling; 文句言う complain	18	2
+	もんだい	問題	N	problem	10	6
	モンペア	モンペア	N	from モンスターペアレント monster parent	21	5
	や	〜や	Particle	things like	17	7R
+	やかましい	やかましい	Adj	noisy, boisterous, annoying	8	5
	やぎ	八木	N	[family name] (Ms. Yagi is Sasha's supervisor)	1	11
+	やきとり	焼き鳥	N	yakitori	2	3
+	やきにく	焼肉	N	yakiniku (grilled meat)	10	3
	やきゅう	野球	N	baseball	10	1
	やく	焼く (-U; 焼いた)	V	fry, grill, burn X	14	3
	やく	約 + Quantity	Sp. Exp.	about, approximately	22	2

	やくいん	役員	N	executive, officer, official; Scene 22-4 役員会 officers' meeting	15	1
+	やくしゃ	役者	N	actor, actress	19	2
+	やくそく	約束	N	promise	15	6
+	やくにたつ	役に立つ	Sp. Exp.	be useful, be helpful	15	4
	やける	焼ける (-RU; 焼けた)	V	get roasted, grill, brown; 焼けるまで until it browns	14	3
+	やさい	(お)野菜	N	vegetable	10	3
+	やさしい	易しい	Adj	easy	2	7
+	やさしい	優しい	Adj	kind, nice, gentle; 優しそう(な) looks nice, looks kind	8	5
+	やすい	安い	Adj	inexpensive, cheap	2	7
	やすい	〜やすい	Adj	easy to X; 使いやすい easy to use	4	5
+	やすこ	安子	N	[given name]	12	9R
+	やすだ	安田	N	[family name]	12	9R
+	やすむ	休む (-U; 休んだ)	V	take a break, go on vacation/holiday; Scene 3-2 (お)休み day off, vacation; Scene 8-6 休みの時 during one's vacation; when one is on vacation	6	5
+	やせる	痩せる (-U; 痩せた)	V	get thin	20	4
	やちん	家賃	N	rent (charge)	23	5
	やつ	やつ	N	thing/person (informal)	14	3
	やっきょく	薬局	N	pharmacy	7	6
	やった！	やった！	Sp. Exp.	Done! I did it!	14	4
+	やっつける	やっつける (-RU; やっつけた)	V	beat (an opponent)	23	2
	やってくる	やって来る (やって来た)	V	come along	24	5
+	やっと	やっと	Sp. Exp.	narrowly, at last	19	5
	やっぱり	やっぱり・やはり	Sp. Exp.	as expected, sure enough	3	2
+	やど	宿	N	inn	17	8R

+	やとう	雇う (-U; 雇った)	V	hire, employ	23	3
	やばい	やばい	Adj	troublesome, dangerous, awesome, extreme (as an interjection, 'awful, crap, oh no')	9	5
+	やぶる	破る (-U; 破った)	V	tear, break X, beat (someone in a game)	14	6
+	やぶれる	破れる (-RU; 破れた)	V	get torn, get beaten	14	6
+	やま	山	N	mountain; also in Scene 23-1	9	9R
	やまぐち	山口	N	[family name]	3	9R
	やましたさん	山下さん	N	Mr/s. Yamashita	4	3
	やまだ	山田	N	[family name]	3	9R
+	やまなか	山中	N	[family name]	9	9R
	やまもと	山本	N	[family name]	3	9R
+	やむ	止む (-U; 止んだ)	V	X stops	19	7R
	やめる	止める・辞める・やめる (-RU; 止めた・辞めた・やめた)	V	stop, quit X	8	2
	ややこしい	ややこしい	Adj	confusing, perplexing	19	1
	やる	やる (-U; やった)	V	do (less formal than する); Scene 14-4 やった！ Done! I did it!; Scene 18-3 やるしかない have no choice but to do X; Scene 20-5 やればやるほど the more I do it, the more . . . ; Scene 22-6 やる気を出す become enthusiastic	5	2
+	やる	やる (-U; やった)	V	give	12	6
+	やわらかい	柔らかい	Adj	soft, tender, gentle, flexible	14	4
+	ゆ	(お)湯	N	hot water	14	3
+	ユーモア	ユーモア	N	humor	19	2
+	ゆうがた	夕方	N	evening	9	2
+	ゆうきゅうきゅうか	有給休暇	N	paid vacation	23	3

+	ゆうしゅう	優秀(な)	N	superiority, excellence	16	6
+	ゆうじん	友人	N	friend; also in Scene 24-5	13	8R
+	ゆうびんきょく	郵便局	N	post office	5	4
	ゆうめい	有名(な)	N	famous; Xで有名 well-known for X; Scene 18-6 有名人 celebrity, public figure	9	4
+	ゆうり	有利(な)	N	advantageous, profitable	23	7R
+	ゆき	雪	N	snow	3	6
+	ゆきこ・せつこ	雪子	N	[given name]	12	8R
	ゆずる	譲る (-U; 譲った)	V	turn over, concede	23	4
	ゆっくり	(ご)ゆっくり	N	slow, relaxed; ゆっくりする relax, take it easy	8	3
+	ユニットバス	ユニットバス	N	modular bath	14	2
+	ゆび	指	N	finger	11	5
+	ゆびわ	指輪	N	ring	11	2
	ゆめ	夢	N	dream; 夢を見る have (see) a dream	10	6
+	ゆるい	緩い	Adj	loose, lax	23	1
+	ゆるす	許す (-U; 許した)	V	forgive, allow	18	6
	よ	〜よ	S. Particle	[sentence particle indicating certainty]	2	2
+	ヨーロッパ	ヨーロッパ	N	Europe	8	4
	よう	よう	N	like, similar to; Scene 14-2 料理するようにして(い)る make sure to cook; Scene 15-4 使えるようになる become able to use; Scene 16-5 どのように in what way; Scene 16-6 高すぎるように思います。 I think it's too expensive.	14	2
+	よう	要 X	N	X needed	19	7R
+	よう	X 用	N	for the purpose of X	22	7R
	よう(び)	〜曜(日)	Classifier	days of the week	4	6

+	ようい	用意(する)	N	preparation; also in Scene 24-2	22	7R
+	よういち	洋一	N	[male given name]	14	9R
+	ようがある	用がある	Sp. Exp.	have something to do	22	7R
+	ようがく	洋楽	N	Western music	19	8R
+	ようこ	洋子	N	[female given name]	14	9R
	ようこそ	ようこそ	Sp. Exp.	welcome (greeting)	8	3
+	ようじ	用事	N	something to do, errand	22	7R
	ようす	様子	N	situation, circumstances	19	3
+	ようた	洋太	N	[male given name]	16	9R
+	ようふく	洋服	N	Western clothes, clothes	18	7R
+	ようへい	洋平	N	[male first name]	21	7R
	よかったら	よかったら	Sp. Exp.	if it's all right	2	3
	よこ	横	N	side, horizontal; 横になる lie down	11	5
	よこがき	横書き	N	horizontal writing	1	BTL 3
+	よごす	汚す (-U; 汚した)	V	get something dirty, pollute	22	1
+	よごれる	汚れる (-RU; 汚れた)	V	become dirty	22	1
	よさん	予算	N	estimate, budget	20	1
	よしだ	吉田	N	[family name]	3	9R
	よしだうんそう	吉田運送	N	Yoshida Transport	6	4
+	よしゅう	予習(する)	N	prepare for a lesson	5	6
	よそう	予想(する)	N	prediction, expectation; 予想外 unexpected	19	6
	よてい	(ご)予定	N	plan, schedule	15	3
+	よなか	夜中	N	in the middle of night	21	8R
	よね	〜よね	Particle	[sentence particle indicating shared certainty]	3	6
	よぶ	呼ぶ (-U; 呼んだ)	V	call, invite; Scene 1-1 BTS 2 呼び捨て calling someone without a title; Scene 16-2 呼んでくれれば行った I'd have come to help you if you'd called	5	5

+	よむ	読む (-U; 読んだ)	V	read; Scene 2-2 (Inst. Exp.) 読んでください。 Please read it.; Scene 5-6 読み reading; 読み書き reading and writing	2	3
	よやく	予約(する)	N	reservation	10	3
	より	より	Particle	compared to (particle for comparison; Scene 7-1 それより leaving that aside, apart from that, more importantly; Scene 10-6 思ったより to the extent I thought	6	6
	よる	寄る (-U; 寄った)	V	get close to, drop by, lean on; Scene 17-4 rely; X によると according to X; Scene 17-5 人によって depending on the person	6	3
+	よる	夜	N	evening; Scene 12-4 夜型 night person	9	1
	よろこぶ	喜ぶ (-U; 喜んだ)	V	be delighted, be pleased; 喜んで delighted; Scene 12-6 happily, with pleasure	5	5
+	よろしい	よろしい	Adj	good (polite); よろしく thanks; please treat me favorably; Scene 1-4 どうぞよろしく。 Nice to meet you (casual).; よろしくお願いします。よろしくお願いします。 (formal)どうぞよろしくお願いします。 Nice to meet you. (formal); Scene 2-3 よろしかったら if it's all right (polite); Scene 5-5; よろしければ if you would like, if it pleases you	2	1
	よわい	弱い	Adj	weak; Scene 16-3 弱気 timid, faint-hearted	5	6
	よわる	弱る (-U; 弱った)	V	get weak	20	4
+	ラーメン	ラーメン	N	ramen (noodles)	2	3
+	らい	来 TIME	N	next TIME; 来学期 next semester; 来月 next month; 来週 next week; 来年 next year	4	4
+	らく	楽(な)	N	easy, comfortable	7	1

	ランチ	ランチ	N	lunch, lunch special; ランチよりカレーの方がお勧め curry rather than the lunch is the recommendation	6	6
	り・にん	～人	Classifier	classifier for people	6	2
+	リーダー	リーダー	N	leader	6	2
+	りえ	理恵	N	[female given name]	19	8R
+	りかい	理解(する)	N	understanding	22	4
+	りけい	理系	N	science (type)	17	8R
+	りこん	離婚(する)	N	divorce	24	6R
+	リサイクル	リサイクル(する)	N	recycle	23	1
+	りじ	理事	N	governing board; 理事会 governing board meeting; 理事長 governing board chair	22	4
+	りすうけい	理数系	N	science and mathematics type	20	8R
	りそう	理想	N	ideal; 理想を言えば ideally speaking; 理想的(な) ideal	23	4
+	りっぱ	立派(な)	N	splendid, elegant	12	5
+	リビング	リビング	N	living room	9	5
+	リモコン	リモコン	N	remote control	14	5
	りゃくご	略語	N	contraction	21	5
+	りゆう	理由	N	reason, motive	19	4
+	りゅうがく	留学(する)	N	study abroad; 留学生 study abroad student; 留学生センター International Student Center	6	1
+	りょう	寮	N	dormitory	2	5
+	りょう	量	N	quantity, amount	16	5
+	りょう	利用(する)	N	making good use	22	7R
	りょうかい	了解(する)	N	understanding, consent, agreement	5	1
+	りょうきん	料金	N	fare	14	7R
	りょうしん	(ご)両親	N	parents	8	4
+	りょうり	(お)料理(する)	N	cooking; X 料理 X cuisine; Scene 14-2 料理するようにして(い)る make sure to cook; Scene 14-8R X 料理店 X-style cooking restaurant	9	5

	りょかん	旅館	N	Japanese-style inn	15	2
	りょこう	旅行(する)	N	travel	9	3
	リラックス	リラックス(する)	N	relax; Scene 14-6 リラックスしなくちゃ have to relax	9	4
+	ルームメート	ルームメート	N	roommate	3	6
+	るい	X類	N	X-sort of things	23	7R
	るいはともをよぶ	類は友を呼ぶ	Kotowaza	Birds of a feather flock together.; also in Scene 20-2	8	0
+	るす	留守	N	away from home or work	6	5
	ルビ	ルビ	N	phonetic guide to reading	1	BTL 4
+	れい	(お)礼	N	bow, gratitude	15	9R
+	れいがい	例外	N	exception; 例外的(な) exceptional	21	3
	れいごうごうにい、はちきゅうのななななにいれい	０５５２、８９の７７２０	Sp. Exp.	(0552) 89-7720	6	4
	れいじ	零時	Numbers	midnight (0 o'clock)	3	2
	れいの	例のX	Sp. Exp.	the X that we both know about	13	3
+	れいわ	令和	N	Reiwa era (2019–present)	4	4
	れきし	歴史	N	history; Scene 11-4 歴史的(な) historical	4	2
+	レストラン	レストラン	N	restaurant	4	4
	レセプション	レセプション	N	reception	5	5
+	レタス	レタス	N	lettuce	14	3
+	レポート	レポート	N	report	2	2
	れんしゅう	練習(する)	N	practice, rehearse; Scene 12-4 練習不足 lack of practice	5	6
	れんぞく	連続(する)	N	series, continuation; Xの連続 series of X	24	4
	れんらく	(ご)連絡(する)	N	contact, communication; Scene 6-4 連絡先 contact information; also in 16-8R	4	4
+	ローマじ	ローマ字	N	romanization	12	7R
	ろく	六・6	Numbers	six	3	2

+	ロシアご	ロシア語	N	Russian (language); ロシア人 Russian (person)	3	1
+	ロッキーさんみゃく	ロッキー山脈	N	Rocky Mountains	24	5
+	ロビー	ロビー	N	lobby	3	4
	ロマンチック	ロマンチック	N	romantic	21	1
	ろんぶん	論文	N	thesis	10	2
+	わ	～羽	Classifier	classifier for counting birds and rabbits	12	3
	わあ	わあ	Sp. Exp.	wow; Scene 12-1 わーい wow! (surprise)	2	3
+	ワイシャツ	ワイシャツ	N	dress shirt (for men)	11	2
	わかい	若い	Adj	young; Scene 17-4 若者 young people	12	5
+	わかす	沸かす (-U; 沸かした)	V	boil X	14	3
	わかる	わかる (-U; わかった)	V	understand; Scene 2-4 わかりました。 Understood. Scene 10-5 分からないこと things/matters one doesn't understand	2	1
+	わかれる	別れる (-RU; 別れた)	V	part from, separate from	14	1
	わけ	わけ・訳	N	reason, judgement based on evidence; Scene 19-2 わけでは・もない doesn't mean X; doesn't mean X either; わけ(が)わからない doesn't make sense, has no point; Scene 19-4 ～訳(が)ない there's no reason to suppose that X	19	1
	わける	分ける・別ける (-RU; 分けた・別けた)	V	divide, split X; ２つに分ける divide into two; 分けるとしたら if we . . . ; if it happens that . . .	14	1
	わざわざ	わざわざ	Sp. Exp.	specially	8	4
+	わしょく	和食	N	Japanese food	10	3
+	わすれる	忘れる (-RU; 忘れた)	V	forget; (お)忘れ物 forgotten thing; Scene 18-2 Stem + 忘れる (-RU; ～忘れた) forget to X	8	2
+	わだ	和田	N	[family name]	14	9R

	わだい	話題	N	subject, topic of conversation	8	2
+	わたし	私	N	I (gentle); Scene 11-4 私・僕的(な) like me	1	7
	わたす	渡す (-U; 渡した)	V	circulate, pass along	20	1
	わたなべ	渡辺	N	[family name]	3	9R
+	わふく	和服	N	Japanese clothes, kimono	18	7R
+	わらう	笑う (-U; 笑った)	V	laugh; Scene 21-9R 笑い声 laughter	8	2
	わり	割	Classifier	unit of 10%, ratio	15	5
	わりと	わりと	Sp. Exp.	relatively	4	5
	わる	割る (-U; 割った)	V	break, split X; Scene 14-6 divide X	14	3
+	わるい	悪い	Adj	bad; Scene 10-6 悪い夢 nightmare	7	4
+	われる	割れる (-RU; 割れた)	V	X breaks, splits	14	4
+	わん	(お)椀・碗	N	small bowl	14	4
+	ワンちゃん	ワンちゃん	N	doggy	20	6
	ワンルーム	ワンルーム	N	studio apartment	23	4

Index

academic major 4-2 BTS 6
accent アクセント Introduction
addresses 22-7 BTL 2
address terms 22-9 BTL 5
adjective 2-1 BTS 1; formal affirmative non-past 〜いです 2-1 BTS 1; formal affirmative past 〜かったです 4-1 BTS 1; formal negative non-past 〜くないです・〜くありません 2-1 BTS 1; formal negative past 〜くなかったです・〜くありませんでした 4-1 BTS 1; informal affirmative non-past 〜い 2-3 BTS 15; informal affirmative past 〜かった 4-1 BTS 1; informal negative non-past 〜くない 2-6 BTS 25; informal negative past 〜くなかった 4-1 BTS 1; 〜く＋は・もない 17-2 BTS 4; polite お〜 6-5 BTS 17; 〜さ form 〜さ 7-1 BTS 2; stem 2-1 BTS 1, 12-4 BTS 10; stem〜がる 18-4 BTS 10; stem〜くなる 5-6 BTS 14; stem 〜目 13-4 BTS 10
advice and suggestions sentence＋方がいい 13-1 BTS 4
affirmative/negative: affirmative adjective forms 〜いです、〜かったです 2-1 BTS 1, 2-3 BTS 15, 4-1 BTS 1; affirmative noun *desu* forms です、でした 2-1 BTS 1, 4-1 BTS 1, 2-5 BTS 18, 3-4 BTS 18, 4-3 BTS 14; affirmative verb forms 〜ます、〜ました 2-1 BTS 1, 4-1 BTS 1; imperative 命令形 23-1 BTS 3, 23-1 BTS 1; negative adjective forms 〜くないです・〜くありません、〜くなかったです・〜くありませんでした 2-1 BTS 1, 4-1 BTS 1, 2-6 BTS 25; negative noun *desu* forms じゃないです・じゃありません、じゃなかったです・じゃありませんでした 2-1 BTS 1, 4-1 BTS 1, 2-6 BTS 25;

negative verb forms 〜ないです・〜ません、〜なかったです・〜ませんでした 2-1 BTS 1, 4-1 BTS 1
affirming 2-1 BTS 5
agreeing and disagreeing 通り(に) 13-3 BTS 9
aida (ni) verb〜ている間(に) 14-3 BTS 10
aimai 曖昧 4-2 BTS 12
aizuchi 相槌 8-5 BTS 14
anime, watching アニメ 20-9 BTL 8
apologizing 謝罪 10-2 BTS 5
appearance 8-5 BTS 12
approximation 4-1 BTS 5, 8-6 BTS 16
apps, using アプリ 19-9 BTL 5
assumption つもり 15-5 BTS 11
ato (de) past verb＋あとで 14-4 BTS 13
-au verb stem 〜合う 17-5 BTS 9

bakari/bakkari ばかり・ばっかり: with non-past sentence 22-4 BTS 9; with noun 22-2 BTS 3; with past sentence 22-1 BTS 1; with 〜て form 〜てばかり 22-6 BTS 12
beki non-past affirmative＋べき 16-1 BTS 1
borrowed words 外来語 5-7 BTL 3
bowing お辞儀 Introduction
business cards 名刺 6-4 BTS 14
business emails 11-7 BTL 1
business phone conversations 11-1 BTS 2

calendar 4-4 BTS 18
causative 〜させる 17-3 BTS 5; ＋ verb of giving or receiving 17-4 BTS 7
causative passive 23-3 BTS 5
classifier 数詞 3-2 BTS 9; multiple in a sentence 5-3 BTS 6; naming *vs.* counting 4-6 BTS 29
clothing 衣服 11-2 BTS 4

collaborative planning 15-6 BTS 12
colors 色 6-3 BTS 11
commands: affirmative 5-1 BTS 2; negative 8-2 BTS 4
commuting 7-1 BTS 3
comparison: sentence + 方がいい 13-1 BTS 4; three or more items 〜が一番 9-4 BTS 10; two items より, ほど 6-6 BTS 24, 10-6 BTS 12
compliments 9-6 BTS 18, 11-4 BTS 8
compositions 作文 21-8 BTL 6
compounds 4-5 BTS 25
conditional 〜たら 11-1 BTS 1, 11-2 BTS 5, 11-4 BTS 9, 11-5 BTS 12, 11-6 BTS 15
connectives 22-5 BTS 11
consonants, long 促音 Introduction, 3-9 BTL 2, 5-7 BTL 10
contractions 20-6 BTS 9
creative language 21-1 BTS 1
cuisine 料理 14-3 BTS 8

dake sentence + だけ 17-6 BTS 12, 20-4 BTS 5
daroo だろう 8-5 BTS 13
-dasu verb stem 〜だす 18-1 BTS 3
datte だって 17-6 BTS 14
de wa ikenai / ja ikenai では・じゃ いけない 13-4 BTS 12
de (wa/mo) aru/nai である・でない・ではない・でもない 13-8 BTL 3
dependence 甘え 5-6 BTS 15
deshoo でしょう 4-1 BTS 2, 4-2 BTS 12, 5-2 BTS 3
diacritics 濁点 2-9 BTL 4
dialects 方言 13-9 BTL 4
disagreeing *see* agreeing and disagreeing
discourse strategy だから 21-6 BTS 12; intonation seeking empathy 21-6 BTS 11; その + noun 21-5 BTS 8
double consonants (促音): hiragana (っ) 3-9 BTL 2; katakana (ッ) 5-7 BTL 10
double-*ga* 〜が〜が 4-6 BTS 27

echo question 2-2 BTS 7
email, closing 13-8 BTL 2
embedded question 12-2 BTS 4, 12-3 BTS 6, 17-8 BTL 2
-eru 〜える 22-9 BTL 6

existence (inanimate) 2-8 BTS 29
explanation *no de* 〜ので 10-1 BTS 3

family 家族 7-2 BTS 6, 11-4 BTS 11, 12-5 BTS 15
family terms, impersonal 13-9 BTL 5
female speech style 8-3 BTS 9
fonts フォント 3-9 BTL 5
formal/informal 2-1 BTS 1, 7-1 BTS 1, 7-3 BTS 10; formal adjective forms 2-1 BTS 1, 4-1-BTS 1; formal noun *desu* forms 2-1 BTS 1, 4-1-BTS 1; formal *-te* form 〜まして 6-4 BTS 16; formal verb forms 2-1 BTS 1, 4-1-BTS 1; informal adjective forms 2-3 BTS 15, 2-6 BTS 25, 4-1 BTS 1; informal noun *desu* forms 2-1 BTS 1, 2-5 BTS 18, 2-6 BTS 25, 3-4 BTS 18, 4-3 BTS 14; informal verb forms 2-6 BTS 25, 7-1 BTS 1, 7-3 BTS 8
fractions 分数 9-2 BTS 6
frequency expressions 8-6 BTS 15
frustration/anger expressing 22-1 BTS 2
furigana ふりがな 1-15 BTL 4
fuu (ni) description + 風(に) 18-5 BTS 11

genkooyooshi how to use 原稿用紙 21-8 BTL 5
genkooyooshi 原稿用紙 1-15 BTL 5
gifts 8-4 BTS 11
giri 義理 24-6 BTL 1
gurai minimizing significance ぐらい 17-9 BTL 4

haiku 俳句 18-8 BTL 3
hajime for listing 始め 24-3 BTS 6
handaku-on (hiragana) 半濁音 3-9 BTL 4
handwritten characters 2-9 BTL 3
hazu はず 17-2 BTS 3
headlines and titles 21-7 BTL 3
health (describing) 13-5 BTS 15
hearsay sentence + そう 14-2 BTS 4
hesitation noises 2-2 BTS 8
hiragana 平仮名 2-9 BTL 1
holidays 4-4 BTS 18
honorific お + verb stem + になる 20-1 BTS 1
hot springs 温泉 15-2 BTS 4
humble nouns 謙譲語 22-3 BTS 7
humble verb 謙譲語 6-5 BTS 21

humor ユーモア 8-2 BTS 6
hypothetical statements 〜としたら 14-1 BTS 3

imperative affirmative 命令形 23-1 BTS 3
imperative negative 命令形 23-1 BTS 1
informal *see* formal/informal
innovative vocabulary 19-8 BTL 2
inns 旅館 15-2 BTS 4
intention つもり 15-2 BTS 2
interjections 9-6 BTS 16
internet language 14-9 BTL 2
intransitive verb *see* transitive/intransitive verb
inverted sentence 3-6 BTS 32
invitations 2-2 BTS 1, 16-1 BTS 2; declining invitations 16-1 BTS 2

ja nai sentence + じゃない 14-5 BTS 17
job hunting 22-7 BTL 2

-kakeru with verb stem 〜かける 20-1 BTS 2
kanarazu shimo かならずしも 21-3 BTS 5
kango (Chinese borrowed words) 漢語 9-8 BTL 3
kanji 漢字: associated with temperature 18-8 BTL 4; identifying and describing 20-8 BTL 5; multiple for one word 13-9 BTL 6; multiple readings 14-7 BTL 1; names 13-8 BTL 1; place names 13-8 BTL 1; radicals 部首 7-9 BTL 15; readings 1-5 BTL 2, 7-7 BTL 10, 7-8 BTL 11, 7-8 BTL 13, 7-9 BTL 15, 8-7 BTL 2, 8-8 BTL 3
katakana 片仮名 5-7 BTL 1
ka to omotta sentence + かと思った 14-5 BTS 16
ka to omou かと思う 14-1 BTS 2
keyboard input 4-7 BTL 3, 7-8 BTL 14
ki 気 13-4 BTS 13
kiri きり 23-4 BTS 6
-kiru verb stem〜きる 17-6 BTS 13
kishootenketsu 起承転結 20-7 BTL 1
ko-so-a-do series こそあど 2-1 BTS 2, 2-4 BTS 17, 2-7 BTS 28, 3-5 BTS 22, 8-1 BTS 2, 10-6 BTS 15
koto こと 10-5 BTS 9; ことになる 12-6 BTS 19; ことにする 11-3 BTS 7; *X no koto* 〜のこと 3-1 BTS 5; relaying information とのことです 15-3 BTS 5; sentence + *koto* ことが

ある・ない 8-4 BTS 10; sentence + ことは + sentence 14-2 BTS 5; *sono koto* そのこと 4-4 BTS 16; って・ということ 12-1 BTS 2
kotowaza ことわざ 20-3 BTS 4
kun-yomi 訓読み 1-15 BTL 2
kurai with a sentence くらい 23-5 BTS 7
kuse くせに 19-3 BTS 6
kuurubizu クールビズ 18-8 BTL 2

loanwords 外来語 3-3 BTS 14

mae (ni) non-past verb + 前(に) 14-3 BTS 9
male speech style 8-3 BTS 9
manga, reading 20-9 BTL 8
manner expression 4-1 BTS 3, 5-1 BTS 2
-mashoo form 〜ましょう 3-2 BTS 8, 10-1 BTS 2
mata wa for alternatives または 24-4 BTS 9
mitai (ni/na) sentence + みたい(に・な) 16-3 BTS 8
mono からいいようなものの 19-5 BTS 9
mono 9-5 BTS 14
mora 拍 Introduction
multiplication 9-6 BTS 17

-nagara 〜ながら 17-1 BTS 1
names 名前 1-4 BTS 8, 1-7 BTS 14, 3-9 BTS 6; kanji for 13-8 BTL 1; キラキラネーム 21-7 BTL 4; popular 21-8 BTL 4
nanka なんか 13-1 BTS 2
-nari ni/-nari no 〜なりに・〜なりの 21-2 BTS 2
narration 21-5 BTS 9
n desu んです 6-5 BTS 19, 7-2 BTS 4, 7-6 BTS 18, 7-7 BTL 2, 8-2 BTS 5, 9-1 BTS 2, 12-4 BTS 14
necessity negative verb 〜なくてはいけない・ならない 14-6 BTS 18
negating 2-1 BTS 5
negative *see* affirmative/negative
negative questions 3-2 BTS 12
news stories listening to and reading 19-9 BTL 3
ni shite wa/mo にしては・も 18-1 BTS 2
ni yoru による 17-5 BTS 11
ni yoru to によると 17-4 BTS 8

ningenkankei 人間関係 18-6 BTS 14
no ni: non-past verb + のに 19-1 BTS 1; sentence + のに 16-1 BTS 3
noun 名詞 2-1 BTS 1
noun *desu*: formal affirmative non-past です 2-1 BTS 1; formal affirmative past でした 4-1 BTS 1; formal negative non-past じゃないです・じゃありません 2-1 BTS 1; formal negative past じゃなかったです・じゃありませんでした 4-1 BTS 1; impersonal である・でない・ではない・でもない 13-8 BTL 3; informal affirmative non-past だ・ゼロ 2-5 BTS 18, 3-4 BTS 18; informal affirmative past だった 4-3 BTS 14; informal negative non-past じゃない 2-6 BTS 25; informal negative past じゃなかった 2-6 BTS 25; noun では・じゃいけない 13-4 BTS 12

occupations 9-3 BTS 7
okurigana 送り仮名 7-8 BTL 12
omoiyari 思いやり 3-4 BTS 16, 7-4 BTS 11
on 恩 24-6 BTL 1
online resources 21-7 BTL 2; search strategies 21-7 BTL 1; using 19-9 BTL 5
onomatopoeia オノマトペ 11-5 BTS 14; in manga 20-7 BTL 2
on-yomi 音読み 1-15 BTL 2
opinion, expressing ように思う 16-6 BTS 11

papers (essays) 小論文 21-8 BTL 6
particle 3-1 BTS 4; だけ 4-2 BTS 9; で (means) 5-4 BTS 9; で (place) 3-4 BTS 15; でも 14-6 BTS 20; が 4-3 BTS 13; が (double が) 4-6 BTS 27; か (noun か noun (か)) 6-6 BTS 23; から 4-4 BTS 22; から (reason) 5-5 BTS 12; まで 4-4 BTS 22, 5-5 BTS 13; までに 5-5 BTS 13; も 3-6 BTS 31; multiple 4-2 BTS 10; な (noun な noun) 3-1 BTS 2; など 22-2 BTS 5; に……に for listing 24-2 BTS 3; に (decisions) 6-6 BTS 28; に (location) 3-6 BTS 30; に (time) 3-4 BTS 20; にて in business writing 22-7 BTL 1; に・へ (location) 5-4 BTS 8; の (noun の noun) 3-1 BTS 2, 3-6 BTS 29; ので 10-1 BTS 3; non-past verb + まで(に) 14-3 BTS 11; [noun + particle] as question 4-2 BTS 7; を 4-5 BTS 24, 4-7 BTL 2; を (location) 7-6 BTS 17; Particle + です 4-4 BTS 23, 6-2 BTS 5; question word + か 6-5 BTS 18; question word + も 6-6 BTS 22; さ 12-3 BTS 7; し (sentence し) 9-3 BTS 9; と (negative non-past sentence と sentence) 13-4 BTS 11; と (noun と noun) 3-2 BTS 10; と (noun と Sentence) 6-6 BTS 25; と (sentence と sentence) 12-4 BTS 13; と *issho ni* と一緒に 3-4 BTS 17; と・って (quotations) 7-3 BTS 9; と・って言うか 18-3 BTS 9; とか 4-2 BTS 8, 10-6 BTS 11; って 3-1 BTS 4; は 2-6 BTS 22, 3-2 BTS 7; や 17-7 BTL 1; のみ 23-8 BTL 4; まで in business writing 22-7 BTL 1; より 23-8 BTL 3
particle (sentence particle) 2-1 BTS 3; が・けど・けれど・けども・けれども 2-4 BTS 16; か, ね 2-1 BTS 3; っけ 14-5 BTS 15; multiple, かなあ, かねえ 2-6 BTS 24, 3-6 BTS 33; ねえ 2-3 BTS 14; ねえ、なあ 2-6 BTS 23; よ 2-2 BTS 6; かしら 22-2 BTS 6; わ 20-6 BTS 8; ぞ 21-4 BTS 7; ぜ 23-2 BTS 4
passive 受け身形 18-1 BTS 1; for general description 受け身形 21-3 BTS 4; honorific passive 尊敬の受け身形 13-1 BTS 1
permission 〜て(も)いい 5-1 BTS 2
physical condition, describing 20-4 BTS 6
place names, kanji for 13-8 BTL 1
plural nouns たち・ら 17-1 BTS 2
polite adjective *see* adjective
politeness 敬語 5-5 BTS 10, 6-4 BTS 15, 10-3 BTS 6
polite prefixes 8-3 BTS 8
polite request 〜ていただけますか 5-3 BTS 5
potential: 〜える 22-9 BTL 6; 〜うる 22-9 BTL 6
potential 可能形 15-1 BTS 1
-ppanashi verb stem〜っぱなし 18-2 BTS 5
prohibition 〜てはいけない 13-1 BTS 7
provisional 〜れば・えば 16-2 BTS 4; 〜れば……ほど 20-5 BTS 7; さえ……えば 22-3 BTS 8
punctuality 15-3 BTS 6
punctuation 句読点 2-9 BTL 2, 10-9 BTL 1

questions without *ka* 4-4 BTS 15
question word: だれ 2-6; どっち 2-7 BTS 28; どちら 2-4 BTS 17; どこ 2-5, 2-7 BTS 28; どうして・なぜ・なんで 7-3; どれ 2-1 BTS 2; いつ 4-3; なに・なん 2-3; question word + か 6-5 BTS 18; question word + も 6-6 BTS 22; question word + particle + でも 15-4 BTS 10
quotation marks 9-8 BTL 1
quotations 7-3 BTS 9

radicals (kanji radicals) 部首 7-9 BTL 15
rashii: noun + らしい 18-3 BTS 8; sentence + らしい 18-2 BTS 6
reading strategies 19-9 BTL 4
recall strategy 16-2 BTS 6
rei 例の noun 13-3 BTS 8
relaying information sentence + とのことです 15-3 BTS 5
repetition: for dramatic effect 14-6 BTS 19; of symbols 々 15-7 BTL 1
requirement negative verb 〜なくてはいけない・ならない 14-6 BTS 18
resume 履歴書 22-8 BTL 3
ritual language 1-4 BTS 7, 1-6 BTS 13
romanization ローマ字 Introduction
rules and regulations 23-1 BTS 2

sae: noun さえ 22-4 BTS 8; with 〜て form 〜てさえ 22-6 BTS 13; with verb stem さえ 22-4 BTS 10
script choice 19-7 BTL 1
sekkaku せっかく 13-1 BTS 6
self, words for 1-7 BTS 15
self-directed comments sentence + か 13-1 BTS 5
self-introduction 自己紹介 1-4 BTS 7, 1-10 BTS 20, 6-1 BTS 4
self promotion 22-9 BTL 4
self reference 20-9 BTL 6
seniority 15-3 BTS 6
senryuu 川柳 18-8 BTL 3
sentence: creative endings 20-7 BTL 3; +か as a noun 18-5 BTS 12; ending with a noun 20-8 BTL 4
sentence modifier 7-5 BTS 14, 9-1 BTS 1
shika しか 13-1 BTS 3

shika nai non-past verb + しかない 18-3 BTS 7
speech スピーチ: formal farewell 24-3 BTS 5; gratitude 24-1 BTS 1; impromptu farewell 24-4 BTS 7; toast 24-2 BTS 2; workplace introduction 24-5 BTS 10
spoken language (*vs.* written language) 話しことば 4-7 BTL 1
storytelling 11-6 BTS 15, 19-6 BTS 10, 20-6 BTS 10
style written 21-8 BTL 7

-(ta)garu verb/adjective stem〜(た)がる 18-4 BTS 10
-tai たい 6-5 BTS 20
tame ため 16-5 BTS 10
-tara form *see* conditional
-tari form 〜たり〜たり 13-6 BTS 16
tategaki (vertical writing) 縦書き 1-15 BTL 3
tatoe...-te mo たとえ...〜ても 18-5 BTS 13
-tatte 〜たって 22-6 BTS 14
-te form 〜て 5-1 BTS 1, 2, 5-2 BTS 4; informal command 6-3 BTS 10; manner expressions 5-1 BTS 2; 〜てある 9-1 BTS 3; 〜てばかり・ばっかり 22-6 BTS 12; 〜てほしい 12-5 BTS 17; 〜ていく 21-4 BTS 6; 〜ている 6-1 BTS 1; 〜ていただけますか 15-4 BTS 7; 〜てから 9-6 BTS 15; 〜てくる 17-5 BTS 10; 〜てくる・いく 5-4 BTS 7, 9-2 BTS 5; 〜てみる 8-1 BTS 1; 〜ても 5-1 BTS 2, 18-5 BTS 13; 〜て(も)いい 5-1 BTS 2; 〜てもらえますか 15-4 BTS 7; 〜ておく 10-1 BTS 1; 〜てさえ 22-6 BTS 13; 〜てしまう 12-2 BTS 5; 〜てやった 21-6 BTS 10
tejun 手順 15-4 BTS 8
time, relative 4-4 BTS 18
time expressions 3-2 BTS 9
titles 1-1 BTS 2, 1-7 BTS 14
togetherness 10-3 BTS 7
to iu to というと 21-2 BTS 3
toki (ni) sentence + とき(に) 13-4 BTS 14
tokoro: non-past + ところ 16-2 BTS 5; past + ところ 16-3 BTS 7; past + ところ + particle 16-4 BTS 9
to negative non-past sentence と sentence 13-4 BTS 11

to shite wa/mo としては・も 19-1 BTS 3
to/tte iu ka と・って言うか 18-3 BTS 9
totomo ni とともに 24-4 BTS 8
transitive verb *-te aru* ～てある 9-1 BTS 3
transportation *see* commuting
trash protocols 23-7 BTL 1
travel plans 旅行 15-2 BTS 3
tsui: つい + sentence 14-2 BTS 6; つい + time 14-2 BTS 6
tsumori: つもり (assumption) 15-5 BTS 11; つもり (intention) 15-2 BTS 2

uchi (ni) non-past negative verb + うち(に) 14-4 BTS 14
-uru ～うる 22-9 BTL 6
usernames 20-9 BTL 7

verb 動詞 2-1 BTS 1; causative ～させる 17-3 BTS 5; causative + verb of giving or receiving 17-4 BTS 7; causative passive 23-3 BTS 5; formal affirmative non-past ～ます 2-1 BTS 1; formal affirmative past ～ました 4-1 BTS 1; formal negative non-past ～ないです・～ません 2-1 BTS 1; formal negative past ～なかったです・～ませんでした 4-1 BTS 1; giving and receiving 12-1 BTS 1, 12-4 BTS 9, 12-6 BTS 18; giving and receiving: いってやった 21-6 BTS 10; honorific passive 尊敬の受け身形 13-1 BTS 1; imperative, negative and affirmative 23-1 BTS 1, 23-1 BTS 3; informal affirmative non-past ～る 7-1 BTS 1; informal affirmative past ～た 7-1 BTS 8; informal negative non-past ～ない 2-6 BTS 25; informal negative past ～なかった 7-1 BTS 8; intransitive verb～てくる 14-4 BTS 12; negative imperative 命令形 23-1 BTS 1; negative in ～ないで ～ないで 20-2 BTS 3; negative in ～ず（に） ～ず（に） 20-2 BTS 3; non-past + 前(に) 14-3 BTS 9; non-past + のに 19-1 BTS 1; non-past negative + うち(に) 14-4 BTS 14; passive 18-1 BTS 1; past verb + あとで 14-4 BTS 13; potential 可能形 15-1 BTS 1; provisional ～れば・えば 16-2 BTS 4, 20-5 BTS 7, 22-3 BTS 8; receiving verb in potential for request ～てもらえます・いただけますか 15-4 BTS 7; root 7-1 BTS 1; stem 3-2 BTS 8; stem as noun 7-5 BTS 13; stem～合う 17-5 BTS 9; stem～だす 18-1 BTS 3; stem～がる 18-4 BTS 10; stem ～かける 20-1 BTS 2; stem～きる 17-6 BTS 13; stem～っぱなし 18-2 BTS 5; stem ～さえ 22-4 BTS 10; stem～たい 6-5 BTS 20; transitive and intransitive 14-1 BTS 1; verb～れば verb ほど 20-5 BTS 7
visiting 訪問 8-3 BTS 7
voiced consonants 濁音 2-9 BTL 4; hiragana 2-9 BTL 4; katakana 5-7 BTL 9
vowels, long 長音: hiragana Introduction, 2-9 BTL 5; katakana (ー) 5-7 BTL 2

wago 和語 17-8 BTL 3
wakannai わかんない 19-2 BTS 5
wake: わけ(が)ない 19-4 BTS 8; わけでは・もない 19-2 BTS 4; わけに(は・も)いかない 19-3 BTS 7; わけ 19-1 BTS 2
weather expressions 天気・天候 18-1 BTS 4
word order 語順 4-6 BTS 28
written language (*vs.* spoken language) 書きことば (話しことば) 4-7 BTL 1, 12-7 BTL 1

yojijukugo 四字熟語 18-7 BTL 1
yokogaki (horizontal writing) 横書き 1-15 BTL 3
yoo: sentence + よう(に・な) 16-3 BTS 8; ように言う 17-3 BTS 6; ようになる 15-4 BTS 9; ように思う 16-6 BTS 11; ようにする 14-2 BTS 7
yoo-on 拗音: hiragana (ゃ, ゅ, ょ) 3-9 BTL 3; katakana (ャ, ュ, ョ) 6-7 BTL 5